LOGIC:

THE ART OF REASONING

LOGIC:

THE ART OF REASONING

by

David Hugh Freeman
Professor of Philosophy
University of Rhode Island

DAVID McKAY COMPANY, INC.
NEW YORK

LOGIC: THE ART OF REASONING

LIBRARY OF CONGRESS CATALOG CARD NUMBER: 66–23077

MANUFACTURED IN THE UNITED STATES OF AMERICA

To Deanna,
Renée, and Irénke

Preface

This text is designed to introduce the beginning student to the art of reasoning. Traditional and modern approaches are combined. Little attention is paid to the philosophy of logic, since philosophical issues can best be raised for the beginning student by utilizing selections from primary sources.

Many of the exercises deal with current topics. There is no intention on the part of the author to take sides on any issue, but we have tried to capture the student's interest.

I am indebted to my colleagues William Oliver Martin, John F. Peterson, Stephen D. Schwarz, Ralph L. Smilde, and William Young for their encouragement and criticism. And I am especially grateful to Dr. Hugh M. Curtler, my former colleague. Dr. Curtler not only read the first draft with painstaking care but also provided the printer with completed drawings used in the text. I would also like to express my appreciation to Estelle Boisclair, for her endless patience with the revision and typing of the manuscript, to Mrs. Bruce Slader, for assistance in proofreading, and to Mary Johnson for her assistance in preparing the Index. Finally, a word of thanks to the many students who have been in my classroom. Their stimulation and interest in logic is the source from which textbooks grow.

DAVID HUGH FREEMAN

Table of Contents

ix

LOGIC:

THE ART OF REASONING

CHAPTER ONE

The Importance of Logic

Tweedledum and Tweedledee
Agreed to have a battle;
For Tweedledum said Tweedledee
Had spoiled his nice new rattle.

Through the Looking Glass—LEWIS CARROLL

1. A Remark to the Student

For most of you logic will not be a battle, nor will it spoil your academic year. It may even improve your standing in other courses, but it will not solve all your problems. The study of logic will not tell you whom to date or how to behave; it has nothing to say about what is good or bad, beautiful or ugly; it supplies no information about love, marriage, and surfing. Logic will not provide you with factual information in any field, whether it be mathematics, physics, chemistry, biology, psychology, history, sociology, aesthetics, linguistics, ethics, jurisprudence, or theology. And yet none of these areas of human knowledge would be possible if we could not form concepts, make judgments, and deduce consequences. In short, our capacity to do what is called reasoning is an essential part of human experience. Everyone practices logic; not everyone studies it. You have been forming concepts, expressing judgments, and arguing all your life. And now you are about to study what you have been doing. You are about to become a logician. The logician simply studies what

concepts, judgments, and arguments are. The result of his study is
the science of logic.

Like any other science, logic is the study of an aspect or mode of
our experience. It is not made up; it does not deal with fictions, nor
is it identical with any other discipline. It has a subject matter of
its own. Logic is not concerned with how we feel when we think; it
is not psychology. Nor is it involved in doing sums or proving
theorems; it is not mathematics, although mathematics cannot dispense with it. Nor is it concerned with the way all people do in fact
think, for it is not a descriptive science; it is rather a normative
science. It can teach you how to reason correctly. It provides the
norms, the rules, by which people *ought* to think, that is, if they
want to think clearly, be able to formulate true propositions and
reason soundly.

2. The Scientific Character of Logic

2.1   The first principles of logic

Like any other science, logic accepts certain first principles—principles that no one in his right mind seriously doubts: namely, the
principle of noncontradiction: that at the same time and in the
same respect, it is impossible for the same proposition to be true and
not to be true; the principle of excluded middle: that the same
proposition is either true or false; and the principle of identity: that
if a proposition is true, then it is true.

Logic does not seek to demonstrate its first principles. If it did,
the principles in question would not be first. Any formulation of
their denial simply takes them for granted. We are immediately
aware of their truth as soon as we understand what they mean. Try
to imagine a situation that contradicts them. The very notion of
contradiction assumes the principle of noncontradiction.

Consider, for example, the proposition "You are presently enrolled in a college course in logic." There is nothing contradictory
about the fact that you did not take logic last semester and are taking
it now, nor is it contradictory that you will not take it again next
semester. What would be contradictory would be to hold that you
are now enrolled and that you are not now enrolled, using the term

enrolled in the very same univocal sense. Can you imagine what this could possibly be like? To deny the principle of noncontradiction is to make no sense; it is to utter a nonsensical statement—a statement without an intelligible or sensible meaning: NONSENSE.

The first principles of logic are also held on the level of common sense. The logician simply makes explicit what is implicit in our experience. As first principles, these norms are not simply inventions of the mind; they are not mere constructs, without any basis in the world of nonmental experience. They are more than mere verbal formulations, more than conventions. We do not simply agree to use them; they force themselves upon us. We are intuitively aware of them.

2.2 *The subject matter of logic*

Every science is constituted as a special science by the fact that it has its own subject matter. Logic is no exception. Of course, the same subject matter may be studied from different perspectives. The perspective or interest of the logician differs, for example, from that of the grammarian. The latter is also interested in the structure and usage of a given language. It will become evident that the logician is not interested in language as such, but is concerned rather with language from the *logical point of view*. Exactly what the "logical point of view" means will become evident in the succeeding chapters. Our present concern is with the subject matter of logic.

Our knowledge is always of something. When someone claims to know, we can ask what it is that he knows. Everyone utilizes words to express concepts, formulates propositions to express judgments, and combines propositions into arguments. The logician, however, seeks to formulate a concept of a concept; he seeks to formulate a proposition stating what a proposition is, and he notes what constitutes a valid argument in contradistinction to an invalid argument. In short, the subject matter of logic consists of concepts, propositions, and arguments.

2.3 *The continuity and systematic character of logic*

Like every science, logic does not simply list disconnected statements about its subject matter. It proceeds rather in a systematic and orderly fashion, thereby disclosing the interrelationship between its parts.

Logic, as a science, has a long history, dating from Aristotle. Its recent development does not destroy the past, but simply expands and utilizes what has gone before. Throughout this text an effort has been made to preserve the past and to integrate the more recent developments into a systematic whole.

2.4 The theoretical and practical aspect of logic

Logic is a science, but it is not a laboratory science. Its laws are normative; they can be and frequently are violated, thereby giving rise to unwarranted and fallacious inferences. To the extent that logic deals with the subject matter simply for the sake of knowing the nature of concepts, propositions, and arguments, it is theoretical. To the extent that what is known is put to use in practice, logic becomes an art and is practical. The numerous exercises in this book provide the student with the opportunity of using what he has learned about concepts, propositions, and arguments, so that at the end of the course, the student ought to be able to give clearer definitions, draw valid inferences, and construct valid arguments, as well as detect the errors of others.

3. Logic and the Other Sciences

Logic is a tool by which we gain knowledge in various fields. It constitutes the method of the various sciences. By studying its role in the sciences, we gain some idea of its importance.

3.1 What is science?

The technological results of the development of science are everywhere in evidence. No one is unfamiliar with rockets, robots, airplanes, cranes, sputniks, telescopes, penicillin, computers, guns, bombs, and contraceptives. Technology is here to stay. Technology, however, is not science, and the sciences which make technology possible are not the sum total of the sciences. To see the product of science is easy; to understand what science is requires some effort. The difficulty is intensified because the word *science* is ambiguous; it is used to refer to more than one concept. When we think of what science is, we may form a concept of its technological results; we may think of such sciences as physics and chemistry or of the science of history, sociology, or psychology. We may also think of all that we know, of knowledge in general, or we may conceive of a special kind of knowledge. At times we think of a body of useful and practical knowledge, and at other times we think of the art of inquiry, of the method of obtaining such knowledge. Our concepts of what science is may or may not comprehend what science actually is. The word *science* may be used arbitrarily, and we can think whatever we wish. Science, however, is not a figment of the imagination; it is rather an actual product of civilization. It is what it is, and our description of science can be formulated in propositions about it, and propositions are true or false.

What science is, is not arbitrary. Of course, our concepts may fail to grasp the actual states of affairs that have developed in the course of human history. Science is one such state of affairs; it is the product of human action, aimed at the satisfaction of our desire to know —a desire that is a fundamental part of our human nature. *Logic is the means by which we come to know.*

There are actually many different sciences. The word *science* in the singular is misleading unless used to refer to the sum total of the special sciences, ranging from physics to linguistics. *Science* is frequently used to refer to the physical sciences. Such a restriction may simply be an arbitrary matter of word usage, but if it intends to imply that human knowledge is confined to the physical sciences, it is not only misleading but factually false. Mathematics and logic are kinds of knowledge. What is the atomic weight of the number 2? Can you check the blood pressure of a syllogism? Such questions make no sense because mathematics is not chemistry and logic is not physiology, and yet they are both kinds of knowledge.

3.2 Philosophy and the sciences

The very question "What is science?" is not a question *of* any special science. It is rather a question *about* each of them, considered both individually and collectively. The question "What is science?" is a philosophical question. The same person may be both a scientist and a philosopher, but neither the question "What is science?" nor the answer is a statement of a special science.

There is a sense in which philosophy is also a science—namely, insofar as it has its own data, object of study, evidence, and systematic development—but philosophy is not a special science, limited to a particular aspect of our world. Philosophy is, among other things, the science of the sciences. Philosophy asks and answers questions not dealt with in a special science. Philosophy raises questions about each of the sciences, it supplies their assumptions about the nature of the world, and since logic is a part of philosophy, it provides the method of science. The sciences seek to know the world as it appears to us from certain abstract perspectives. Philosophy offers alternative assumptions about its ultimate origin and the nature of its unity and diversity.

Philosophical assumptions are indispensable to the various sciences. Without them the sciences would not have come into being, nor could they continue to develop. This does not mean that philosophy should make the mistake of dictating what the results of a scientific investigation must be. Philosophy does not enter constitutively into the domain of the sciences. Philosophy is not a substitute for the special sciences, nor can the latter be a substitute for philosophy.

That philosophy is indispensable for the sciences is readily evident. Simply consider the fact that although there is in principle a general agreement within the physical sciences concerning the method to be followed, there is, for example, no such unanimity concerning what constitutes a physical theory. Does the latter provide an image of reality, so that perceptible phenomena are effects of a really existing, although not directly perceptible, atomic structure? Or is a physical theory simply a human device that systematically records our many experiences in an easily remembered manner, without telling us anything about what is really real? The question "What is a physical theory?", like the question "What is science?", cannot be answered in physical concepts, nor can it be solved by the methods of the physical sciences.[1]

The physical sciences as such do not reflect upon their own nature. A judgment about a scientific theory is a philosophical judgment, for it is the task of philosophy to reflect upon the nature of science as well as upon itself. The affirmation or the denial that a physical

[1] See Andrew G. Van Melsen, *Science and Technology* (Pittsburgh, Duquesne University Press, 1961), pp. 10–16.

theory enriches our knowledge of nature is not expressible in the language of science. Concepts about what is real and what is knowledge belong to metaphysics and epistemology; that is, to philosophy.

In practice, the scientist can pursue his immediate goals by simply following a particular procedure. The scientist need not reflect upon what he is doing to gain practical results. The moment that he reflects upon the foundations of his pursuit, upon the nature of his results, and upon his cognitive capacities, he ceases to act as a scientist and becomes a philosopher. The *nonreflective* nature of the sciences is in part what makes philosophy indispensable to the sciences. The very effort to eliminate philosophical reflection and to declare it meaningless itself requires philosophical reflection.[2]

The failure to distinguish propositions *about* science which are philosophical from propositions *of* science has led to many confusions, including the naïve assumption that all human problems will be solved by the various sciences. We need only note that the discovery of the answer to the question "What causes cancer?" does not tell us whether or not we should utilize this knowledge to spread cancer through bacteriological warfare.

Without philosophical reflection, we would be unable to distinguish the different special sciences. What is it that gives rise to the many sciences? Why are there many and not one? How do they agree? In what do they differ? Such questions are not questions *of* science; they are *about* science.

3.3 The origin of science

The sciences *originate* because of our desire to know. The satisfaction of this desire may be for its own sake, or one may seek to know in order to utilize what we know. The desire itself, however, is apparently as old as the history of mankind. Man finds himself in a world that he did not make. On the level of ordinary, everyday experience there is an indissoluble coherence between the numerical, spatial, physical, and organic aspects of our world. We have feelings, form concepts, use language, engage in social intercourse, buy and sell, form aesthetic and moral judgments, make laws, and entertain religious beliefs. Our experience takes place within a historical

[2] *Ibid.,* p. 13.

context; the past is different from the present, and the future course of events may produce the unexpected. In our pretheoretical attitude, we crudely note the various aspects of our world in a vague, unanalyzed, instinctive manner. And yet on this level we know our world directly and immediately. We observe that different kinds of things function in different ways, are subject to different laws, have different patterns of behavior. To common sense, stones are numerable, spatial, and physical, but they do not grow, reproduce, feel, form concepts, or develop a civilization. Plants, in addition to their numerical, spatial, and physical modes of existence, function as subjects in the organic aspect of experience. They are subject to growth; they live and die. Animals, in contrast, function in the numerical, spatial, physical, organic, and psychical modalities. It is possible to count them, state where they are, and describe their physical properties, their organic processes, and their feelings of pleasure and pain.

Man alone actively functions as subject in the analytical, historical, linguistic, social, economic, aesthetic, juridical, moral, and religious dimensions. Man alone forms concepts, consciously and purposively introduces changes in language, social intercourse, economics, in art forms, in legal, moral, and religious systems. Stones, plants, and animals may be the object of concept formation; they may be named, valued, contemplated aesthetically, or worshiped, but they are never actively engaged in logical analysis, the formation of history, language, society, economics, art, law, ethics, or religion.

Man is also subject to physical, organic, and psychical laws. And here he cannot exercise any choice. He cannot avoid being subject to the necessities of the physical, organic, and psychical aspects of the world. However, when he exercises his analytical function, he can reason validly or invalidly; he can form history in keeping with the continuity of a tradition, or he can act in a revolutionary manner. He can conform his language to the customary conventional patterns, or he can violate the rules of grammar. He can follow the accepted patterns of social behavior or disregard them; he can respect or violate an economic principle, aesthetic style, a legal principle, or a moral principle; and finally he can believe or disbelieve in God.

On the pretheoretical everyday level a person simply *knows* all this immediately and directly, without reflection. He takes the diversity and the unity of his experience for granted. His experience is concrete, naïve, pretheoretical. The *knowledge* that he has is immediate and practical. He has no carefully formed theories about his experience. *It is logic that enables him to move from this naïve level to the theoretical plane of scientific theory.*[3]

The scientific attitude, the scientific perspective or outlook, focuses upon a limited aspect of the fullness of our experience. The sciences originate in a theoretical, abstract perspective. Unlike our ordinary naïve way of knowing, the scientific way of knowing tears apart by abstraction what constitutes a unity in actual everyday experience. *It is man's ability to use logic that makes this abstraction possible.*

The sciences may be classified according to different principles. For convenience, we shall divide them into the physical and nonphysical. *It is the application of logic that enables us to classify the sciences.*

The different kinds of science originate because of the nature of the field under investigation and because of the interests of the investigator. The physical sciences deal with the spatial, physical, organic, and psychical aspects of our world. The nonphysical sciences investigate the spheres of experience in which man alone functions as subject; for example, the historical, linguistic, social, economic, aesthetic, moral, juridical, and religious. The difference in subject matter gives rise to a different kind of knowledge. The special sciences originate to the extent that each has a different object of study. What they share (and this is why such diverse subjects as physics and history are both sciences) is a *common method. Logic is what the sciences share; namely, a common method.*

Every science utilizes logic as the instrument by which it acquires a special kind of knowledge of the world in which we live. All our knowledge begins in some form of experience, whether it be of our world, ourselves, or God. The physical sciences limit themselves to objects as they appear to the external senses: to the eye, the ear, or our sense of touch. By limiting themselves to what is externally observable, the physical sciences are able to be *objective*, and their "facts" are in principle the same for every observer; that is, they

[3] See Herman Dooyeweerd, *A New Critique of Theoretical Thought*, trans. by David H. Freeman *et al.* (Philadelphia, Presbyterian and Reformed Publishing Co., 1953), Vol. I.

are *intersubjective*. Of course, there are complications, since observations do not occur without intellectual activity and individual observers may see different things; nevertheless, observation is of primary importance.

By abstracting from the fullness of concrete experience, the physical sciences are able to form diverse concepts in order to attain a theoretical comprehension of material phenomena.[4]

The sciences are generated by our desire to explain and to make predictions about the world in which we live. Scientific explanations seek to be systematic and controllable by factual evidence. The sciences organize and classify our knowledge on the basis of explanatory principles. They discover and formulate the conditions under which events occur by isolating certain properties in the subject matter under consideration.[5]

Thus the different sciences originate because we want to know different things. The "facts" can neither be expressed nor described without abstraction from the fullness, the totality, of our ordinary experience. The perception of any object takes place from a determined standpoint, and by a determined means, by one or more of the senses. By abstraction, the concrete material objects of our experience may be placed in different conceptual contexts; prescientific concepts are refined, made more precise, and new concepts are developed. What is irrelevant to the interest of the investigator is simply left out of consideration.[6]

3.4   The role of logic

The various special sciences share a common method, known as the scientific method. Essentially the scientific method is simply the application of deductive and inductive logic to our experience. The classification of the sciences into the physical and nonphysical does not imply a sharp dichotomy or opposition. The physical sciences, however, exhibit a greater degree of exactness. Both the physical and the nonphysical sciences are based on sense experience, but the

[4] Van Melsen, *op. cit.*, pp. 27 ff.
[5] See Ernest Nagel, *The Structure of Science* (New York, Harcourt, Brace & World, 1961), pp. 15–28.
[6] See Van Melsen, *op. cit.*, pp. 38–52.

latter are concerned with man insofar as he is capable of acting consciously and purposively; for example, in forming history and social groups. The physical sciences deal with man solely to the extent that he is of a material nature.

The greater degree of exactness of the physical sciences arises in part because of the application of mathematical methods. The concern of mathematics is with quantitative aspects of our world in abstraction from qualitative properties. The sciences are empirical in the sense that they are concerned with reality as it is experienced. The quantitative data of the physical sciences are obtained, however, by measurements which presuppose something qualitative. Within the physical sciences there is a tendency toward perception which excludes ambiguities, so that a sense perception is reduced to an unambiguous datum, such as "This pointer is on 2." Moreover, the experimental procedure frequently leading to the appearance of the datum is also unambiguous and can be controlled by any trained investigator. Such exactness is not characteristic of the sciences which deal with man as he voluntarily develops the civilization of which he is a part.[7]

Consider, for example, the report that a person has been found stabbed to death in a dark alley. To the police investigator, the corpse is an observable fact. The coroner's report may yield an exact description of the physiological causes of death, but the matter is not ended here. Whether a crime has been committed is a legal matter; whether moral guilt is involved is an ethical consideration; the study of the motive may be of interest to the psychologist; and an investigation of the social conditions that constituted the environment of the killer may be of concern to the sociologist. The legal, moral, psychological, and social aspects of the event hardly lend themselves to the same degree of exactness as the physiological investigation of the coroner.

Our probings beyond the realm of physical science do not lend themselves to the same degree of exactness as can be attained in the physical realm. This does not imply any inferiority on the part of the nonphysical disciplines. They are simply different because they view the data from a different perspective.

[7] *Ibid.*, pp. 53–73.

3.5   The aims of science

The purpose of the sciences is twofold. First, they aim at the satisfaction of our desire to know. When such knowledge is pursued solely for the sake of knowing, without reference to its application in technology, the result is frequently called pure science or theoretical science. When knowledge is pursued for its use value, for the sake of doing, rather than knowing, it is frequently identified as practical. Theoretical knowledge enables us to develop material tools and to utilize the sources of energy.

Knowing is an intellectual act, whereas *making* changes something outside of ourselves. Our cognitive and technical abilities may approach each other, but they are not to be confused. The physical sciences are characterized by the discovery of what already exists; technology is characterized by the invention of what previously did not exist. Discovery and invention, however, are closely related, for the knowing which characterizes physical science includes the finding of new models, and the invention of new technical constructions requires the knowing of new possibilities. And yet the distinction between knowing and making cannot be eliminated if we are to understand the aims of the sciences. In their pure form, the sciences aim at increasing our knowledge of the world of nature and of man's role in civilization. In its practical application in technology, applied science arranges what is given in nature in such a manner that it leads to the effective control and mastery of nature.[8]

The sciences are concerned with observable events or happenings. They seek to employ sophisticated and systematic methods for understanding and managing what happens. Wherever possible, they may manipulate and control events to observe what happens under certain circumstances. The sciences are concerned with "facts"—with the "facts" of nature and the "facts" about human behavior. They seek to ascertain what happens and why it happens. Thus their task is both descriptive and explanatory: descriptive to the extent that they deal with what happens, explanatory to the extent that they deal with why something happens.

The physical sciences seek to deepen our understanding and control of nature. The term *nature,* however, is equivocal. In its broad-

[8] Van Melsen, *op. cit.,* pp. 229–248.

est sense it may designate whatever happens, apart from the influence of man, to the whole cosmos as it exists independently of man. More narrowly:

Nature may refer to that aspect of material things, whether artificial or natural, which is outside the sphere of man's influence. It is not to be forgotten that the scientist can only work by following the procedure prescribed by the properties of nature as they are in the external world. He must take nature as it is, so that in a sense every technical product is natural simply because it can be produced.[9]

3.6   The scientist and "fact"

The scientist seeks to discover what the "facts" are, and he seeks to explain the facts by construction of theories and the formulation of laws. *It is logic that enables theories to be constructed and laws to be formulated.*

There are different uses of the word *fact,* and there are different assumptions concerning what constitutes a theory and a law. The word *fact* is ambiguous. First, it may refer to certain selected elements in sense perception, and it may or may not be assumed that there is a direct correspondence between the events of the universe and our sense impressions of them. The sensory elements of experience are sought out in order that we may find reliable signs that enable us to check the inferences we make. Such "facts" are facts of observation, and here it is possible to reach a general agreement.

Secondly, the word *fact* is used to denote propositions interpreting what we observe in our sensory experience. For example, "This glass is brittle," "This is a chair," assert facts. Scientific investigation presupposes a large number of facts in this second sense. Of course, subsequent investigation may show that certain of these propositions are false. The glass in question may be shatterproof.

A third sense of the word *fact* refers to propositions asserting an invariable sequence or conjunction of properties, such as "The volume of a fixed mass of gas at constant pressure is proportional to the absolute temperature." Whether or not we believe such a proposition to be true depends on the evidence we have to support it. We cannot observe the fact, the generalization, that all salt is soluble, but we

[9] *Ibid.*, pp. 284 ff.

can observe particular instances of salt dissolving. Whether or not a proposition is here called a fact or a hypothesis depends on the evidence we have at hand.[10]

A fourth sense of "fact" refers to the actual existing states of affairs in the external world in virtue of which a proposition is true. Such states of affairs simply are what they are. A proposition in the third sense of fact is true when it does state what is actually the case in the real world.[11]

The "facts" which appear in sensory experience contain an element of being-found-there, of being-so-as-a-matter-of-fact. What we sense forces itself upon us in a way we cannot change; nevertheless, we do not simply receive such sense data passively, but we try to understand. We try to explain what we see; we think about it and try to make it intelligible. Our explanation, our attempt to understand, does not alter the givenness of what we sense; it simply places what we see in a theoretical context. Not only do we see colors, shapes, and forms but we are also aware of connections and interrelationships between the sense data. A theoretical interpretation accompanies our awareness of sense data. There is an intentional aspect in our knowing. Our theoretical knowledge is always of and about something, but we do not know concrete reality in its full concreteness; we know it as it has been taken apart in abstract perspectives. *It is by utilizing logic that we are able to gain such abstract perspectives or concepts of things as they are.*

Our theoretical knowledge is a synthesis of abstract perspectives; it is to a degree a model, an interpretation, a theory projected by ourselves. Our interpretative models, our theories, try to understand the various aspects of our world in their unity and diversity; they are constructs composed of familiar conceptual elements. However, the subjective aspect of knowledge does not eliminate objectivity, the fact that we are oriented to reality as it is in itself.[12] Skepticism is frequently the result of a choice between knowing everything and knowing nothing. Such a disjunction is not forced upon us. Actually

[10] See J. O. Wisdom, *Foundations of Inference in Natural Science* (London, Methuen, 1952), p. 24.
[11] See Morris R. Cohen and Ernest Nagel, *An Introduction to Logic and Scientific Method* (New York, Harcourt, Brace, 1934), pp. 217–219.
[12] Van Melsen, *op. cit.*, pp. 74–79.

the dichotomy between omniscience and complete ignorance is not the alternative. We cannot know everything about anything, but we can know something about some things. We can utilize our ability to form concepts to describe what we experience. And our concept of something may be of and about something outside ourselves.

3.7   Description and explanation

The sciences begin with ordinary experience, with what happens in the external world. They then try to give a precise description of what happens. They may ascribe a property to a definite thing or to a class of things or individuals. Such a description involves the selection of something to be described and the recognition that it belongs to a certain kind or possesses a certain property. A description is successful when an appropriate linguistic expression is found which refers to the object intended and when the object does have the property or belongs to the class we say it does. *Logic analyzes the kind of categories according to which things and properties may be classified.*

A description may be definite, referring to only one object, or it may be general, referring to every member of a class.[13] Our knowledge is partial because our descriptions and explanation of things are related to specific contexts and are thus incomplete. A description that is adequate for everyday purposes may be insufficient for more esoteric purposes. No single science is able to give a complete description of its subject matter. However, although a completely comprehensive description is unattainable, still, within a specific science, a description may be more or less comprehensive. The preciseness of a description tends to vary in inverse proportion to the wideness of the range of contexts over which it extends.

We are able to describe in a scientific manner because of our ability to form *concepts* of what things are. Our descriptive knowledge is a knowledge of the "facts" as they occur to our senses. It corresponds to the explanatory stage of a science where data are gathered, grouped together, and named. The occurrents, the "facts," may be clearly given to the senses, so that their qualities

[13] See R. Harre, *An Introduction to the Logic of the Sciences* (London, Macmillan, 1960), pp. 4–8.

may be immediately noted, or we may utilize instruments, devices for producing an occurrent. Our concern may then be with the needle on a dial or the image seen in a microscope. By experimentation we may place an occurrent in a situation in which it would not occur without our intervention.[14] (We do more than merely record sense impressions, however, for we conceptualize what is given to us by the senses.)

Our description of what is the case is not the same as an explanation as to why something is the case. The distinction between description and explanation may be relative and for the sake of convenience, but to describe something is not ordinarily identical with explaining something.

One of the basic aims of physical science is to give adequate descriptions of extended objects having general properties and structures. Such objects are built up of component parts which may themselves be described. Our scientific descriptions aim at specifying the structure of extended objects by describing the arrangement and connections of their parts. Our descriptions specify the observable properties of things by utilizing descriptive predicates. When possible, the property selected is quantified, expressed as a cardinal number, and assigned a unit of measure. The expression "is hot," for example, may be replaced by "has a temperature of $x°C$." [15] *Logic studies how such predicates can be assigned to a subject.*

Our explanations answer the question "why?" Different sorts of answers are relevant in different contexts. In our ordinary experience we may describe such individual facts as follows: "This is water." "This is being heated." "This boils." When we describe in this manner, we state what we see. But if we ask, "Why does this boil?" and answer "Because it's heated," we then offer an explanation of what is before us. Actually the very success of science is in part due to the repeated asking of the question "Why?" By asking "Why?", theories are generated to explain the facts. Science begins with observed facts and ends with observed facts, but in between it offers theoretical explanations and makes deductions and predictions enabling the scientist to check his theories with observed facts. *Logic*

[14] See A. Cornelius Benjamin, *The Logical Structure of Science* (London, Kegan Paul, Trench, Trubner, 1936), pp. 267–289.

[15] See Harre, *op. cit.*, pp. 43–49.

provides the scientist with the valid forms in which he can make his deductions.

3.8   *The role of deduction in scientific explanation*

As previously stated, the scientific method is primarily the application of logic to a given subject matter. We combine our concepts into propositions when we describe in science, and we combine propositions into arguments when we explain in science. There are different kinds of explanations. The *deductive model* has the form of a deductive argument. The fact to be explained is the logical conclusion of the explanatory premises. To ask "Why is the sum of any number of consecutive odd integers beginning with one always a perfect square?" leads to a deductive explanation. Deductive explanations are not limited to propositions of mathematics; they may be given of individual events, of historical facts, and in terms of general law like statements.[16]

To explain an individual event, it is necessary to formulate at least one universal premise which asserts an invariable connection between certain properties. Such a *universal law,* together with singular statements asserting that given objects have certain properties or have occurred under specific conditions, makes a deductive explanation possible.

To explain why a stone falls when dropped, we must already be in possession of a well-established general theory; namely, that whatever is heavier than air falls when unsupported. Accepting this generalization as a law, together with the fact that this stone is heavier than air, it is clearly deducible that this stone falls when dropped.

The repeated asking of the question "Why?" generates a hierarchy of explanations. By asking "Why?", Newton derived an improved law of planetary motion and constructed a theory which explained Kepler's three laws describing the motion of planets, Galileo's law of free fall, and the law of the tides. Einstein's general theory of relativity enabled him to deduce not only Newton's laws but laws concerning the motion of rays of light. By continuing the process of explanation, an ever wider application is given to scientific

---

[16] Nagel, *op. cit.,* pp. 16–21.

theories, and greater accuracy is attained.[17] *The study of the various forms of deduction is an integral part of logic.*

4. Summary

In this chapter we have noted the scientific nature of logic and seen that it is indispensable to the other sciences. We have observed that while the science of logic does not provide factual information in any field other than logic, logic is indispensable to every field. The scientific character of logic, its first principles (the laws of non-contradiction, excluded middle, and identity), its subject matter (concepts, propositions, and arguments), its continuity with the past and systematic character, as well as its theoretical and practical aspects, have been noted. Special attention has been given to the role of logic in the other fields of knowledge. Our examination of the sciences disclosed something of their nature: that they develop by abstraction, by the formation of concepts, of various kinds of propositions, and of arguments.

It has become evident that the subject matter of logic is concepts, propositions, and arguments. The perspective in terms of which the logician views his subject—the logical point of view—will become evident in the remainder of the book.

EXERCISES

Part I

1. In what sense does logic have a subject matter of its own?
2. How does logic differ from mathematics?
3. What is meant by saying that logic is a normative science?
4. Why is it impossible to demonstrate the first principles of logic?
5. Why are the first principles of logic more than mental constructs?
6. What is the subject matter of logic?
7. Does every science have a theoretical or practical aspect? In what sense is logic practical?
8. What different uses does the word *science* have?

[17] John G. Kemeny, *A Philosopher Looks at Science* (New York, D. Van Nostrand, 1959), pp. 167–169.

9. Can science dispense with philosophy? If so, how? If not, why not?
10. What role does logic fulfill with respect to the sciences?
11. Can science dispense with presuppositions?
12. How many different uses of the word *fact* can you distingush?
13. What is the difference between description and explanation?
14. Why is the study of logic important?

Part II

Test your skill in using logic. Be sure to give reasons in support of your answers.

1. *Given:* Either the queen will not punish the prince or if war is not inevitable, then the prince's lover will not be jealous; but if the jealousy of the prince's lover implies that war is inevitable, the king will be angry, and if the queen's punishing the prince implies that the king is angry, then the king is bald, but he's not bald.
   a. Will the queen punish the prince?
   b. Will the king be angry?

2. *Given:* Albert, Bill, Charlie, and David are storekeepers and that either Albert or Bill must go shopping every day, but never on the same day, and that when Albert stays home, Charlie always goes shopping, and when Bill stays home, David always goes shopping.
   a. Can David stay home when Charlie stays home?
   b. When David stays home, does Charlie go shopping?
   c. If Bill goes shopping, can Charlie stay home?
   d. If David does not go shopping, can Albert still go shopping?

3. *Given:* A hunter shot either a daddy bear or a mother bear, and not both. If he shot the daddy bear then he did not shoot either a black bear or a red bear, and if he shot a mommy bear then he did not shoot a teddy bear. But he shot a teddy bear.
   a. Did he shoot a mommy bear?
   b. Did he shoot a daddy bear?
   c. Did he shoot a black bear?
   d. Did he shoot a red bear?

4. *Given:* Five dogs—a cocker, a poodle, a shepherd, a boxer, and a dachshund—were entered in a show. The first letter of the names of their owners, Smith, Brown, Davis, Paul, and Corn, did not correspond to the first letter of the breed name of their dogs. The dogs of the two owners that were neighbors did not win any prize that day. The three other dogs all placed first in their division. The shepherd was lighter than the boxer and the poodle. The dogs that belonged to Mr. Corn and to Mr. Davis were smaller than any of the others. Mr. Paul, the owner of the shepherd, had never previously met anyone who was at the show before. The man that owned the boxer, the only man from out of town, had previously met the owner of the poodle. Who owned each dog?

5. *Given:* On a given night the Yankee Conference title is at stake. To win the conference, Connecticut must beat Maine. Judging from past performances, if Maine loses, Vermont will certainly beat New Hampshire, and assuming that New Hampshire loses, Rhode Island will undoubtedly defeat Massachusetts. A Yankee Conference team never loses at home unless its opponent averages over 6 ft. 6 in., and Rhode Island is well under that. And unfortunately for Rhody fans, Massachusetts is playing at home.
    a. Will Vermont beat New Hampshire?
    b. Will Maine lose to Vermont?
    c. Will Connecticut win the title?
    d. If Connecticut does not win the title, can you determine who does?

6. *Given:* Imagine that Penn State, Boston College, Utah, N.Y.U., Providence College, and Connecticut were engaged in a three-round elimination tournament. Although the team from the Far West did not win the final round or play in the second, it did defeat its opponent in the first round. Boston and Providence could not both win in the first round. Boston never played Penn State. The team that won the final round beat Connecticut in the first round and Boston in the second.
    a. Who won the tournament?
    b. Who played with whom in each round?

7. *Given:* Three Vietnamese were brought to an interrogation center to determine whether they were members of the Viet Cong. The first prisoner spoke a dialect unintelligible to the interrogator, but known to the other two prisoners. When questioned about the first prisoner's testimony, the second prisoner said that the first prisoner denied that he belonged to the Viet Cong. The third prisoner, who was standing by, then testified that the first prisoner really was a Viet Cong. On the assumption that the Viet Cong always lie and the South Vietnamese tell the truth, what can you determine about the identity of the prisoners?

8. *Given:* Three Secret Agents, 0007, 0008, and 0009, were to be executed by a firing squad on the orders of SMOOH. The prisoners were blindfolded. To protect their heads from the sun, they were to be given hats. Three of the hats customarily used were green and two were black. When the hats were placed on the prisoners' heads, none of them could see the color of any of the hats. To add to their torment, they were promised release if they could guess the color of their own hat. By loosening the blindfold, the first prisoner, 0007, managed to see the color of the hats of 0008 and 0009. Agent 0008 only managed to get a glimpse of the hat on the head of 0009. He could not see the hat of 0007. Poor agent 0009 could not loosen his blindfold at all. Can 0009 tell the color of his own hat if 0007 and 0008 could not? If so, how?

9. WE SPY! *Given:* Once upon a time GALAXIE, ZOWIE, and SMERSH were involved in spying and counterspying. Our investigation thus far has disclosed that the SMERSH agent works for the Russians. And we know that if the agent of SMERSH works for the Russians, he must be against China. It is impossible to be against China and not to be the agent who is seeking to prevent China from destroying the world's electric power. If the agent involved is seeking to prevent China from destroying the world's electric power, he must be 0007, who is known to be an agent of GALAXIE. If the SMERSH agent who works for the Russians is 0007, then either 0009 was assassinated or 0007 is working for ZOWIE. Our problem is that we know that the death of 0009 was accidental. Whom is 0007 working for?

10. *Given:* Butch, Charlie, Duty Dan, Edie, and the Fink were sus
pects in a murder case. We know that no one could have com
mitted the crime unless he knew the victim. If the Fink com
mitted the crime, Butch helped, too, but if Butch helpe
Charlie lied when he said he saw Butch leave by the side doo
And if the Fink is innocent, Butch did not know the victir
previously. Charlie did not lie when he said he saw Butch leav
by the side door. Moreover, Duty Dan really told the truth whe
he said that he, Duty Dan, only found the gun and did not ki
the victim; that is, he told the truth, unless the Fink is reall
guilty. We can be sure that if Duty Dan only found the gur
Edie did not know the victim previously. The victim arrive
at the scene of his murder shortly after the clock stopped i
the hallway. Who done it?

CHAPTER TWO

On Concepts

"Speak English!" said the Eaglet. "I don't know the meaning of half those long words, and, what's more, I don't believe you do either!"

Alice in Wonderland—LEWIS CARROLL

The subject matter of the science of logic can be divided into concepts, propositions, and arguments. The present chapter is concerned with the question "What is a concept?"

1. The Origin of Concepts

All knowledge begins in some kind of sense experience. Our five external senses are indispensable to the knowing process, but mere sensation alone is not sufficient for knowledge. A newborn infant may have normal senses, but can hardly be said to know. Our mind combines various sensations into a sense image of an object. By means of abstraction it then forms a general notion or concept of the nature or essence of the object. A concept is thus the result of asking *what something is*. A concept abstracts the notes or characteristics that are common to many particulars. To form a concept of a concept adequately it is first necessary to distinguish a concept from the word or words which we utilize to express our concepts. This leads us to the question: "What is a word?"

2. What Is a Word?

The question "What is a word?" is indeed very odd, since words are used in the very asking. To use a word is to know what a word is. *Fish, fools, cabbages, snails, and, kings, relative, concrete, abstract* —all are words; even *word* is a word. Word lists are helpful, and the explication of a meaning of a word increases our understanding of what a word is. *Words are plastic means of communication;* that is, a single word serves many purposes, has many meanings, none of which are fixed or unchanging. Without words, desires could not be expressed or thoughts made known; rather, without words, we would have no thoughts; feelings, yes, but ideas, no. Grunts, groans, and gestures neither fully describe what we feel nor transmit what we have learned. Words are not simply useful but indispensable.

It is impossible to imagine what our experience would be like if it lacked a linguistic aspect; the very imagining utilizes words. Try to think without words. Can you? Without words we would be lost within the murky walls of blind sensations, unable to advise and consent, incapable of offering suggestions or making amends. We can describe, make appraisals, prescribe the remedy, convey our wishes, give information, and call something by name because we have words, prize possessions of which we are scarcely aware.

Words are indispensable means of communication, and yet in a sense they are arbitrary and artificial, since there is no necessary connection between the word we use and the thing we would describe—between the sounds that we speak or the lines that we write and the meaning that we would convey, the idea that we would impart. Words are simply what they are: *artificial signs* constructed haphazardly or with painstaking care, invented to meet a new situation or to describe what is old; words are transformed consciously or unconsciously, are subject to gradual or sudden change and shifts in meaning, initiated by people at different times and places.

Unlike smoke, which is ordinarily a natural sign of fire, words are *material, artificial signs:* material, in that they can be heard or seen, spoken or written; artificial, in that they are invented; signs, because they represent something, stand for something, are substitutes, not he real thing. Words are signs of things thought of, of concepts, of the operations of thinking, or of other words.

Although written differently in variant characters and in distinctive languages, words are always signs with an intelligible meaning, not just noises or scratches on paper; words mean something to someone. To share meanings, to hold the meanings of the same marks or sounds in common, is to share a language, a network of meanings. As the building blocks of a language and the means of conveying meanings, words are the simplest units of communication that declare intentions and point to things by combining into meaningful expressions, phrases, sentences, and paragraphs. Words combine into a crisscross of interconnected, interrelated patterns of meaning, governed by a common usage, thereby forming a given language. To be meaningful, a word must represent things, express action, stand for ideas or concepts, or serve a function in modifying the meaning of other words.

Words mean what we want them to mean, neither more nor less; the question is who is the master, for with practice even terrible-tempered verbs can be humbled and made as submissive as adjectives without paying them extra.

> 'Twas brillig, and the slithy toves
>   Did gyre and gimble in the wabe:
> All mimsy were the borogoves,
>   And the mome raths outgrabe.

Through the Looking Glass—LEWIS CARROLL

Here are many "hard words" (to quote Humpty Dumpty) which can be given a meaning, but until you realize that "brillig" means four o'clock in the afternoon, "slithy" means lithe and slimy, "toves" are like badgers, lizards, and corkscrews, except that they live on cheese and nest under sundials—until such combinations of letters are given a meaning, they are unintelligible and make no sense, are nonsensical; they are not words at all—at least, not ordinary English words. Thus, while words are artificial signs, arbitrarily constructed, meaning what we want them to mean, once they are chosen they acquire a conventional meaning which must be respected if genuine communication is to take place.

Words take on a meaning by the way they are used within a language. To understand the meaning of a word is to understand how it is used within a given context. The same combination of letters may have more than one meaning. The three-letter word *day* may mean twenty-four hours, a period of daylight, an epoch of indefinite length; or it may simply be used as a literary device to order or arrange events in a logical sequence. The interpretation of the meaning of a word requires the understanding of the intention of the writer or speaker. What is meant is frequently unintelligible and often misunderstood.

Words have a history: they come into being, are used for a while, are frequently modified by their usage, and subsequently may be discarded. Words or groups of words constitute unitary meanings and function as terms which designate or stand for a referent whether real or imaginary, actual or fictional, contingent or necessary, possible or impossible. A single word or a complex linguistic expression, such as a descriptive phrase, may designate an object, a class of objects, a condition, a series of events, or relations between objects or events. A word or combination of words may refer to a word, a concept, an object, or a concrete natural thing. Certain words—*categorematic* words—can stand for the subject or the predicate of a proposition; others—*syncategorematic* words—order, connect, and modify categorematic words. *Concrete* words refer to or name persons or things that exist in a certain way; *abstract* words refer to qualities, properties, or relations between things or persons. When a word or words are utilized as the subject or the predicate of a proposition, they function as *terms;* they then serve as the vehicle by which we express our concepts. Concrete words are utilized to stand for things. That the same combination of letters may have a diversity of meanings is the source of much confusion and invalid reasoning. The disputes that often arise as a result of such diversity can frequently be eliminated by means of adequate definitions; however, before treating the latter, it is necessary to distinguish between a word and a concept.

3. Words and Concepts

There is something puzzling about the question "What is a concept?" It looks like the question "What is a word?", but in answer to the latter, examples can be listed and descriptions given in terms of such physical qualities as length and sound. The word *green,* for example, is a five-letter English word, but how long is a concept of green? Is a concept of green, green? The very question is a confusing source of bewilderment, avoided only by those in possession of an adequate concept of a concept; for concepts, unlike words, are not artificial material signs describable in terms of a sound or marks on paper. Concepts are signs; they are the ideas or notions that we have after we have answered a *what* question such as "What is a word?" From our discussion you should now understand that the word *word* denotes or refers to kinds of individual things that are words and connotes what such individual words have in common that causes us to group them together in our mind. The word *word* is a sign of a concept. In a different language other words (such as *woord* in Dutch, *mot* in French, *logos* in Greek) stand for the same concept, having the same meaning in spite of variant spelling. A concept is not the same as a word. To know what the word *word* means is to form a concept of a word. The words *word, mot, woord,* and *logos* stand for the many individual examples, found in dictionaries and elsewhere constituting an indispensable part of human experience by serving as artificial signs, employed as the simplest intelligible means of communication.

As an answer to the question "What is it?", a concept is an instrument which is indispensable to theoretical knowledge and ordinary experience. Not only do we form a concept of words and of things that caw, coo, moo, roar, scream, and shriek but we can also form a concept of shrieking and screaming. At the moment we are trying to form an adequate concept of what a concept is. Without this ability, without this logical aspect of experience, knowledge and human life would be impossible. It could not even be known that we did not know; we would not be self-consciously aware of God, the world, and ourselves. Concepts point to aspects of our world, enabling us to know its diversity by providing the means of differentiating between tables and trees, plants and stones, monkeys and millionaires. The ability to form concepts is an indispensable and natural part of us, a part of being human. Concepts are the mental furniture of the mind, not of the living room. A concept of hot or cold neither warms nor chills; an idea of a mad dog does not bite;

nor need there be giant Dragmesteeru monsters, with a head at each end, simply because we can name them and conceive of them. Because something can be thought of as actually existing in no way implies its nonmental existence. It makes no sense to ask whether concepts are true or false. As adequate or inadequate tools, enabling us to live and know our world, concepts may be precise or vague, sufficient or insufficient for the task of understanding the mode and manner of what we experience.

Concepts are the instruments by means of which we comprehend what things are. Our concepts are more than the words used to express them, and yet concepts can hardly be imagined to exist except in our heads. My idea or concept of a horse is not running around in my head; and yet without some concept of a horse, we simply would not *know* what horses are.

4. The Extension and Intension of Concepts

Every concept that we have may be approached from two perspectives or aspects. We may think of the kinds of things that fall within the scope of our idea, with its *extension,* or *denotation,* or we may think of the characteristics common to such things, with its *intension* or *connotation.* My concept of a horse refers to or denotes each and every concrete horse, of every kind and possible description, no matter when and where it lives, regardless of its size, shape, color, and breeding. But what does a large draft horse pulling Budweiser have in common with the thoroughbred that wins the daily double? What is a horse, anyway? To know the nature of horses, to know what they are, it is necessary to shift from the extension of our concept of a horse to its intension, to its connotation. Here we consider the common nature of individual horses: that they are animals serviceable to man, of a certain anatomical and genetic structure, with a certain history and importance. Here we attempt to ascertain the class of things to which horses belong and how they differ from other members of the same class, from other animals. Here we seek to determine their properties, the qualities they have because of what they are. In short, we seek to comprehend, to understand, what horses are by abstracting what is essential to them and by disregarding such an accidental quality as color. To be four-legged is a natural, normal property of being a horse, but to be white is accidental.

Every concept that we form has these two aspects. Our concept of a word, for example, has an extension or denotation and an intension or connotation. The extension or denotation of our concept of a word includes or designates the millions of concrete examples partially listed in the various language dictionaries. The extension of the concept *word* has many particular members; it designates what can be found within human experience in its linguistic aspect. Words, the concrete things, are not imaginary, nor are they impossibilities; words are actualities. While it is practically impossible to enumerate every member within the extension of our concept of a word, we can refer to or designate every member. By using the term *word* in its *distributive sense,* each and every existing word, whether spoken or written, is designated or denoted. The extension of our concept of a word can be partially enumerated, divided, classified, and arranged in groups.

Thus, the intension of a concept, sometimes referred to as its connotation or comprehension, lists the set of traits or characteristics that something must have if a certain name is to apply to it. The intension of a term includes the essential properties, constituent notes, or marks of whatever is denoted by the concept in question. The extension of a concept refers to its range of application, to the classes, types, and individuals referred to, denoted, or designated by a concept, whereas the intension refers to the common and peculiar characteristics shared by whatever falls within the extension. Concepts often refer to what things are, to their qualities, to where they are, to what they are doing and how they are acting.

The intension or connotation of a concept states what is common and essential to each and every member included within the extension. To state that *words mean material artificial signs serving as the simplest intelligible means of communication* is to give a conceptual or connotative definition of our concept of words.

Notice that there is an inverse variation between the intension and the extension of concepts. When our intension increases, the extension decreases, and vice versa. The more we say, the fewer things we talk about. The extension of the concept *words* is greater than the extension of *words currently in use,* and by adding the further qualification *technical English words currently in use* to our concept *words,* the new concept, namely, *technical English words currently in use,* designates still fewer actual words. For this principle to hold, a genuine qualification must be added; that is, there must be a genuine variation in the intension of the term in question, and the extension of the term cannot be empty, but must have members in some mode of possible existence.

Consider, for example, the following terms:

a. Books on the history of ancient philosophy, translated into English, written before Aristotle.

b. Books on the history of philosophy.

c. Books on the history of ancient philosophy, written before Aristotle, translated into English, written by Plato.

d. Books.

e. Philosophy books.

f. Books on the history of ancient philosophy, translated into English.

i. Books on the history of philosophy, translated into English.

When they are rearranged in order of their increasing intension and decreasing extension, they need to be written in the following sequence:

d. Books.

e. Philosophy books.

b. Books on the history of philosophy.

i. Books on the history of philosophy, translated into English.

f. Books on the history of ancient philosophy, translated into English.

a. Books on the history of ancient philosophy, translated into English, written before Aristotle.

c. Books on the history of ancient philosophy, written before Aristotle, translated into English, written by Plato.

Thus we see that although concepts have no real and independent existence of their own, they do enable us to know the various aspects of the world, at least to the extent that it is knowable. It is not necessary to choose between knowing everything and knowing nothing, between omniscience and *omni-ignorance;* for we are able to know much about many things without knowing everything about anything. We know where we live and how to get there. Most of us know who our father was.

5. *The Categories*

Our concepts are natural to us; they are instruments by which we know. To express them we utilize *terms,* or verbal means of expressing what we know through concepts. The terms that we utilize are made up of words. A simple term—for example, *dog, building, government*—is made up of a single word. Complex terms are constituted by a combination of words; for instance, "The red books on the third shelf" is a complex term, standing for a single concept. Terms, whether simple or complex, can be used as the subject or the predicate of a proposition. From the point of view of what a term represents, terms may be arranged in certain categories.[1]

Terms may be utilized to stand for different kinds of individual things or structural unities. The same individual thing can be described from different perspectives. We can speak of it in terms of its *quantity:* that it is one, that it is five feet tall or weighs one hundred pounds. We can describe things in terms of certain *qualities:* that they are white and hard. Such qualitative terms may be restricted to physical and spatial concepts, as in the case of stones, for example, or they may need to be widened to include biological concepts, in the case of plants, or psychological concepts, in the case of animals. A description of a human being requires the inclusion of additional qualities. A man can be described as reasoning, as forming history, as using language, as being social; as engaging in economic transactions, making works of art, formulating laws, making moral judgments, and entertaining religious beliefs. A diversity of terms is required to express our concepts about man, for a human being functions potentially in every sphere or aspect of experience; to wit, the numerical, spatial, physical, biotic, psychical, analytic, historical, linguistic, social, economic, aesthetic, juridical, ethical, and religious.

In all such spheres or modes of experience, a thing is either active

---

[1] Traditionally the categories usually referred to substance, quantity, quality, relation, place, time, position, state, action, or affection.

or acted upon. Certain stones, for example, are considered precious and are prized for their value. The stone is passive; it is man that is *active*. Temporal and spatial concepts can also be applied to things and events, for we can always ask *where* something is and *when* did an event occur. The relationship between things can also be expressed. To state that John is superior to Bill in a particular subject is to express a relation between John and Bill. In short, we think about different kinds of things: their quantity, their qualities or modes of existing, how they are related to each other, what they are doing or what is being done to them, and the time and place of an event.

The totality of human experience need not be reduced to a simple list of categories. Nevertheless, it is helpful to note what kind of thing something is. Failure to pay attention to the proper use of categories can result in category mistakes. We note different kinds of things by describing their mode of existence.

Our first question is usually "What is it?" Are we talking about a concrete thing? What kind of thing? What can we say about it? Is it something physical? If it is physical, we can utilize the category of *quantity* and ask, "How big is it? How much does it weigh?" Does it make sense to ask, "How heavy is love?" Metaphorically, a person's heart may be filled with joy or sadness, but emotional states require psychological terms that cannot be measured or weighed in the same manner as wheat on a scale.

5.1   The category of quantity

The following propositions illustrate the category of quantity.

1. The truck *weighs two tons*.
2. The crate *is six feet tall*.

Courage will not mend a wound, simply because courage is not a physical thing, but is rather a moral concept. Courage or cowardice describes in moral terms certain qualities of a person. Not everything can be described in quantitative terms.

5.2   The category of quality

The category of quality is needed to indicate certain habits or dispositions that a person may have. To say that a person is courageous describes a moral habit enabling us to predict that under certain conditions he will overcome his fear and act in a certain way. To describe habits and predispositions to act in a certain way—to describe capacities and powers, sense qualities, figures and shapes— is to refer to the quality of a thing or an event. The following propositions illustrate the category of quality.

1. The house is *square*.
2. The spaghetti is *spicy*.
3. John is extremely *intelligent*.
4. This undertaking is *dangerous*.
5. A bully is a *coward*.

5.3 The category of relation

The category of relation expresses the way two things refer to each other. Examples of terms indicating relations are: greater than, superior to, more beautiful than. The following propositions illustrate the category of relation:

1. The music of Beethoven is *superior to* the songs of the Beatles.
2. New York is *larger than* Philadelphia.
3. Karate masters are *more dangerous than* professional boxers.

5.4 The category of action

The category of action expresses the way in which something behaves; it answers the questions "What is going on?" "What is something or someone doing?" For example:

1. John is *singing*.
2. The dog is *barking*.
3. The basketball player is *shooting*.

5.5 The category of passion

The category of passion expresses the way something or someone is being acted upon. For example:

1. The pedestrian *was struck by a car*.
2. The tree *was struck by lightning*.
3. The village *was bombed*.

5.6 The category of time

The category of time expresses the order of past, present, or future. It answers the question "When did it happen?" For example:

1. The dance was *yesterday.*
2. The meeting is *at three o'clock.*

5.7   *The category of space*

The category of space answers the question "Where is something?" Examples:

1. John is *in Chicago.*
2. My car is *in the parking lot.*

Our list is by no means exhaustive; partial as it is, an awareness of the categories will prove useful in the formulation of definitions and in the classification and division of a subject matter. The categories we have mentioned are simply universal terms that can be applied to many different kinds of things.

6. *Equivocal, Univocal, and Analogical Use of Terms*

6.1   *Equivocal use of terms*

Terms can vary in their meaning as they are used in a different way. The same term may stand for different things. Terms are used *equivocally* when the same term is used to refer to different things. We may assign a common name to things that are quite different. The term *mug,* for example, may bring to mind a large glass used by beer drinkers, or it may refer to a rather tough-looking character in the police line-up. To use terms ambiguously is to employ the same word or combination of words to refer to two or more unrelated classes of objects. It is simply an accident of language that the same linguistic expressions are used to refer to different things and to different concepts. Examples of equivocal usage:

1. The *bat* flew out of the cave.
2. The baseball player picked up the *bat.*
3. Every lunatic has *bats* in his belfry.
4. King George was a *ruler.*
5. A *ruler* is twelve inches.
6. Children play in the *yard.*
7. A *yard* is thirty-six inches.

We shall subsequently note that much confusion results from such equivocal usage. Genuine agreement or disagreement can only occur when two people are referring to the same thing.

6.2   Univocal use of terms

A term is used *univocally* when applied to two or more objects in the same way. To call a man a sentient being and an ox a sentient being utilizes the expression *sentient being* in a univocal sense, for both men and oxen are subject to the same physical and biological principles. To describe a Great Dane and a Dachshund by the term *dog* employs the term *dog* in the same way. In spite of accidental differences in size and shape, what is meant by being a dog would be equally applicable to both. More than a name is shared. Examples of univocal usage:

1. A man is *human.*
2. A woman is *human.*
3. Dogs are *animals.*
4. Cats are *animals.*

6.3   Analogical use of terms

A third use of terms is frequently overlooked. The same term may be used to refer to concepts that are not exactly the same, but are not wholly unrelated. To use a term in such a manner is to use it *analogously.* To state that John is healthy and exercise is healthy uses the term *healthy* in a different, yet related, sense. In the case of John, the term refers to a quality of John's being; that is, he enjoys health, is in a state of physical well-being, free from illness. Exercise is conducive to such a state, so it, too, is healthy. To say John has a healthy complexion means that his complexion is a sign of health in John. To say that exercise is healthy means that exercise induces health in John or in someone else. An analogy may also hold between two beings because of a relation that each holds to something else.[2] A complexion and a summer resort can both be said to be healthy, since the term *healthy* can be referred to human beings to whom the predicate healthy properly belongs.

[2] See E. L. Mascall, *Existence and Analogy* (London, Longmans, Green, 1949), pp. 101–121.

The theologian, for example, uses terms analogously when he speaks about God and about man.[3] The basis of the analogy resides in a relation that the one allegedly bears to the other. To say God is good and Moses is good intends to say that God has goodness in a way that is necessary in order to produce goodness in His creatures. To say that Moses is good is to ascribe certain moral qualities to Moses.

Still another analogical use of terms, again drawn from the field of theology, is the analogy of proportionality.[4] Here the *analogue* (the characteristic under consideration) is held to be in each of the *analogates* (the things being compared) in a mode determined by the nature of the analogate. For example, life (the analogue) applied to cabbages (an analogate), to elephants (an analogate), to man (an analogate), and to God (an analogate) asserts that a cabbage has life in a mode proper to the nature of a cabbage, that an elephant has life in a mode proper to the nature of an elephant, that a man has life in a mode proper to the nature of man, that God has life in a mode proper to the nature of God.

Expressed in a quasi-mathematical form:

$$\frac{life\ of\ cabbage}{essence\ of\ a\ cabbage} = \frac{life\ of\ an\ elephant}{essence\ of\ an\ elephant}$$

$$\frac{life\ of\ man}{essence\ of\ man} = \frac{life\ of\ God}{essence\ of\ God}$$

The word *life* is used here in a way that is not wholly the same nor wholly different. In each instance there is a shift in meaning proportionate to the difference between cabbages, elephants, man, and God.

A further analogical use of terms is metaphorical. To call a lion the king of the beasts does not assert his literal kingship, but it does suggest a relationship of supremacy over other animals not totally different from that of a monarch over his subjects.

[3] *Ibid.*, p. 102.

[4] Whether what the theologian says is true or false is not our present concern. The fact is that most theologians recognize that many of their statements about God are expressed in language taken from ordinary experience and cannot be understood literally. The notion of analogy has, therefore, been treated extensively by those engaged in the theological enterprise.

7. *The Universal, Particular, and Singular Use of Terms*

The failure to distinguish carefully whether a term is used univocally, equivocally, or analogically is not the only way that we become confused. As the outward signs of concepts, terms stand for what we understand. Frequently, our use of language does not make our meaning clear. Each concept has an extension as well as an intension.

At times we may wish to refer to every single individual that falls within the extension of our concept. For example, a person may be talking about politicians. His concept of what it means to be a politician may be adequate, but it may not be clear as to whether the term *politician* refers to each and every individual coming within the scope of our concept of a politician. When a term is used to refer to every single member of the extension of a concept, it is used in a *universal* or *distributive* sense. When it is used to refer to at least one but not every member of the extension of a concept, it is used in a *particular* or *undistributed* sense. Often we can readily ascertain whether a term is *distributed* (used universally) or *undistributed* (used particularly). Certain words act as *quantifiers;* that is, they tell us whether reference is to each and every member of the extension of a concept or to some of them. Terms are used in a distributed or universal sense when they are modified by such words as *every, each, all.* Examples:

> All dogs
> Each person
> Everyone

Terms are used in an undistributed sense when they are modified by such words as *some, many, a few.* Examples:

> Some dogs
> Many people
> A few doctors

The absence of any clear indication of whether a term is used in a universal or in a particular sense makes communication difficult at times.

In addition to being used universally or particularly, a term may be used to refer to a single person, a single event, a single object, or a single place. Such terms are *singular*.[5] Examples:

> George Washington
> The First World War
> New York City

Remember that a term is either a word or combination of words used as the subject or predicate of a proposition. We shall subsequently need to pay careful attention to their usage as they occur in propositions.

8. Collective and Divisive Use of Terms

At this point it is necessary to note two more ways that terms are used: *collectively* or *divisively*. A term is used *collectively* when reference is being made to a given subject considered as a whole, as a unit or group, without referring to each member falling within the extension of the subject. For example, to assert "Man is rational" ascribes rationality to man in a collective sense. It implies that man as such, as an aggregate, as a whole, is capable of reasoning. It does not mean that each and every individual human being is capable of reasoning. There are idiots. To state that the audience cheered does not necessarily mean that each individual cheered, but the group as a whole, the audience in a collective sense, cheered.

To use a term *divisively*, however, is to predicate something about each member of the subject under consideration. Predication is here made of a subject in its distributed sense. To assert "The members of the team weigh over two hundred pounds" ascribes a certain weight to each and every member of the team. The failure to note this distinction may lead to faulty reasoning. Because a Rolls-Royce is an expensive car, it does not follow that each and every part of a Rolls-Royce is expensive.

In summary, we have seen that concepts are the first instruments by which we come to "know" and that we utilize a word or a combination of words to express our concepts. Such words or terms, consid-

---

[5] For practical purposes, we shall subsequently treat singular terms as universals.

ered from the point of view of what they represent, can be arranged in certain categories. Considered from the point of view of their usage, they may be used univocally, equivocally, analogically. Terms may also be used in a universal, particular, or singular sense; and they may be used collectively or divisively. From a practical point of view, one of the first tasks of the logician is to indicate clearly the meaning of a term and the sense in which it is being used. To this end we shall now direct our attention.

EXERCISES

Part I

1. How do we form concepts?
2. Are words indispensable to thought?
3. What is meant by saying words are artificial signs?
4. What is a concept?
5. Distinguish carefully between the extension and intension of a concept.
6. Illustrate what is meant by saying that there is an inverse variation between the intension and extension of concepts.
7. What is the difference between a concept and a term?
8. What is meant by the categories?
9. What is the difference between the univocal, equivocal, and analogical use of terms? Illustrate.
10. Distinguish carefully the universal, particular, and singular use of terms. Illustrate.
11. What is meant by saying a term is used in a distributed or undistributed sense?
12. Distinguish the collective and divisive use of terms. Illustrate.

Part II

To which categories do the italicized terms belong?

1. The stove is *next to the window.*
2. Students are *intelligent.*
3. The meeting is *at 3:30.*
4. Lions are *vicious.*
5. The drawing was *square.*
6. The examination was *difficult.*

7. The furniture was *old*.
8. The horse *jumped* over the fence.
9. The roses are *white*.
10. The wedding was *formal*.
11. The patient was *run over*.
12. The plane *landed*.
13. The freight *weighed 1,600 lbs.*
14. Man of War is *the father of many horses.*
15. The soldier was *courageous*.
16. The tea is *hot*.
17. Cadillacs are *expensive*.
18. The music is *sad*.
19. The legislation is *progressive*.
20. Alcohol is *poisonous*.

Part III

Rearrange the following groups of terms in the order of their increasing intension and decreasing extension.

1. *a.* Animals now living.
   b. Animals now in Europe which are domestic.
   c. Animals now living in Europe.
   d. Animals.
2. *a.* Automobiles built in 1960 in U.S. by General Motors.
   b. Automobiles built in 1960.
   c. Automobiles built in 1960 in U.S. by General Motors costing over $3,000.
   d. Automobiles built in 1960 in U.S.
   e. Automobiles.
3. *a.* European nations with population over 12 million.
   b. Nations.
   c. European nations.
   d. European nations with population over 12 million under Communism.
4. *a.* American authors writing fiction.
   b. Authors.
   c. American authors writing fiction professionally.
   d. American authors.

5. *a.* Advocates of unilateral disarmament in the United States.
   b. Advocates of disarmament.
   c. Advocates of unilateral disarmament.
   d. Advocates of unilateral disarmament in the United States residing in Chicago.

Part IV

Determine whether the italicized terms are used equivocally, univocally, or analogically.

1. *Nut,* as something to eat; as a disparaging term.
2. *Bad,* applied to man; applied to animals.
3. *Bright,* applied to a light; applied to a person.
4. *Cold,* applied to a day of the week; applied to a person.
5. *Good,* applied to man; applied to God.
6. *Tricky,* applied to a lock; applied to a person.
7. *Difficult,* applied to an exam; applied to a person.
8. *Animal,* applied to a dog; applied to a cat.
9. *Pen,* applied to enclosure; applied to a writing instrument.
10. *Sucker,* applied to fish; applied to a person.

CHAPTER THREE

On Definitions

"I know what you're thinking about," said Tweedledum; *"but it isn't so, nohow."*

"Contrariwise," continued Tweedledee, *"if it was so, it might be; and if it were so, it would be; but as it isn't, it ain't. That's logic."*

Through the Looking Glass—LEWIS CARROLL

1. The Predicables

To avoid confusion in our use of terms, it is helpful to arrange and order them in a systematic way. By defining what we mean and by classifying and distinguishing the kinds of things we are talking about, we are frequently able to apprehend our subject matter more simply. Before turning to the subject of division and definition, let us briefly note certain possible ways that the predicate term can be related to a subject term. A concept has a single meaning; and yet it applies to many particular things or instances. In this sense it is a universal. Concepts may be related to each other in different ways. In a proposition the predicate states something about a subject. Suppose we begin by talking about an individual person.

What can we say about John? We could begin by noting that he is a student. There is, however, nothing in the nature of John which requires him to be a student. That he is a student happens to be the case. He might very well have been drafted and would then have been a soldier. His being a student is *accidental,* due to a variety of circumstances outside of his inner being. The facts that John is six feet tall, has brown hair, blue eyes, plays the guitar, studies logic, are *accidents.* Such accidental descriptions do not affect his being.

To express his complete nature or essence, we simply state what kind of a being John is. To what *species* does he belong? John is human; he is a man. But to what class of things does man belong? What is the *genus* of the species *man?* We previously noted that, with other beings, man is subject to physical, biological, and psychological laws. Man is a living, sentient organism. It is of his very nature to be such. But the fact that he has a body, is alive, and has feelings does not express the whole of his essence. Other beings also fall within the range of this description. There are certain distinguishing notes which differentiate a man from an animal: a man is capable of forming concepts, propositions, and arguments; he introduces changes in the historical process, constructs a language, freely forms social groups, exchanges commodities, enjoys beauty, makes laws, formulates moral judgments, and entertains religious beliefs. In short, there are *differentia* which set man apart from other living, feeling organisms. Because of what man is, he has certain *properties* which, although not of his essence, are necessarily connected with his essence. He has a sense of humor, for example, and frequently laughs.

In summary, then, there are different ways that we can talk about something. We can speak either about its essence or about what is nonessential to its nature. If we speak about the essence of something, either we can speak about its entire essence, in which case we state of what *species* it is, or we can speak of a part of its essence. If we take the latter course, we then place what we are talking about into a *genus* and state how the subject under consideration differs from other things within the same genus; that is, we note its *specific differences.* If we do not speak about the essence of a subject, we may refer to certain *properties* it has which are connected with its essence, or we may refer to certain characteristics accidental to its essence. The ways we can speak about a subject, in terms of species, genus, difference, properties, or accidents, are known as the *predicables.* The distinction we have just made is of practical significance in formulating certain kinds of definitions.

2. The Purpose of Definitions

The ambiguity and vagueness of terms frequently require that we state precisely how a word or expression is being used, that we set its definite boundaries and limitations and specify its meaning exactly. Definitions enable us to explain adequately the intension or meaning of a term as well as to identify its extension, although the members of the latter are seldom completely enumerated. By introducing new words and explaining old ones, we find that definitions increase our vocabulary; they inform, persuade, abbreviate, elaborate, clarify, and give the conventional usage of terms, redefining and renaming them, and they influence our attitudes. Whether a definition is adequate depends on its effectiveness in accomplishing the purpose for which it is intended, so that while a good or adequate definition is always intelligible and capable of teaching its recipient what was intended, whether a particular definition is adequate or inadequate is, nevertheless, a relative matter, depending on the given context in which it is formulated.

Certain definitions simply describe the conventional usage of a word; others propose that terms be used in a certain way; some give the meaning of a concept; while still others express propositions, and thus seek to describe certain states of affairs and specify that such and such is so and so.

By explaining and restricting the meaning of a term, adequate definitions provide a mastery over words, promote clarity of thought and precision of expression, and avoid platitudes, slogans, and clichés. To define a word requires that we state how it is to be used; to define a concept, we state what it means; to define a class of things, we state what they are.

Basically, definitions serve three distinct purposes. By establishing the relation between a word and its referent, the intended referent of a word is disclosed; by reference to the intension and extension of a concept, the meaning intended is explicated; and by stating what something is, the nature or essence of something is asserted to exist in a certain way. Definitions are thus of words, of concepts, and of actual states of affairs.

Words are arbitrary, artificial signs; however, *verbal definitions,* which purport to describe the way words are customarily used in a given language, report their usage either accurately or inaccurately. The adoption of the word *automobile* in English to refer to a self-propelled vehicle, commonly used as a means of ground transportation, is the result of an arbitrary conventional decision; however, any definition that purports to give the customary English usage of the word *automobile* by defining it as a jet-propelled vehicle capable of flying through the air at high speed simply fails to report its customary conventional usage, and in certain situations such a definition amounts to a false report. Of course, it is possible to propose that an old word be used in a different way by stipulating that when we use the word *automobile,* we shall refer to what everyone else calls by the word *airplane.* Such a procedure would hardly serve a useful function; nevertheless, when we wish to introduce new terminology or to remove ambiguity, such definitions are of importance.

3. Kinds of Definition

Definitions are of words, concepts, and actual states of affairs; that is, they are verbal, conceptual, and real. The type of definition to be employed depends on the situation.

3.1   Verbal definitions

Verbal or nominal definitions are concerned with the use of words in a given language. In learning a language, for example, a new word may be adequately defined in terms of other words synonymous to it. Such definitions frequently give the usage of a word either by actually pointing to examples of its referent or by mentioning such examples. Dictionaries describe the various ways that words are customarily used; however, old words may be used in new ways, and new words may be introduced by stipulation. *Stipulative* definitions are proposals or declarations of the way a word is to be used. Such definitions are nominal; they are either reports or resolutions concerning the use of words. They do not claim to analyze the essential nature of a referent and tell us what something is; rather they tell us how to use a word correctly in a given context. It is possible to offer an explanation of a word by simply stating that *paard* in Dutch means horse in English, and it is possible to stipulate that *Dragmesteeru* means a two-headed animal with a head at each end.

To introduce new words when they are not needed and to obliterate important distinctions by redefining old ones may be an effective means of spreading confusion, but it does not serve to enlighten. Nevertheless, when new vocabulary is needed because of new discoveries and when existing vocabulary is filled with ambiguities, stipulative definitions are extremely serviceable.

To formulate a verbal definition, what is to be defined is called the *definiendum,* and the words used to state the usage or meaning to be understood is called the *definiens.* At times definitions can be formed by stating ———— conventionally means ————, or simply by "We shall employ ———— to mean ————."

When verbal definitions are reports of usage, they are accurate or inaccurate. As artificial signs, words are arbitrary constructs; but the reports given about the way words are used may be complete or incomplete, accurate or inaccurate. Stipulative definitions, however, are neither true nor false, since the predicate "true" or "false" is inapplicable to a proposal of any kind. To decide to use a particular symbol or set of symbols to mean what is meant by another symbol or set of symbols may be wise or foolish, helpful or confusing, but not true or false. In short, a verbal definition is lexical, reporting what is meant by an expression at a certain time and place, in which case the report may be true or false; or it is stipulative in that it assigns a meaning to a word, in which case it is useful or confusing.

Pseudo-communication, a source of verbal disputes, a faulty reasoning due to ambiguity, arises when the word chosen by a speaker is erroneously understood to refer to a referent not originally intended by the speaker.

When the word or words in question are crucial to communication, when they are key words in a discussion or argument, they may give rise to verbal disputes and lead to genuine difficulties.

Imagine a situation in which Jack and Jill are not thinking of climbing a hill, but they are considering marriage instead.

Jack says, "Before we get married there are several things you ought to know. I shall never make a *lot of money,* I want a *large family,* and I am *quite religious.*"

Jill says, "That's fine, Jack; I've never had a *lot of money* any-

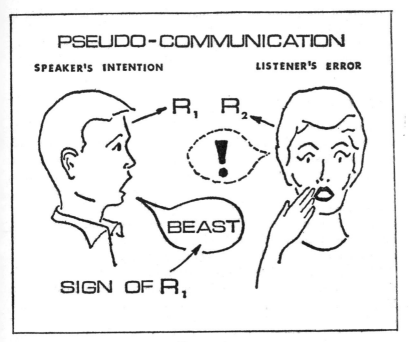

Figure 1.

way. I've always thought it would be nice to have a *large family,* and I'm *quite religious* too. We should get on very well together."

Suppose that after Jack and Jill are married they discover that when Jack used the expression a *lot of money* he meant more than $6,000 a year, by a *large family* he meant ten or twelve children, and by *quite religious* he meant that he went to church twice every Sunday. Jill, however, understood a *lot of money* to mean more than $25,000 a year; by a *large family* she meant four children; and by being *quite religious* she meant going to church at least once a month. Such confusion can be avoided if adequate definitions are given.

To resolve a verbal dispute, it is necessary to clarify the key words by stating precisely how certain terms are used to stand for different things or concepts.

Real disputes are not so readily resolved. For example, different concepts of the nature of man may arise from confusing what is essential to being human with what is simply an accident; and if, to be fully human, it is considered necessary to be a German Aryan, the resulting confusion may lead to the extermination of "sub-human" types.

3.2 Conceptual definitions

To define the usage of a word is to formulate a verbal definition, whereas to define the meaning of a concept is to give a conceptual definition. And since the meaning of a concept is disclosed under two aspects, the extensional and intensional or the denotative and connotative, there are also two basic types of conceptual definitions. The extensional or denotative definition wholly or partially enumerates, classifies, or divides the extension of a concept, whereas an intensional or connotative definition employs various techniques to explicate the intensional meaning of the concept.

3.21 Denotative definition. A denotative or extensional definition simply refers to the extension of a concept by indicating the kinds of thing which are designated or intended whenever the concept is brought to mind. Concepts as such are neither true nor false; they simply are. When what is understood or grasped by our concepts actually has a basis in the world that we experience, more than one person can conceive of the same individual things, so that when two or more adults of average intelligence use the word *horse* to stand for their concept of a horse, they usually understand the extension of their concept to include the same kinds of things, although, of course, they need not think of the same individual horses. It is possible for someone, especially a child, to use a word such as *horse* to refer to a concept other than what is commonly conceived of when the word *horse* is employed. A small child may have a vague notion of four-legged animals over three feet tall, and by *horse* he may wish to refer to any example of such a creature, including what adults call cows, reindeer, and zebras. The child's concept is neither true nor false; it is simply different from what is conventionally understood. The child has a different concept, and that such is the case may be evident when a denotative definition makes it clear that in saying "horse" a child includes animals with horns or with black and white stripes.

By pointing to the extension of a term, whether ostensively or demonstratively (that is, by physically pointing to concrete examples or simply by mentioning examples), a denotative definition clarifies what is understood when a concept is formed. A denotative definition indicates the variety of kinds or species in which a common character is exhibited; it does not explicate the nature of the characteristic held in common. At times it is sufficient simply to mention examples included within a concept's extension; however, it may also be desirable to classify and divide the members of the extension of a concept in the manner already indicated.

It is to be noted that the kinds of things included in the extension of a concept may be real or imaginary; they may be concrete things, such as horses or unicorns, or complex events, such as battles, or wars, whether historical or fictional. We can even mention what is impossible or contradictory, such as round squares or holes that are both empty and filled to the brim, and we can refer to what is both necessary and actual and to what is impossible and nonexistent. Singular terms designate a single example that can be described, but of course cannot be enumerated, whereas general or common terms stand for concepts which include more than one example. To define the extensional meaning of a concept, it is not necessary to enumerate every possible member included within its extension. A few representative examples are usually sufficient. At times it is also helpful to mention examples that are not to be included. An extensional definition of a democratic form of government might indicate that the kinds of government to be included are like those found in the United States, in the British Commonwealth, and in western Europe, but not in the Soviet Union, in the Satellites, in Red China, nor in Cuba.

The giving of examples of what is included within the extension of a concept does not yet state what characteristics are held in common. A denotative definition does not explicate the intensional or connotative definition of a concept. The enumeration of illustrative instances given above might lead to the confusion that there is a connection between the geographical location of a country and whether or not it has a democratic form of government. Also it might not be clear as to how to classify the governments of Spain, South America, and Africa. Our enumeration is incomplete and does not explicitly state what is essential to a government before we understand it to be a democracy. Knowledge of the extension of a concept, even when complete, does not guarantee an understanding of the essential characteristics that warrant inclusion in a concept's extension. To list the names of the Senators and Representatives of the Congress of the United States does not explain what it means to be a member of Congress in terms of the Constitution.

3.22 Connotative definition. To understand what it means to be a member of Congress requires the formulation of an intensional or connotative definition. It is frequently helpful to state the connotation or intensional meaning of a concept by utilizing the notion of *genus, species,* and *specific differences* and by making reference to the modality of experience and the mode of functioning of what is to be defined. The *definiens,* or defining part of the definition, may also make reference to the use, composition, and process of construction or the cause, origin, and purpose of the *definiendum.* Certain characteristics are *common* to many individual things, and certain characteristics are *peculiar* to an object or a group of objects. Stones, for example, function in the physical and numerical modality of experience, and can be counted and described in physical terms but they do not possess any biological qualities and cannot be meaningfully described, except negatively, in biological terms. A clear concept of what something is grasps or comprehends the nature of what is experienced. It is, of course, possible to conceive of stones as growing, reproducing, feeling, and thinking, but such a concept has no basis in our nonmental experience. To define the intensional meaning of stones in a way that indicates an understanding of what stones are, it is necessary to ascribe only such qualities to stones as actually belong to them. A *subjective* intensional concept of stones may include qualities which do not belong to stones; however, such a concept, while neither true nor false, is simply inadequate as a means of understanding what stones are. By stones a person may mean large physical objects which are silently contemplating their surroundings. Such a concept simply lacks a basis in the real world; stones may think and feel in works of fiction, but the stones in a rock garden do not. An *objective* intensional concept of stones includes such characteristics as are held in common by the many individual objects included within its extension. An intensional definition of stones is adequate when the *definiens* succeeds in making clear what is conventionally understood by stones and what is not understood by stones.

Consider the following definition: "The word *stones* is a sign of our concept of *concrete objects* which are *natural;* the highest modality in which they function as subjects is *physical;* they are *hard* and *solid* to our sense of touch and *visible* to the eye and may be of a diversity of *sizes* and *shapes.*"

Such a definition is not necessarily adequate for a geologist, but together with the partial enumeration of the extensional meaning of the concept, preferably by physically pointing to certain specimens, it is adequate in order to understand what is conventionally understood by stones. This is what stones mean to most people of average intelligence. The *genus* or the larger class to which stones belong is that of concrete existing objects. This *genus* is predicable of stones; in part it tells what they are. Not all concrete existing objects are stones, but every stone is a concrete existing object. The *genus* is that part of the essence of something which can also be predicated of other things, different in kind or species. Horses, automobiles, tables, and chairs are also concrete existing objects, whereas numbers, circles, and squares, in contrast, do not exist concretely outside the realm of mathematics. To define something in terms of its *genus* is to predicate a universal common to many things that differ specifically.

To state what something is, is to state its essence or the basic qualities necessary and sufficient to constitute a thing as of a certain type. A formulation of a definition in terms of the *genus* of something mentions what is necessary to what is being defined; however, the *genus* is not convertible with the *definiendum,* so that the mere fact that something is a concrete existing object is not sufficient to constitute it as a stone. The specification that stones are *natural* indicates something further about the kind of things or the *species* of things in question, thereby eliminating human artifacts, such as automobiles and tables and chairs, but still including horses and human beings. A *specific difference,* a further qualification, is provided by the restriction that the highest modal function of a stone is physical; that is to say, a stone does not itself grow, feel, think, or self-consciously engage in cultural activities. Mention of such qualities as being hard to the touch, solid, and of a wide diversity of sizes and shapes, within certain arbitrarily imposed limits, in contradistinction to grains of sand, large rocks, and coral reefs, constitutes further a part of the comprehension, or what is meant by stones. It is extremely difficult, if not impossible, in the case of a stone, to find a *property* that belongs solely to stones and to nothing else. The size, shape, and weight of a particular stone is of course *accidental* to it, but that a stone is of a certain size or shape is implied in its very nature as a concrete physical body.

Ideally a connotative definition strives to give the essence of what is to be defined, so that the *definiens* is convertible with the *definiendum*. When possible, the *definiens* is positive rather than negative, avoiding synonyms and obscure expressions. However, a definition is adequate when it serves its purpose, so that any evaluation of its adequacy should not slavishly follow a rigid set of rules. For completeness, however, the following directives are useful in the formulation of intensional or connotative definitions.

1. Seek to formulate a *definiens* which is convertible with the *definiendum*.

2. Find a *genus* or larger class to which the *definiendum* belongs.

3. Differentiate between the kinds of thing within the extension of the *definiendum* and other things which are similar, by examining the mode and manner of their existence, pointing to differences and similarities.

4. Make mention of the cause, composition, purpose.

5. Avoid ambiguity and obscure and unnecessary technical language.

6. Rely as little as possible on negative and synonymous qualifications.

7. Always keep in mind the purpose for which a definition is offered.

3.3 Real definitions

Connotative definitions are of the form S (*definiendum*) means P (*definiens*). The *definiens* states the comprehension, or what is understood by the *definiendum*. Such a definition is, strictly speaking, adequate or inadequate, precise or vague, for the purpose of communication. However, the *definiens* has understood the nature of the *definiendum* either correctly or incorrectly. And when, instead of merely stating what the *definiendum* means subjectively to the definer, the word *means* is replaced by *is,* the sentence now asserts the proposition "The *definiendum* is the *definiens,*" or S is P. Propositions are true or false (as we shall subsequently see in detail), and statements offered as definitions, but formulated in propositional form, are also true or false. They are *real definitions.* A real definition asserts the comprehension or intensional meaning of a connotative definition as the predicate of a proposition.

Suppose when asked what he understands by the word *God* a person replies, "When I use the word *God* I refer to a term which has no nonmental reference; that is, it fails to designate anything outside of my mind. Thus God means what is erroneously believed to exist, a projected symbol, a reified name." Undoubtedly this is what atheists understand by God. As long as someone states what God means to him, what he understands by God, such a statement is autobiographical; it is about the mental furniture of his own mind. And while it is true or false that he has such a concept, the mere having of a concept does not determine the existence or nonexistence of any nonmental state of affairs. By changing the word *means* to *is,* however, an intensional, connotative definition is transformed into a real definition, which now reads: "God *is* what is erroneously believed to exist, a projected symbol, a reified name." To decide whether God is simply a pious fiction, a word like *unicorn* or *centaurs,* is beyond the scope of a logic text; but obviously the dispute between theists and atheists cannot be decided by definition, by the question-begging assertion of the point at issue. To make an assertion by means of a definition is not to supply evidence in support of an assertion. Definitions do have a persuasive power, however, and may be uncritically offered as a substitute for an objective examination of the evidence relevant to a given issue. Examples of question-begging and of uncritically deciding issues by assertion, by definition, will be given in Chapter Thirteen, on fallacies.

In summary, then, definitions remove ambiguity, introduce new terms, and increase our understanding. Verbal definitions report or stipulate the usage of words; conceptual definitions exemplify either the extensional or intensional meaning of a concept; whereas real definitions assert the comprehension or intensional meaning of a concept as the predicate of a proposition and are thus true or false.

4. Division

We have noted that a denotative definition refers to the kinds of things which fall within the extension of a concept. At times it is of practical significance to arrange or order such a diversity of things. The extension of a term should be divided according to a *single fundamental principle*. The extension of our concept of living sentient organisms, for example, may be divided, on the basis of physical structure, into vertebrates and invertebrates. The vertebrates in turn may again be divided on the basis of one of their functions into mammals and nonmammals, and the mammals may again be divided into the human and nonhuman.

To insure that a division takes into account the whole extension of a concept, it should be complete (*jointly exhaustive*) and free from overlapping (*mutually exclusive*). To attain such exhaustive and exclusive divisions, the extension of a class can be divided into one kind of thing and into everything else which is not of that particular kind. Such a dichotomy can be achieved by utilizing the prefix *non*. For example:

books	nonbooks
mortal	nonmortal
rational	nonrational
sensible	nonsensible
physical	nonphysical

Certain divisions are simply physical, in that they divide a natural whole into its parts. A tree, for example, may be divided into its branches, trunk, roots. Obviously the parts of such a division cannot be equated with the whole. A trunk of a tree is not a tree. Other divisions are logical. Dogs may be divided into thoroughbreds and mongrels, in which case it can be said that a thoroughbred is a dog and a mongrel is a dog. Logical divisions are made on the basis of an essential distinction or in terms of some accident or property. The division of mammals, for example, into the human and the nonhuman is made in part on the basis of an essential difference in heir functioning; a man forms concepts, makes history, and so on, whereas whales do not.

Man may also be divided in terms of certain accidental features, such as height, weight, size, and shape; in qualitative terms (intelligent–nonintelligent) ; in terms of age or geographical location.

The mistaken identification of an accidental division with an essential division is frequently the source of prejudice. A person's humanity is not changed by his being six feet tall, weighing 210 pounds, and having blue eyes and blond hair. City dwellers are no more human than cave dwellers. Where, when, and how a person lives does not change what he is, insofar as he is a human being.

The principles governing a good division can be formulated in terms of two general rules:

  1. Keep the basis of the division uniform.
  2. Make the parts of the division coextensive with the whole.

The first rule is violated when man is divided into Americans, non-Americans, and wealthy. The distinction between American and non-American is made on the basis of nationality, whereas the notion of being wealthy introduces a new basis: economic status. Different principles of division may be used in different divisions, but within any one division a single principle should be employed. A violation of Rule 1 automatically violates Rule 2. The division of man into American and non-American is coextensive with man; that is, the entire extension of man is exhausted. Unfortunately, being wealthy is not coextensive with man, since there are also the non-wealthy. The study of division will prove useful to the student in arranging material in outline form.

EXERCISES

Part I

A. Rearrange the following terms in the order of their increasing intension and decreasing extension.
  1. *a.* American professional baseball players.
     b. Baseball players.
     c. American professional baseball players playing for the Yankees.
     d. Professional baseball players.

    2. *a.* College students opposed to the draft who are 1A.
      b. Students.
      c. College students opposed to draft.
      d. College students.

B. To which categories do the italicized terms belong?
    1. The building is *rectangular.*
    2. The boy is *running.*
    3. The ship *was sunk.*
    4. The dinner is at *four o'clock.*
    5. John is *at the table.*
    6. The books weigh *ten pounds.*
    7. Bach *is superior to* Go Go.
    8. Students are always *intelligent.*

C. State what is meant by the predicables. Illustrate each.

D. Very briefly enumerate at least five directives that are useful in the formulation of connotative definitions.

E. State briefly two general rules which govern a good division.

Part II

A. Note the basis of the following divisions:

1. Sciences:	Exact and inexact.
2. Nations:	Communist and non-Communist.
3. Man:	Wealthy and nonwealthy.
4. Laws:	Just and unjust.
5. Religious institutions:	Christian and non-Christian.
6. Arguments:	Valid and invalid.
7. Animals:	Domestic and nondomestic.
8. Furniture :	Modern and nonmodern.
9. Art:	Visual and nonvisual.
10. Languages:	English and non-English.
11. History:	Modern and nonmodern.
12. Judaism:	Orthodox and non-Orthodox.
13. Substances:	Organic and inorganic
14. Horses:	Pedigreed and nonpedigreed.
15. Man:	Male and female.
16. Books:	Fiction and nonfiction.
17. Governments:	Democratic and nondemocratic.

18. Religions: Theistic and nontheistic.
19. Human acts: Moral and nonmoral.
20. Sport events: Professional and nonprofessional.

B. Note the defects in the following divisions:
1. Books: Historical, nonhistorical, modern.
2. Sports: Outdoor, indoor, dangerous.
3. Academic subjects: Graduate, undergraduate, scientific.
4. Women: Moral, immoral, beautiful.
5. Animals: Wild, nonwild, vicious.
6. Automobiles: Expensive, inexpensive, operational.
7. Whisky: Domestic, imported, old.
8. History: Ancient, nonancient, political.
9. Illness: Curable, incurable, painful.
10. Philosophy: Consistent, inconsistent, practical.
11. Articles: Published, unpublished, well written.
12. Courses: Difficult, nondifficult, well taught.
13. Boats: Powered, nonpowered, over twenty feet.
14. Food: Fattening, nonfattening, tasty.
15. Groups: Authoritative, nonauthoritative, large.
16. Crowds: Orderly, nonorderly, teen-agers.
17. Music: Classical, nonclassical, loud.
18. Theories: Confirmed, unconfirmed, interesting.
19. Transportation: Rapid, nonrapid, expensive.
20. Nations: Democratic, nondemocratic, large.

Part III

Definitions

A. Read the first and second chapters of the book of Genesis. How many different possible senses can you assign to the words *day, heaven, earth?* What possible verbal disputes can arise from the different uses you have noted? What real disputes can arise?
B. Define what is meant by "a word."
C. Invent a word. Define it in as many different ways as you can and use it in a sentence.
D. Define each of the following verbally, conceptually, and really.

1. God	7. Education	13. Democracy	19. The limits
2. Man	8. Religion	14. Communism	of the State
3. Sin	9. Science	15. Divorce	20. Justice
4. Evil	10. Abortion	16. Faith	21. Birth control
5. Love	11. Courage	17. Morality	22. Temperance
6. Hope	12. Sex	18. Wisdom	23. Humility
	24. Justice		25. Pride

What real disputes can arise from your definitions?

Part IV

Disputes

Which of the following disputes are verbal and which are real. When they are verbal, show how they can be clarified by specifying the precise meaning of the terms. When the dispute is real, indicate the direction that their resolution would take, the kinds of issue that are involved, and the kinds of evidence that would be relevant to the solution of the problems raised.

1. *a.* In the beginning God created the heaven and the earth.
   b. The world has evolved over the course of countless centuries.
2. *a.* The presence of evil in the universe is incompatible with the existence of God.
   b. There is no problem of reconciling God and evil.
3. *a.* Religion is simply an expression of feeling, a projection of human hopes and fears, without any foundation outside of human interests, so that every religion is true if it satisfies man's needs.
   b. Religion is man's relation to the omnipotent God, the creator of the heaven and the earth, whose nature is revealed to man in nature and in the Scriptures of the Old and New Testaments.
4. *a.* Not only has the universe always existed but it has always been expanding and has looked the same at any point in time. New galaxies are constantly being formed out of hydrogen that is created. As the galaxies move farther away from each other, the new galaxies fill the gaps, keeping the expanding universe at a constant density.

b. Ten billion years ago, when the universe began, there was a big explosion of densely packed matter. The galaxies are the fragments of that explosion. Either the galaxies will continue to move outward and away from each other forever, or they may eventually overcome their outward motion and converge in a cataclysmic collision that will bring the universe to an end.

c. The universe expands after a big bang, then slowly contracts, then explodes, in a never-ending cycle which is repeated every 80 billion years.

a. It is evil to separate an act, which pursues a vitally important good, from its natural end. By the use of contraceptives, the marriage act is always frustrated from its natural end, so that it is morally evil to use them.

b. A married couple who for good physiological, economic, or psychological reasons should have no more children may find that the use of contraceptives is essential to the well-being of their marriage and is therefore morally permissible.

CHAPTER FOUR

Propositions

"By-the-bye, what became of the baby?" said the Cat. . . .
"It turned into a pig," Alice answered. . . .
"I thought it would," said the Cat, . . . and this time it
vanished quite slowly, beginning with the end of the tail, and
ending with the grin, which remained some time after the rest
of it had gone.

Alice in Wonderland—LEWIS CARROLL

1. The Nature of a Proposition

Words, the simplest units of language, stand for other words, serve
as names, stand for concepts, and combine usefully into sentences
expressing commands, wishes, questions, and intentions. To define a
concept is to state what we mean; to formulate a proposition is to
assert that such and such is so and so, that something exists in a certain mode and manner. Concepts answer such questions as "What
are you talking about?" "What do you mean?" "To what do you
refer?" "What do you intend by that?" By themselves concepts are
what they are, neither true nor false; simply adequate or inadequate,
vague or precise, useful or a hindrance in enabling us to know ourselves and our world.

A proposition does more than state what we mean: it declares
that what we intend by our concepts exists in a certain way—that
things are or are not. A proposition states whether or not what we in-

end in our concepts exists; and when existence is predicated by a subject, the proposition may affirm how the subject exists. To answer *whether* something is and *how* it is is to specify a proposition.

Propositions are about something; they are simple or complex—simple when a single concept is expressed both in the subject and in the predicate, complex when simple propositions are combined into larger units.

To the questions "And do elves exist? Are they real?" a small boy, or an adult with the simple profundity of the child, might reply, "Of course!" The expression *of course* then asserts the simple proposition "Elves exist, elves are real, elves exist in story books, there are elves in the wonderland of fantasy." Where? In fantasy land—in the imagination, in fiction, on paper. And what are elves like? Elves are wee folk, not too tall; very clever, full of mischief; not mean or wicked, a bit of a nuisance at times, still pleasant enough companions of the mind during sojourns of fancy. Both the simple expression *of course* and the more complicated description of elves express a proposition. The first simply states in a cryptic way that there are elves; the second proceeds to tell about them, indicating their mode and manner of existence.

Propositions are expressed by sentences, but not every sentence expresses a proposition. A gesture or a facial expression may be used to assert a proposition in ordinary experience, but gestures (whether socially acceptable or morally reprehensible) do not lend themselves to logical analysis. Whereas words are employed as a sign of a concept, a sentence is utilized to formulate a proposition, to assert the mode and manner of existence of something. What propositions assert to be the case may be the case—that is, a proposition may be true; or what is asserted to be the case may not be the case, in which instance a proposition is false.

To express a proposition, a sentence must be either true or false. Sentences uttering commands, exclamations, and questions do not express propositions. "Do you approve of making birth control retroactive?" asks a question, and it may be true or false that such a question is asked, but the question itself does not declare or assert anything to be true or false.

Different sentences may assert the same proposition. "Blessed is the man that walketh not in the counsel of the ungodly" and "The man that walketh not in the counsel of the ungodly is blessed" are two different sentences, but the same proposition. Both sentences mean the same thing. Both assert that blessedness belongs to a certain type of individual, that God looks favorably upon a certain class of persons. The word order of the sentences differs; the proposition is the same.

The linguistic vehicle employed to express a proposition is arbitrary to the extent that the words, their order, the style of the sentence, and the language used may be freely chosen. The same proposition may be stated in Greek or in Latin, in German or in French, in English or in Hebrew; the words may be well chosen, befitting a well-educated person, or they may betray a crippled vocabulary and a diseased mind; the proposition, however, is simply what the sentence means to assert. A proposition is a composite expression; all its parts may signify separately, but when they are taken together, the resulting proposition tells whether something is and may indicate what a thing is.

The terms within a proposition *designate* something somehow existent. A proposition may simply express existence, as in "Elves exist," or it may express a relation between subject and a predicate, as in "Elves are mischievous." The word *existence* is ambiguous to the extent that it may refer to what exists outside the mind or to fictional entities or events that exist solely within our own fantasy. Elves and the present bald king of China do exist, but solely within our imagination.

A proposition is not identical with a sentence. Propositions are concerned with the relationship between concepts. The grammarian is concerned with the structure of a sentence, whereas the logician is concerned with the meaning intended by the terms of the proposition.

The word or words that stand for the concepts expressed in the subject of a proposition are called the *subject term,* and those that stand for the concept expressed in the predicate of a proposition are called the *predicate term*. Not every word or combination of words can stand for the subject or predicate of a proposition; certain words —*syncategorematic* words—are functional; they order, connect, and modify *categorematic* words that can stand for the subject or the predicate of a proposition.

2. *The Truth or Falsity of Propositions*

Whether a proposition is true or false is not a question as to whether it is useful and interesting or useless and dull; nor is the question of truth or falsity identical with the question "How do you know that a proposition is true or false?" For example, the proposition "When the king Ahasuerus sat on the throne of his kingdom, which *was* in Shushan the palace, . . . he made a feast unto all his princes and his servants" is recorded in the Old Testament in the book of Esther (1:2–3). It purports to be historical; it claims to describe what happened during the reign of a certain specific king. Whether or not the reader is interested in king Ahasuerus or whether what the king did is useful or how you first learned about the old gentleman has nothing whatever to do with the factual assertion made by the proposition. Of course, if the assertion had never been transmitted we would not now know it, but whether what is described by the words in question is true or false does not depend *on us*, on our knowing, but *on what happened.*

The proposition is true if there was a king Ahasuerus who, at the time indicated—that is, during his reign at Shushan—did invite the persons mentioned to a feast. The proposition is false if the term *king Ahasuerus* does not designate the historical person described or if king Ahasuerus, although living and reigning at Shushan, never invited his princes and servants to a feast. Unless we first understood what it means to state that a proposition is true or false, we would not know if the available evidence is sufficient to warrant the conclusion that a particular proposition is true or false.

There are at least two reasons why a proposition is false. When the subject term fails to designate the mode of existence indicated, a proposition is false by reason of *designational falsity*. When the predicate term ascribes to the subject what does not belong to the subject, the proposition is false by reason of *predicational falsity*.

The proposition "The Russians invaded England during World War II" is false because of *predicational falsity;* the activity of invading England during World War II is not truly predicable of anyone, including the Russians. Of course, the subject term *The Russians* does designate a historical people, whereas in the proposition "World

War IV actually began yesterday," the term *World War IV* fails to designate a historical actuality, and the proposition is false by reason of *designational falsity*. If what was intended, however, was to designate within a work of fiction, it might very well be true that within a particular novel World War IV began yesterday. To determine whether a proposition is true or false, it is necessary to know the context in which it is stated. In other words, to comprehend *the proposition*, it is necessary to understand what is intended by the terms employed. Often confusion results when the intention, the meaning, of a sentence is not clear. It is frequently not clear as to what mode of existence is intended and what kind of proposition is being asserted.

The terms of a proposition may designate different universes of discourse, different realms: the sphere of history, of actual concrete existence; the sphere of fiction—the world of imagination, art, literature; or even the world of mental disorder. A proposition is true when what it asserts to be the case does in fact correspond to or conform to things as they are. Before any discussion of truth or falsity can be useful, however, the realm or sphere of discourse must be clearly delineated. Is the proposition one of mathematics, physics, biology, history, logic, aesthetics, theology, or any other science—or is it a proposition of fiction, of the realm of fact and fantasy? What mode of being, what realm or sphere, is designated by its terms?

Certain propositions assert a relation between the subject term and the predicate term; others attribute or predicate a property to or describe an aspect of the subject term. It is, moreover, sometimes important to distinguish the mode or the manner in which something is asserted by a proposition. The predicate may seek to state what is essential to an object; it may state that something is the case, that it may be the case, or that it must be the case. It may set forth with absolute certainty that such and such is necessarily so and so or with virtual certainty, that is, it is beyond reasonable doubt that such and such is so and so; it may simply assert that something is likely, that is, to a certain degree it is probable that . . . ; or it may speak of a toss-up, of equal probability, or of what is possible, of what is virtually impossible, of what is absolutely impossible. The terms of a proposition may refer to what is necessary, to what is actual, to what is possible, and to what is impossible. We may assert that a proposition is necessarily true, that it is possibly true, that it is contingently true, that it is known to be true, that it is undecided whether it is true, that it is known to be false. Propositions may assert what we ought to do, what is permitted to do, and what is not allowed. And without due consideration of the many different types of propositions, varying because of their structure and subject matter, there can be no adequate discussion of truth or falsity.

A proposition truthfully or erroneously asserts the mode and manner of existence: of things that are, that they are; of things that are not, that they are not. Propositions are structures of identity in that they assert that a specific subject is such and such, for example, "Black is the color of my true love's hair," "The ink stand is here," and so forth. The concepts they contain are different in meaning, different in their intension; but the parts of a proposition have a separate signification. In the case of a true proposition, however, what is designated by the subject term and the predicate term is one and the same thing.

Consider the proposition "Abraham Lincoln was a President of the United States."

Let S = The subject term: Abraham Lincoln.
Let P = The predicate term: President of the United States.

Diversity of Signification

Identity of Designation

What is designated by the term *Abraham Lincoln* and what is designated by the term *a President of the United States* are in one instance one and the same. Of course, there are individuals other than Lincoln who also fall within the extension of the term *President of the United States*. Considered individually, the terms *Abraham Lincoln* and *President of the United States* are not identical. There is a diversity in their signification. It is their designation that is identical.

Now consider the *false proposition* "Benjamin Franklin was a President of the United States."

Let S = The subject term: Benjamin Franklin.
Let P = The predicate term: a President of the United States.

Diversity of Signification

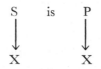

Nonidentity of Designation

The singular term *Benjamin Franklin* designates a historical individual, but it does not designate any individual who is one and the same as any individual designated by P. Such an instance of falsity is predicational, since the predicate purports to describe a relation of identity when in fact it fails to do so. The predicate *President of the United States* simply does not truly belong to Benjamin Franklin.

3. *Differences in Propositions because of Their Content*

There are at least two basic reasons why propositions differ; the first is because of their subject matter, the second is because of their structure. As previously stated, a proposition may simply assert the mere existence of a subject or it may assert something about a subject. In the latter instance, a proposition contains at least two concepts: the one serving as the *subject term,* the other as the *predicate term.* Different types of concepts give rise to a diversity of kinds of propositions. In our ordinary, everyday experience we pay little attention to the formation of concepts.

Our usual concepts of a plant and of an animal, for example, are adequate for our ordinary, naïve experience, but they are much too vague for the trained microbiologist. Confronted as we are by the many things in the world, we can examine them from many different perspectives: in terms of their numerical, physical, biological aspects;

n terms of their history, names, social function, economic value, aesthetic qualities, legal status, moral propriety, and religious significance. We can speak of their *quantity* and their *qualities;* of *where* and *when* they are found; of *what they are doing, what is happening to them;* and of the *relation* some things have to other things. In short, we can speak of *things,* of their *quantity,* their *quality,* their *interrelationships,* their *actions,* and their being *acted upon.* The richness of experience and the ability to abstract different kinds of concepts give rise to the formulation of different kinds of propositions. In combining numerical concepts, propositions of mathematics are formed; for instance, one, two, three, and four are natural numbers. The concepts of one, two, three, and four belong to the numerical aspect of experience, as does the concept of a natural number. Such a statement is a proposition *of* mathematics, and the evidence for its truth or falsity will be found in the domain of mathematics; whereas the proposition "Mathematics trains the mind to be logical" is not a statement *of* mathematics, but a statement *about* mathematics, and the evidence for or against its truth or falsity will have to be sought elsewhere. It is not always easy to determine a *type* of proposition. However, when a particular field is mentioned as the subject term of a proposition, then the proposition is not *of* that field. It is rather *about* the field mentioned in the subject. Thus the evidence for the statement "Physics is important" is not itself a statement of physics, nor is the proposition "Sociology is a science" a statement of sociology. There are as many different kinds of propositions as there are domains of experience.

Numerical concepts form numerical propositions; physical concepts, physical propositions; psychological concepts, psychological ones; historical, linguistic, juridical, economic, aesthetic, moral, and religious concepts, respectively, form diverse kinds of propositions. Our listing is by no means complete, for there are many possible combinations. The situation is further complicated by the diversity of the kinds of things we actually experience in the world. Consider the difference between a stone, a plant, an animal, and a man. You will note that certain kinds of predicates are applicable to all such entities; stones, plants, dogs, and human beings are capable of being described in numerical terms—in terms of *quantity;* there is no shift in the meaning of *ten* when it is used to describe them. The notion of quantity is applicable to whatever we experience. Numbers themselves have no qualities other than mathematical ones; they may be natural, irrational, negative, and imaginary, but they are never green or irritable; they do not get angry, do logic, form unions, or go to church. In addition to being described in numerical terms, stones, in contrast, can also be truly described in physical and chemical terms: in terms of *position, age, size, shape;* in terms of atomic structure and chemical analysis. A stone may be the *object* of awe, of religious devotion, of litigation, and have economic value, but the stone itself is *subject* solely to physical laws; it does not grow, nor does it feel pain nor study logic. The limitation of the kinds of true propositions that can be formulated about stones is not a matter of arbitrary convention. The proposition "The stone in my back yard took a deep breath and slowly unfolded its newspaper" simply fails to describe a possible state of affairs; little stones just are not like that.

Besides being capable of being described in numerical and physical terms, plants may also be truly spoken of in categories appropriate to living organisms: in terms of growth, nourishment, cell structure, and photosynthesis. Here, too, plants may be the *object* of logical analysis; they may be acted upon in many ways, but they feel neither pain nor pleasure. Imagine forming a society for the prevention of cruelty to rose bushes. "Poor dears, having their buds snapped without anesthetic." Preventing unnecessary cruelty to animals is a worthy concern because animals do have feeling; plants do not. Besides being numerable, physical, and biological, some animals, at least, are subject to physical laws; they feel pain, modify their behavior by conditioning, are capable of learning, and give expression to their feelings. What they apparently lack, however, is the ability to form elaborate concepts.

The past development of animals can be the subject of investigation, but animals do not consciously initiate historical changes that unfold an evolving pattern of civilization, with complex legal and economic systems; nor are their actions properly praiseworthy or blameworthy in any moral sense. Dodoes and mice organize caucus races and award prizes solely in Wonderland, not on Main Street.

A person, however, can be the subject of a true proposition in which the predicate employs a wide variety of categories, since human beings, as a class, are capable of functioning in every mode of experience; to wit, in the numerical, physical, biological, psychical, logical, historical, social, linguistic, economic, juridical, aesthetic, ethical, and religious. In addition to functioning actively in the numerical, physical, biological, and psychical spheres, a human being can form concepts, employ logic, and actively develop a complicated civilization.

The complexity of the world and of human activity is the source of a wide diversity of propositions, varying because of types of concepts employed and because of the types of things being discussed. The neglect of this diversity and the artificial attempt to narrow the range of human experience is, as we shall see in Chapter XIII,[1] a source of much confusion.

4. Differences in Propositions because of Their Structure

Besides merely asserting the fact of existence, as in "Crows exist" —that is, S exists, where S stands for *crows*—the predicate term of a proposition may also assert something about S, about the subject term: that is, that S exists in a certain way, S is P, "Crows are black," where P stands for the predicate term of the proposition. When the term that occurs in the predicate of a proposition is asserted of the subject term without qualification, the proposition is *categorical*. Although categorical propositions are *simple,* containing two and only two terms—the subject term and the predicate term —the linguistic expressions employed may be exceedingly involved. The sentence "High on the middle of the back of the circus elephant, toward its left side, was a hole three inches in diameter" locates the position of the subject S, *a hole three inches in diameter,* by asserting the predicate P, *high on the middle of the back of the circus elephant, toward its left side.* That the predicate P belongs to S is stated unconditionally; P is explicitly attributed to S without restriction or qualification. That elephants usually do not have holes, that such a hole is an *accident,* and not a *property* (like hav-

---

[1] Fallacious reasoning frequently occurs when the various domains of experience are reduced to one another and when categories of one sphere are inappropriately applied to things which do not actively function in that sphere.

ing a trunk), is here of no concern; that there is such a hole is asserted *categorically*. Instead of talking about holes, assertions can be about elephants. The word *elephant* refers to a concept, the connotation of which may include the largest extant land animal of the pachydermate order, with a long memory, a fear of mice, a high level of intelligence, and a prehensile proboscis. Its denotation refers to animals that are natural to Africa and India and else where are readily seen in zoos and circuses.

When the term *elephant* occurs as the subject of a proposition reference may be made to *every* single elephant falling within its extension, in which case the term is *distributed;* or to some elephants but not all, in which case the extension of the term is *undistributed*.

Propositions vary as to *quantity,* depending on whether their *subject term* is distributed or undistributed. In the proposition "All elephants love peanuts," the subject term *elephants* is qualified by *all,* a *universal quantifier,* indicating that each and every elephant, without exception, is to be included among some of those who are fond of peanuts.

To understand what is involved, let us conceive of the whole world in terms of elephants and in terms of everything other than an elephant; that is, as nonelephants. Let us also think of the whole world in terms of peanut-lovers and nonpeanut-lovers. We know from experience (so there is no use pretending that we do not) that there are actual elephants and, of course, nonelephants as well as actual peanut-lovers and nonpeanut-lovers.

Within this frame of reference, we can speak of four different kinds of things. If we let E stand for elephants, $\bar{E}$ for nonelephants, P for peanut-lovers, and $\bar{P}$ for nonpeanut-lovers, we can then speak of elephants which are nonpeanut-lovers, $E\bar{P}$; of elephants which are peanut-lovers, EP; of peanut-lovers which are nonelephants, $\bar{E}P$; and of those which are neither elephants nor peanut-lovers, $\bar{E}\bar{P}$. By interlocking two circles, we can visualize a universe of discourse about which assertions can be made.

Area 1 represents elephants which do not love peanuts.

Area 2 represents elephants which love peanuts.

Area 3 represents nonelephants who do love peanuts.

Area 4 (everything in the square, but outside the two circles) rep-

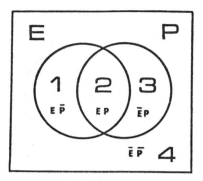

FIGURE 2.

resents everything else in our universe of discourse, namely, non-elephants who are nonpeanut-lovers.

Now, suppose we are told that the proposition "All elephants love peanuts" is true; that for every x, if x is an elephant, then it loves peanuts, and that there is at least one x, which is an elephant that loves peanuts. The proposition "All elephants love peanuts" is *universal*, and it is *affirmative*; the predicate asserts something about every single elephant; namely, its fondness for peanuts. The given proposition "All elephants love peanuts" we shall abbreviate EaP (the lower-case *a* indicates a categorical proposition which is universal in *quantity* and affirmative in *quality*). Our universe of discourse deals with actual existing things: elephants, nonelephants, peanut-lovers, and nonpeanut-lovers. Their existence is contingent, not necessary; but that they exist is beyond a reasonable doubt. The proposition EaP asserts that "No elephants are nonpeanut-lovers"; that for every x, if x is an elephant, then x is not a nonpeanut-lover. Our universe of discourse presupposes actual, concrete, contingent existence—that the things we are talking about exist. In other words, Area 1, $E\bar{P}$, has no members (expressed in an equation as $E\bar{P} = 0$). All the elephants are in Area 2; Area 3 contains nonelephants which love peanuts, and Area 4 contains neither peanut-lovers nor elephants. To indicate that $E\bar{P} = 0$, that it has no members, we shall shade Area 1. EaP asserts that "No E is a non-P," which means the same as "No non-P is an E," indicated by the shading of Area 1; Area 2 tells us that every E is a P, that some P's are also E's, and

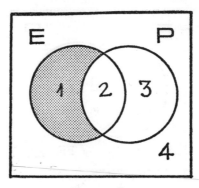

Figure 3.

that at least one P is not a non-E. Area 4 indicates that every non-P is a non-E and that some non-E's are non-P's. From Area 4 we also know that there is a non-E which is not a P. In other words, EaP tells that either something is not an elephant or it loves peanuts, that it is not the case that something is an elephant and does not love peanuts. Note carefully that when we state "All elephants love peanuts," the term *elephants* is distributed; it refers to every individual elephant, to each and every member within the extension of the term. Reference is not made to every member of the predicate; the term *peanut-lovers* is not distributed. We are saying that each and every elephant loves peanuts. We are not saying that every creature who loves peanuts is an elephant. You may love peanuts, but you are not an elephant. To state that every elephant loves peanuts implies no more than that some creatures who love peanuts are elephants. Area 3 contains peanut-lovers other than elephants. The predicate of a universal affirmative proposition of the A-type is undistributed.

Let us now change the type of categorical proposition to a proposition which is still universal in quantity but is *negative* in *quality,* because the individuals falling within the extension of the subject term are excluded from the predicate term: "No elephant wears sneakers to catch mice." The subject term *elephants* is still distributed, but instead of the predicate's affirming something of the subject, the proposition denies that the act of wearing sneakers to catch mice is ever performed by elephants. In other words, there is not a single solitary elephant to be found among those who do wear sneakers to catch mice.

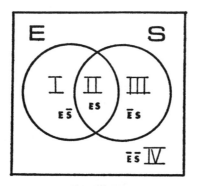

FIGURE 4.

Universe of discourse: contingent, actual elephants, E; nonelephants, $\bar{E}$; those who wear sneakers to catch mice, S, and those who do not wear sneakers to catch mice, $\bar{S}$.

By asserting "No elephant wears sneakers to catch mice," abbreviated EeS (using lower-case e to indicate that the proposition is universal and negative, of the form E), by shading we affirm that Area II is empty; in an equation, ES = 0.

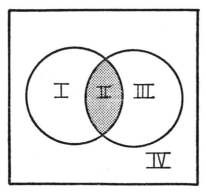

FIGURE 5.

"No elephant wears sneakers to catch mice" means that for every *x,* if *x* is an elephant, then it does not wear sneakers to catch mice, and there is at least one *x*, such that it is an elephant and it does not wear sneakers to catch mice. By asserting "No E is S," we mean that "whatever wears sneakers to catch mice is other than an elephant" and that some nonelephants do wear sneakers to catch mice; that some nonelephants are not those who do not wear sneakers to catch mice; that every elephant is other than one of those that do wear sneakers to catch mice. Since universal negative propositions exclude the entire extension of the subject term from the entire extension of the predicate term, the predicate as well as the subject of the E-type proposition is distributed. The subject term and the predicate term are thus interchangeable. "No elephant wears sneakers to catch mice" tells us exactly the same thing as "No creatures who wear sneakers to catch mice are elephants."

Two other basic types of simple categorical proposition are possible: the first is particular in quantity and affirmative in quality; the second is also particular in quantity, but negative in quality. A particular affirmative proposition is of the form "Some S is P," where S is the subject term and P the predicate term; it is called an I-type proposition, abbreviated SiP. Both the subject and the predicate of a particular affirmative proposition are undistributed, since both the subject and the predicate terms designate at least one but not every possible individual included within their respective extensions. To state "Some spiders are pretty" does not refer to every spider, and the term *pretty* is undistributed.

A diagram of an I proposition asserts that Area II is not empty;

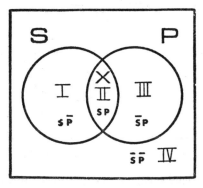

Figure 6.

there is an S that is also a P and a P that is also an S; there is a P that is not non-S and an S that is not non-P. "Some S is P" may be expressed by an inequation, SP is not equal to 0, or SP $\neq$ 0.

A particular negative proposition of the form "Some S is not P," called a 0-type proposition, abbreviated as SoP, does not distribute its subject term, but it does distribute the predicate, since a part of the extension of S is excluded from the entire extension of P. To state "Some women are not pregnant" does not refer to every member of the class *women,* but the term *pregnant* does refer to every member of that class. No one is just a little pregnant.

A 0 proposition when diagramed asserts that Area I has a member, that there is an S that is not a P, or that there is a $\bar{P}$ that is an S, or that there is a non-P that is not a non-S. "Some S is not P" affirms that S$\bar{P}$ is not equal to 0, or S$\bar{P}$ $\neq$ 0.

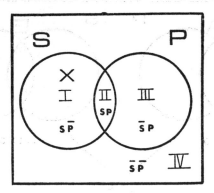

FIGURE 7.

In summary, then, there are four basic types of categorical propositions, of which two are universal in quantity and two are particular in quantity; of the two universal propositions, one is affirmative in quality (the A-type) and the other negative (the E-type); of the particular propositions, the I proposition is affirmative and the O is negative in quality.

Each of the four categoricals is composed of four constituent parts: a *quantifier,* a *subject term,* a *copula* (that is, some form of the verb *to be*), and a *predicate term.* Whenever we formulate sentences as propositions, we distinguish these four elements.

Universal propositions, both A and E, distribute their subject; particular propositions I and O do not. Affirmative propositions A and I do not distribute their predicate, while negative propositions always distribute their predicate. The following table may help us to remember the distribution of each of the four basic types of propositions.

Type	*Distributed*	*Undistributed*
A	S	P
E	S and P	—
I	—	S and P
O	P	S

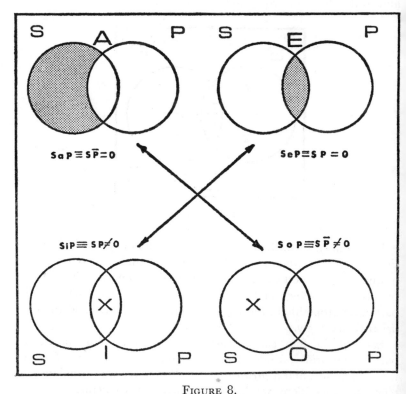

Figure 8.

The four categorical propositions A, E, I, O, can be expressed in the form of an equation or inequation. All S is P, SaP, is equivalent to asserting that "No S is non-P," or $S\bar{P} = 0$. "No S is P," SeP, is equivalent to the assertion that $SP = 0$. "Some S is not P," SoP, is equivalent to asserting that $S\bar{P} \neq 0$. "Some S is P," SiP, is equivalent to asserting $SP \neq 0$. The preceding diagram also makes it clear that A and O propositions contradict each other and that E and I propositions contradict each other.

5. Difficulties in Translation

At times neither the quantifier nor the verb *to be* is explicitly stated and must be supplied. Frequently, the order of the subject and predicate terms are hard to find and the quality of the proposition is not easy to determine. To reduce a sentence to its standard logical form requires skill and the understanding of its meaning.

Problems of quantification occur when it is not clear whether a proposition is universal or particular. Affirmative sentences employing such words as *everyone, every, each, everybody, all,* when used as quantifiers, usually indicate a universal A-type proposition. "Each person with a ticket will be admitted" reduces to:

S
All (persons with a ticket) are
P
(among those who will be admitted)

or, more simply, SaP.

"Everyone at the game had a good time"

becomes

S   P
All (persons at the game) are (among those who had a good time).

Notice that when the verb *to be* does not appear in the original sentence, the verb that does appear is considered as a part of the predicate term and the verb *to be* is inserted.

"Each horse entered in the race can run faster than a billy goat"

becomes

S   P
All (the horses entered in the race) are (some of the things that can run faster than a billy goat).

Further difficulties arise when the quantifier or a part of the subject term is suppressed. "Income tax frauds will be prosecuted" means "All income tax frauds that are caught will be prosecuted," even though the word *all* does not appear. "Dogs snapped angrily at the baby leopard," however, does not refer to all dogs, but to

S
some dogs, and thus reduces to "Some (dogs) are (those which
  P
snapped angrily at the baby leopard)," SiP. "A child requires sleep" and "The adult elephant is a large animal" mean that "All
    S   P
(children) are (among those who require sleep)" and "All (adult
S   P
elephants) are (large animals)."

Universality is also indicated by such terms as *always, whenever,* and *never;* while *frequently, seldom, at times, almost always, nearly always, on most occasions, a few, few, many,* and *most* indicate particular propositions.

S
"Children always love to play" becomes "All (children) are
          P
(among those who love to play)." "Whenever it rains; it pours"
              S   P
means "All (occasions when it rains) are (occasions when it pours)."

S
"Snakes never smile at crocodiles" means "No (snake) is (among
          P
those that smile at crocodiles."

The word *frequently* is ambiguous; it may mean on most occasions and perhaps on every occasion, or it may mean on most occasions but not on every occasion. Without a context clearly indicating that the latter interpretation is intended, we shall interpret *frequently* to mean most of the time and perhaps always, so that "Little girls frequently loathe snakes" means "Most little girls, and perhaps

S

all of them, loathe snakes" or, in standard form, "Some (little girls)

P

are (among those who loathe snakes)," SiP.

A similar ambiguity occurs with respect to *seldom, few, a few,* and *several.* The word *seldom* may mean very infrequently, if at all, or very infrequently, but on occasion. Again in the absence of a context unequivocally to the contrary, we shall interpret *seldom* to mean very infrequently, if ever, so that "Children seldom are born with

S

two heads" means "Most (children) are not (among those things

P

born with two heads)," that is, SoP. *Few* may mean most are not and some are. Again without a context to the contrary, we shall interpret *few* to mean *few, if any,* so that "Few dark streets are safe at night" means "Most dark streets are not safe at night" or "Some

S   P

(dark streets) are not (safe at night)," that is, SoP.

A few and *several* may mean at least some are and perhaps all or some are and some are not. Without a context to the contrary, however, we shall interpret *a few* and *several* to mean at least some are and perhaps all, so that "A few students or several students studied

S   P

hard" means "Some (students) are (among those who studied hard)," that is, SiP. Of course whenever *a few* or *several* is used together with the word *not* modifying the verb *to be,* the result will be a particular negative or O proposition, "A few students are not cheats" then means at least some and perhaps no student is a cheat,

S   P

or simply "Some (students) are not (cheats)," without implying that some students are cheats.

Likewise *on most occasions* and *usually,* without a contrary context, will be interpreted to mean at least on most occasions and perhaps on every occasion, so that "On most occasions a coward will

S   P

run" means "Some (cowards) are (among those who will run)," that is, SiP. *Almost always* and *nearly always* we shall interpret to mean most are and perhaps a few are not, so that "Sheep are nearly always white" at least asserts the proposition "Some sheep are white," and, depending on the context, it may also assert that some sheep are not white. It ought to be evident that *most, many, nearly all,* are simply translated with the bare minimal meaning of *at least one* or, more simply, *some.*

There are many pitfalls of translation. The mere presence of a word in a sentence is not sufficient to determine the quantity and quality of the proposition; *it is always necessary to understand what the sentence means;* that is, what proposition is being asserted and what kind of existence is intended. For example, the sentence "All students are not geniuses" does not assert that "No student is a genius," but rather that "Not all students are geniuses" or, more simply, "Some students are not geniuses." The word *not* here belongs with the quantifier *all.*

Further perplexities arise in connection with the words *only, none but, alone, except, unless,* and *equivalent.*

The sentences "Only women are mothers" and "None but men are priests" do not assert that all women are mothers or that all men are priests; rather they assert, respectively, that all mothers are women and all priests are men. The procedure here is simply to invert the word order of the sentences.

The sentence "No one will pass a course unless he passes the final" means "No one who passes a course fails the final." Whereas the sentence (1) "To pass the course is equivalent to passing the final" and the sentence (2) "No one passes the course except those who pass the final" respectively assert the two propositions:

(1) "All who pass the course pass the final" and
"All who pass the final pass the course";

(2) "No one who passes the course failed the final" and
"No one who passed the final failed the course."

A further difficulty may be occasioned by the arrangement of the subject and predicate term within a sentence. "Callous to suffering

s he who is unkind" and "Blessed is the man that gives to the poor"
$$S$$
respectively mean "All (those who are unkind) are (among those
$$P \qquad\qquad\qquad\qquad S$$
that are callous to suffering)," and "All (men who give to the poor)
$$P$$
are (among the blessed)."

Not every proposition consists of a quantifier, a subject term, a predicate term, and a part of the verb *to be*. Besides simple existence propositions (such as S exists) and simple categorical propositions of the A, E, I, O type, there are propositions whose primary intention is to express a special relation or a modality as well as compound propositions composed of two or more simple propositions. Not every proposition has a general term as its subject; some have singular terms as subject terms; for example, "John is running." Such singular propositions can be treated as universals by regarding the subject term as including one individual in its extension.

EXERCISES

Translate the following propositions into their standard A, E, I, O forms by noting the subject and predicate terms, their distribution, and the quality and quantity of the proposition. Symbolize each and express as an equation or inequation.

Example: All dogs are vicious.   S = dogs
$$P = \text{vicious, } SaP \equiv S\bar{P} = O.$$

1. Nobody knows you when you are down and out.
2. Whenever I get my hands on money again I'll hold it until the eagle screams.
3. Mommy don't allow no guitar playing around here.
4. It is always unwise to argue with a porcupine.
5. There are no special problems for people over sixty-five, except those imposed by retirement.
6. Riddles are always quibbles.
7. Whenever rain-tail tomcats are on the fence, all other cats are on the ground.

8. Everyone who turns the heat up ought to turn the damper down.

9. Brand X with the superduper filter gives you more lung cancer than any other leading poison.

10. Born into a hostile world, guilty, fearful, and vacillating, modern man is afraid.

11. Medical science is concerned with all health problems.

12. The encouraging progress in dermatology results from a growing fund of medical knowledge coupled with continuing research.

13. A few rotary blades whirl at an incredible 3,500 revolutions per minute.

14. The years are hurrying by.

15. This car can be yours for only eighteen thousand dollars and ninety eight cents.

16. This is one reason why you get so many more cavities with Zest.

17. The *première* of a new drama that will appear every other week is tonight.

18. Best sellers are frequently poor literature.

19. Good novels are almost always made into movies.

20. A few Buddhists prefer gasoline to tea.

21. Tea seldom burns when struck by a match.

22. Barrels are seldom changed when going over Niagara Falls.

23. Wars against jungle guerillas are almost always long, nasty affairs.

24. In setting a deadline for victory in the battle against the Viet Cong, the administration was not making a military judgment.

25. Many a studious observer has seen that male insects use special tricks to woo reluctant females.

26. Crickets and grasshoppers are musically inclined.

27. A few May flies spice up their seductions with dancing.

28. Butterflies lean to perfume.

29. The males of Malachudae, a family of tiny beetles usually found in the tropics, sometimes slip the females an aphrodisiac to loosen their inhibitions.

30. Beetles usually bring candy when they go courting.

31. Only motherless children have a hard time at Thanksgiving.

32. None except motherless chickens are prey to roosters.

33. Bald-headed women alone are mean.
34. All theologians are not theists.
35. A few students object vigorously to administration policy.
36. On most occasions administrations censor what might possibly be detrimental to the reputation of the University.
37. Long strikes usually cause delays in building schedules.
38. Students are forbidden to drink alcoholic beverages.
39. At times the best team does not win.
40. With one minute to go, the visitors scored the winning goal.
41. High-spirited undergraduates seldom place the Dean's car on the roof of the girls' dormitory.
42. The beanie unites the new students with the old.
43. Frequently, faculty members without backbones bend over backward to please their students.
44. Students never show enthusiasm unless they are aroused.
45. He fears life who is most afraid.
46. Politicians occasionally win elections without campaigning.
47. Never have so few owed so much to so many.
48. The student is seldom able to grade his own work fairly.
49. Happy is the bandersnatch that plays cricket.
50. Few snarks speak to boojums.
51. Nonliars are never Communists.
52. Heartless is he who never gives to beggars.
53. Puppies always play with bones.
54. A few of the wise are humble about their achievements.
55. Bond issues frequently achieve popular support.
56. Engineers crossed the bridge.
57. Diligent students are often successful.
58. Only bandersnatches are frumious.
59. Lions are carnivorous.
60. Only a few millionaires are active in politics.
61. Major political upsets seldom occur.
62. Olympic contestants are happy whenever they win a gold medal.
63. Logic examples not arranged in regular order like the ones I am used to are always difficult.
64. Each member of the team is a star player.
65. Only boojums are snarks.

66. Every nonboojum is other than a snark.
67. A few nonsnarks are nonboojums.
68. Few nonsnarks are boojums.
69. Few bandersnatches are frumious.
70. Bandersnatches are happy whenever they play cricket.
71. Bandersnatches alone stop at the crossing.
72. Every Communist is a liar.
73. Some liars are Communists.
74. Some liars are not other than Communists.
75. No Communist is other than a liar.
76. Only liars are Communists.
77. Communists alone are liars.
78. A few liars are Communists.
79. Few Communists are liars.
80. Few non-Communists are liars.
81. No liar is a Communist.
82. Only non-Communists are liars.
83. Few nonliars are non-Communists.
84. A few nonliars are Communists.
85. Blessed is the man that walketh not in the counsel of the ungodly.
86. On the good and faithful God has set his love.
87. The wicked like the driven chaff are swept from off the land.
88. All the high hills that were under the whole heaven were covered.
89. Whosoever slayeth Cain, vengeance shall be taken on him sevenfold.
90. Professing themselves to be wise, they became fools.
91. The poison of asps is under their lips.
92. Whosoever shall say, Thou fool, shall be in danger of hell fire.
93. Whosoever shall marry her that is divorced committeth adultery.
94. The just shall live by faith.
95. Except a man be born again he cannot enter the kingdom of heaven.
96. Only the meek shall inherit the earth.
97. Many people who are interested in science enjoy trips to the moon.

98. Whoever does not approve of U.S. foreign policy objects to armed intervention.
99. That man is blest who, fearing God, from sin restrains his feet.
100. The way of sinners, far from God, shall surely be overthrown.
101. A city that is set on an hill cannot be hid.
102. Bread-and-butter flies never drink weak tea with cream.
103. The sun was shining on the sea.
104. All of us are not fat.
105. All the King's horses couldn't put Humpty Dumpty in his place again.
106. Over his own sweet voice the stock dove broods.
107. Nearly all Tennesseans are mighty partial to their hunting dogs.
108. All Tennesseans are not mighty partial to their hunting dogs.
109. Lots of folks claim there's nothing lighter on its feet than a a bluetick hound.
110. The matter of a categorical proposition consists of its subject and predicate terms.
111. Men are not all musicians.
112. Many persons who are not unexpected are not unwelcome.
113. Everything that is irrelevant is beside the point.
114. Trains are frequently late.
115. Rosy cheeks are not always a sign of health.
116. Unjust intervention is not something to be condoned.
117. Not to eat is to starve.

CHAPTER FIVE

Immediate Inference

*"Well! I've often seen a cat without a grin," thought Alice;
"but a grin without a cat! It's the most curious thing I ever saw
in all my life!"*

Alice in Wonderland—LEWIS CARROLL

The previous chapter disclosed the basic structure of categorical
propositions. Our present concern is to show how propositions are
related to each other.

1. Independent Propositions

Two propositions are independent when the truth or falsity of the
one does not permit any inference to be drawn with respect to the
truth or falsity of the other. Independent propositions can be noted,
but they cannot be logically opposed to each other. Two propositions are independent when they can both be true. For example, the
truth of the proposition "To be just is to give everyone his due" is
in no way related to the truth of the proposition "To know her is to
love her." Propositions that have a different subject and/or predicate
term are independent: both can be true, both can be false, or the
one can be true and the other false.

Comparable Propositions

Two simple propositions are comparable when they both contain the same subject and predicate terms. Comparable propositions may differ in quantity (the one may be universal, the other particular) and in quality (the one may be negative, the other affirmative), but the concepts expressed by the subject and the predicate terms of the one proposition must be identical with the concepts expressed by the subject and predicate terms of the other.

The proposition "All snakes are poisonous" (SaP) is comparable with three propositions: "No snakes are poisonous" (SeP), "Some snakes are poisonous" (SiP), "Some snakes are not poisonous" (SoP). When we know the truth or falsity of a proposition, we can infer the truth or falsity of certain other comparable propositions. For example, the E proposition: "No pigs have wings" (SeP) is comparable with the three propositions: "Some pigs have wings" (SiP), "All pigs have wings" (SaP), "Some pigs do not have wings" (SoP).

Before we can begin to draw inferences, we must make explicit certain tacit assumptions. We must select a universe of discourse; that is, we must decide what it is we are talking about. We must decide what we mean. If in our original proposition we restrict the designation or reference of the subject term *pigs* to actual animals and restrict the designation of the predicate term to actual animals with wings, we cannot shift our reference to fictional animals in the wonderland of fantasy. Inferences between propositions can be drawn when the terms involved designate in the same way. To infer that no real pigs have wings says nothing about pigs in fairy tales. We must decide the mode of existence that we intend to designate.

Assuming that we are talking about real pigs and real animals with wings, given the truth of the proposition "No pigs have wings," it is false to hold that some pigs do have wings; and certainly if none of them have wings, it is false to hold that all of them do. Obviously, since no pigs have wings, the pigs on Old MacDonald's farm, which are only some of the pigs of this world, do not have wings. In short, given an E proposition as true, we can infer that the comparable I proposition is false, the comparable A proposition is false, and the comparable O proposition is true.

Suppose, however, that we start by assuming that an E proposition is false. For example, it is a reasonable assumption that the proposition "No student in this class is honest" is false. Unfortunately, however, the admission of the falsity of an E proposition does not permit us to draw any certain inference about the corresponding A and O propositions. Given the falsity of the proposition "No student in this class is honest," we can infer the truth of the proposition "Some students in this class (at least one) are honest." Whether every student in the class is honest or whether some students in the class are not honest is still an open question. On the basis of what is given, we just do not know. Given an E proposition as false, the truth of the corresponding A and O propositions are undetermined.

The following table summarizes the inferences that can be drawn when the truth or falsity of an E proposition is known.

Given	Inferences that can be drawn		
SeP true	SiP false	SaP false	SoP true
SeP false	SiP true	SaP undetermined	SoP undetermined

Instead of beginning with an E proposition, let us now assume the truth of the A proposition "All the members of the Freshman class are over two feet tall." Here again we are talking about real beings, not possible or imaginary creatures. There are Freshmen and if all of them are over two feet tall, some of them are. It is certainly false to hold that some of them are not over two feet tall, and equally false to maintain that none of them are over two feet tall. When an A proposition is true, the comparable I proposition is also true, whereas the comparable E and O propositions are false. Here again we cannot shift the designation of our terms from the possible to the actual or from the real to the imaginary.

Let us now begin with the assumption that an A proposition is false. Given as false "Every student in this room is a millionaire," we can infer that it is true that some students in this room are not millionaires. But we do not know that no student in this room is a millionaire, nor do we know that some students present are millionaires. When an A proposition is given as false, the comparable O

roposition is true, but the comparable E and I propositions are
ndetermined.

The following table summarizes the inferences that can be drawn
hen the truth or falsity of an A proposition is known.

Given	*Inferences that can be drawn*		
SaP true	SoP false	SeP false	SiP true
SaP false	SoP true	SeP undetermined	SiP undetermined

Thus far we have begun our analysis with a universal proposition:
ith an A or an E. It is also possible to draw inferences when we
now the truth or falsity of a particular proposition—of an I or an
. For example, given as true "Some students in this room are Re-
ublicans," we can immediately infer that it is false to say that no
:udent in this room is a Republican. But we do not know whether
ll are Republicans or some are not Republicans. Given an I propo-
tion as true, the comparable E proposition is false, but the com-
arable A and O propositions are undetermined. Suppose, however,
e knew that it was false that some students in this room are Repub-
cans. If that is the case, it is true that no student here is a Re-
ublican. If none of them are, we can then conclude that it is false
 hold that all of them are Republicans, and since none of them
re Republicans, those on the first row are not Republicans; that
, we can infer that some students in this room are not Republicans.
iven an I proposition as false, the comparable E proposition is
ue, the comparable A is false, and the comparable O is true.

The following table summarizes the inferences that can be drawn
hen the truth or falsity of an I proposition is known.

Given	*Inferences that can be drawn*		
SiP true	SeP false	SaP undetermined	SoP undetermined
SiP false	SeP true	SaP false	SoP true

Let us now begin by assuming the truth of an O proposition:
Some students in this room are not dishonest." We can immediately
nfer that it is false to hold that all students in this room are dis-
onest, but we do not know whether some students present are dis-
onest or none of them are. When an O proposition is given as

true, the comparable A proposition is false, but the comparable and I propositions are undetermined.

Suppose we now begin by assuming that an O proposition is fals Given as false "Some students in this room are not Democrats," w can infer that every student in this room is a Democrat, and everyone is a Democrat, those in the first row are, too, so some them are, and it is obviously false that none of them are. Thus whe an O proposition is given as false, the comparable A is true, the is true, and the E is false.

The following table summarizes the inferences that can be draw when the truth or falsity of an O proposition is known.

Given	Inferences that can be drawn		
SoP true	SaP false	SeP undetermined	SiP undetermined
SoP false	SaP true	SeP false	SiP true

3. Relationships between Comparable Propositions

3.1 Contradictories

The relationship between the various kinds of comparable propo sitions can be summarized and given names for the sake of cor venience. A and O propositions and E and I propositions are *con tradictories*. An A proposition is contradicted by an O propositior and conversely an O proposition is contradicted by an A. An E proposition is contradicted by an I proposition, and an I proposi tion is contradicted by an E. *Two propositions are contradictory i and only if they both cannot be true and they both cannot be false* In other words, when an A proposition is true, the corresponding C proposition is false, and conversely when an O proposition is true the corresponding A proposition is false. A and O propositions can not both be true, and they cannot both be false. The one must b true and the other false. Likewise, E and I propositions are contra dictory. Both cannot be true, and both cannot be false; when E i true, I is false, and when I is true, E is false. Either E is true or is true, and both cannot be true. Either E is false or I is false, an both cannot be false.

3.2 Contraries

Contradictory propositions are frequently confused with contrary propositions. Arguments in bull sessions are often fruitless because both parties to a dispute are wrong. Each sees the falsity of the other person's position, but fails to see the falsity of his own. When two propositions contradict, one of them must be true; but when two propositions are merely contrary, they cannot both be true, but both may be false. The contrary proposition of an A proposition is an E proposition, and conversely the contrary of an E proposition is an A proposition. When an A proposition is true, its contrary is false, and when an E proposition is true, its contrary is false; but as we have seen, an A and an E may both be false. The propositions "All snakes are poisonous" and "No snakes are poisonous" are in fact both false. Of course, if one were true, the other would be false. It certainly could not be the case that every snake is poisonous and that none of them are. The contradictory of "All snakes are poisonous" (SaP), namely, "Some snakes are not poisonous" (SoP), and the contradictory of "No snakes are poisonous" (SeP), namely, "Some snakes are poisonous" (SiP), are both true.

3.3 Subcontraries

I and O propositions are related to each other as subcontraries. "Some snakes are poisonous" and "Some snakes are not poisonous" are both true. Certain people are fond of ridiculing logic by stating that life is more than logic and life is filled with contradictions. What they may mean, if they mean anything at all, is the simple truism that people do other things besides studying logic. By "contradictions" they may mean to say that "life is filled with subcontraries." There is nothing contradictory about being alive on Monday and dead on Tuesday. "Some days we are healthy" and "Some days we are not healthy" may both be perfectly true. I and O propositions are frequently both true; however, both cannot be false. If the I proposition "Some students in this room are millionaires" is false, then it must be true that "No student present is a millonaire," and if none of them are, those on the first row are not millionaires, so the comparable O proposition "Some students in this room are not millionaires" is also true. Subcontrary proposi-

tions can both be true, but if one is given as false, the other must
be true.

3.4 Superimplication

We have previously noted that given an A proposition as true, we
can infer the truth of the corresponding I proposition, provided
that there is no shift in designation from the possible to the actual
or from the imaginary to the existential. Some logicians restrict
propositions asserting actual existence to particulars and utilize universal propositions to express possible existents. To state "All the
apples in my desk are rotten" then means that every apple in my
desk is rotten, if there are any. If this is what is intended, we cannot
conclude that there are some actual apples in my desk. From a discussion of possible apples, we cannot draw inferences about actual
apples. However, if we state, "All the apples in my desk are rotten,"
and we assume that there really are apples in my desk, then if all
of them are rotten, some of them are.

We may formulate whatever conventions we wish, but in dealing
with language as it occurs in everyday experience we must always
seek to ascertain the intended meaning of the speaker or writer.
Inferences are not made in a vacuum. Unless there is a clear context to the contrary—that is, a shift in designation—we shall continue to infer that when an A proposition is true, the corresponding
I is also true, and when an E proposition is true, the corresponding
O proposition is also true.

For the sake of convenience, the relationship between A and I
propositions and between E and O propositions is called *implication*.[1] A is the superimplicant of I, and I is the subimplicant of A.
E is the superimplicant of O, and O is the subimplicant of E. When
A is given as true, we can immediately infer that I is true; but when
I is given as true, A is undetermined. When E is given as true, we
can infer that O is true; but when O is given as true, E is undetermined. It is to be remembered, however, that when I is given as
false, its superimplicant, the corresponding A, is also false; and like-

---

[1] Frequently the relation of implication is called subalternation, in which
case A is the superalternate of I and E the superalternate of O while I is
the subalternate of A and O the subalternate of E.

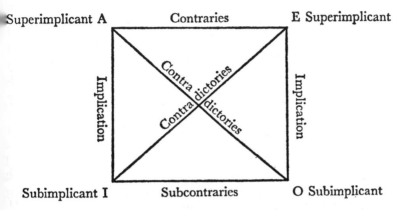

Superimplicant A   Contraries   E Superimplicant

Implication   Contradictories / Contradictories   Implication

Subimplicant I   Subcontraries   O Subimplicant

wise when O is given as false, its superimplicant, the corresponding E proposition, is also false.

The diagram at the top of this page, known as the *square of opposition,* summarizes Implication, Contraries, Contradiction, and Subcontraries.

Notice carefully that contradictories are always opposites in truth value; if one contrary proposition is given as true, the other is false; if one subcontrary proposition is false, the other is true; when a superimplicant is given as true, the subimplicant is true; and when the subimplicant is given as false, the superimplicant is false. See diagram at bottom of pg. 94.

EXERCISES

Part I

In each of the following sets of propositions, assume that the first is *true;* what do you then know about the second?

1. *a.* Few hedgehogs read the *New York Times.*

    b. A few hedgehogs read the *New York Times.*   T   F   U

2. *a.* Every Dodo loves to run a caucus-race.
    b. Few Dodos love to run a caucus-race.   T   F   U

3. *a.* Rabbits never carry watches in their pockets.
    b. A few rabbits carry watches in their pockets.   T   F   U

4. *a.* Anyone who falls down a rabbit hole is dreaming.
    b. At least one person fell down a rabbit hole who
        wasn't dreaming.   T   F   U

5. *a.* Students never study early in the morning.
    b. Some students do not study early in the morning.   T   F   U

6. *a.* Many supporters of unilateral disarmament are
        Communist sympathizers.
    b. Many supporters of unilateral disarmament are
        not Communist sympathizers.   T   F   U

7. *a.* Only treaty-breakers are Communists.
    b. Few Communists are treaty-breakers.   T   F   U

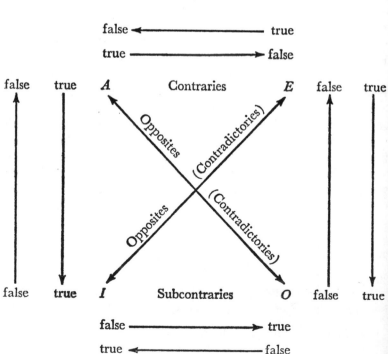

8. *a.* All that glitters is not gold.
   b. Some glittering objects are gold.   T   F   U
9. *a.* Babies cannot manage crocodiles.
   b. Few babies can manage crocodiles.   T   F   U
10. *a.* Every supporter of Castro is disloyal.
    b. No supporter of Castro is disloyal.   T   F   U
11. *a.* No marriage is unsuccessful.
    b. Some marriages are unsuccessful.   T   F   U
12. *a.* Every Yankee Conference game is easy.
    b. Some Yankee Conference games are not easy.   T   F   U
13. *a.* Some students are lazy.
    b. All students are lazy.   T   F   U
14. *a.* Some ducks cannot swim.
    b. Every duck can swim.   T   F   U
15. *a.* A few logicians are logical.
    b. No logicians are logical.   T   F   U
16. *a.* Some students cheat.
    b. Some students do not cheat.   T   F   U
17. *a.* No professors make mistakes.
    b. All professors make mistakes.   T   F   U
18. *a.* Old soldiers never die.
    b. Some old soldiers do not die.   T   F   U
19. *a.* Every dog has its day.
    b. Some dogs have their day.   T   F   U
20. *a.* Few cats swim.
    b. No cats swim.   T   F   U
21. *a.* Some wives are not unfaithful.
    b. Some wives are unfaithful.   T   F   U
22. *a.* Few labor leaders fail to be sympathetic to the problems of unemployment.
    b. Labor leaders never fail to be sympathetic to the problems of unemployment.   T   F   U
23. *a.* Only supporters of strong labor unions advocate a closed shop.
    b. Many advocates of a closed shop support strong labor unions.   T   F   U
24. *a.* Peaceful demonstrations frequently lead to violence.
    b. Peaceful demonstrations always lead to violence.   T   F   U

25. *a.* Students never fail to be diligent before finals.
    b. A few students fail to be diligent before finals.   T   F   U
26. *a.* Only the brave march in Alabama.
    b. None of the marchers in Alabama are brave.   T   F   U
27. *a.* A few of the wise lack a formal education.
    b. Many of the wise do not lack a formal education.   T   F   U
28. *a.* Never have so few owed so little to so many.
    b. So few have frequently owed so little to so many.   T   F   U
29. a. Civil Rights workers seldom fail to calculate the risks.
    b. Civil Rights workers occasionally fail to calculate the risks.   T   F   U
30. *a.* A few indignant citizens reacted wisely.
    b. None of the indignant citizens reacted wisely.   T   F   U
31. *a.* All that sparkles is not a diamond.
    b. Only diamonds sparkle.   T   F   U

Part II

Assuming that the first of each pair of propositions is *false,* what can you infer about the second?

1. *a.* Whatever is fun is fattening.
   b. What is fun is seldom fattening.   T   F   U
2. *a.* Few of the great lack humility.
   b. Many of the great lack humility.   T   F   U
3. *a.* Almost everyone favors liquor on campus.
   b. Few favor liquor on campus.   T   F   U
4. *a.* Whoever is just never fails to be happy.
   b. The just always fail to be happy.   T   F   U
5. *a.* Babies never smile at crocodiles.
   b. Few babies smile at crocodiles.   T   F   U
6. *a.* Witchcraft is seldom practiced legally.
   b. Witchcraft is always practiced legally.   T   F   U
7. *a.* Logic exercises are never easy.
   b. Logic exercises are always easy.   T   F   U
8. *a.* Only disaster can result from failure to withdraw our armed forces.
   b. Failure to withdraw our armed forces will never lead to disaster.   T   F   U

9. *a.* A few Presidents are trigger-happy.
   b. Presidents are always trigger-happy. T F U
10. *a.* Campaign promises are seldom kept.
    b. Campaign promises are frequently kept. T F U
11. *a.* Euclidean triangles necessarily have three sides.
    b. Euclidean triangles can have three sides. T F U
12. *a.* At least a few exercises in logic are difficult.
    b. At least a few exercises in logic are not difficult. T F U
13. *a.* Many unemployed are disabled.
    b. No unemployed are disabled. T F U
14. *a.* Whoever does not get sufficient exercise is in danger of a heart attack.
    b. Some who do not get sufficient exercise are not in danger of a heart attack. T F U
15. *a.* Everyone who does not study hard is in danger of failing logic.
    b. No one who does not study hard is in danger of failing logic. T F U
16. *a.* All students are not dishonest.
    b. A few students are dishonest. T F U
17. *a.* Not every rogue is in prison.
    b. Every rogue is in prison. T F U
18. *a.* Exceptions can be made under no circumstances.
    b. Exceptions can sometimes be made. T F U
19. *a.* Arguments are never won.
    b. Arguments are always won. T F U
20. *a.* A few acts of aggression are not unjustified.
    b. At least one act of aggression is unjustified. T F U
21. *a.* Not every commuter belongs to a fraternity.
    b. Some commuters belong to a fraternity. T F U
22. *a.* Walruses never smile at crocodiles.
    b. Walruses always smile at crocodiles. T F U
23. *a.* To know her is to love her.
    b. Some who know her love her. T F U
24. *a.* Blessed is the man who gives to the poor.
    b. The man who gives to the poor is never blessed. T F U
25. *a.* All soldiers are not brave.
    b. Some soldiers are brave. T F U
26. *a.* Several hearts are asleep in the deep.

		T	F	U
b. Every heart is asleep in the deep.		T	F	U
27. *a.* Many boojums are snarks.				
b. Some boojums are not snarks.		T	F	U
28. *a.* Under certain circumstances exercises can be fun.				
b. It is impossible for exercises to be fun.		T	F	U
29. *a.* Geniuses are never dull.				
b. Geniuses are always dull.		T	F	U
30. *a.* Universal affirmative propositions always distribute the predicate.				
b. Most universal affirmative propositions do not distribute the predicate.		T	F	U
31. *a.* At least one proposition is true and false.				
b. A proposition cannot possibly be true and false.		T	F	U
32. *a.* A few lions are not vicious.				
b. No lion is vicious.		T	F	U

Part III

1. "Every Republican is a conservative." Assuming that this is *true,* what can you infer about each of the following?
   a. Republicans are never conservatives.   T   F   U
   b. A few Republicans are conservatives.   T   F   U
   c. Republicans are seldom conservatives.   T   F   U
2. "Many Democrats are liberals." Assuming that this is *false,* what can you infer about each of the following?
   a. Few Democrats are liberals.   T   F   U
   b. Democrats are always liberals.   T   F   U
   c. Democrats are never liberals.   T   F   U
3. "Monkeys never read the *Times.*" Assuming that this is *true,* what can you infer about each of the following?
   a. Monkeys seldom read the *Times.*   T   F   U
   b. Every monkey reads the *Times.*   T   F   U
   c. At least one monkey reads the *Times.*   T   F   U
4. "At least one Prime Minister cannot coo like a dove." Assuming that this is *false,* what can you infer about each of the following?
   a. At least one Prime Minister can coo like a dove.   T   F   U
   b. No Prime Minister can coo like a dove.   T   F   U

    c. Every Prime Minister can coo like a dove.   T   F   U

5. "Only reactionaries oppose selling wheat to Russia." Assuming that this is *false,* what can you infer about each of the following?
    a. A few of those that oppose selling wheat to Russia are reactionaries.   T   F   U
    b. Those that oppose selling wheat to Russia are never reactionaries.   T   F   U
    c. Some of those who oppose selling wheat to Russia are not reactionaries.   T   F   U

6. "No Supreme Court decision is challenged by constitutional law experts." Assuming that this is *false,* what can you infer about each of the following?
    a. Many Supreme Court decisions are not challenged by constitutional law experts.   T   F   U
    b. Supreme Court decisions are always challenged by constitutional law experts.   T   F   U
    c. Supreme Court decisions are occasionally challenged by constitutional law experts.   T   F   U

7. "Most drugs are habit-forming." Assuming that this is *true,* what can you infer about each of the following?
    a. Many drugs are not habit-forming.   T   F   U
    b. Every drug is habit-forming.   T   F   U
    c. Drugs are never habit-forming.   T   F   U

8. "Some Senators are honest." Assuming that this is *true,* what can you infer about each of the following?
    a. A few Senators are not honest.   T   F   U
    b. Every Senator is honest.   T   F   U
    c. Senators are never honest.   T   F   U

Part IV

Assuming that the first proposition is *true,* what do you know about each of the following?

1. Draft dodgers will be prosecuted.
    a. Few draft dodgers will be prosecuted.   T   F   U
    b. Most draft dodgers will be prosecuted.   T   F   U
    c. Draft dodgers are never prosecuted.   T   F   U

2. Only mortals are men.

    a. Many men are mortal.   T   F   U

    b. No men are mortal.   T   F   U

    c. Few men are not mortal.   T   F   U

3. Most students like logic.

    a. Few students like logic.   T   F   U

    b. Every student likes logic.   T   F   U

    c. No student likes logic.   T   F   U

4. All students are not geniuses.

    a. Many students are geniuses.   T   F   U

    b. Every student is a genius.   T   F   U

    c. Students never are geniuses.   T   F   U

5. Millionaires frequently enter politics.

    a. Millionaires seldom enter politics.   T   F   U

    b. Millionaires always enter politics.   T   F   U

    c. Millionaires never enter politics.   T   F   U

6. Only liberals are fair-minded.

    a. All who are fair-minded are liberals.   T   F   U

    b. Few of the fair-minded are liberals.   T   F   U

    c. Many of the fair-minded are liberals.   T   F   U

7. Conservatives are never intolerant.

    a. Whoever is a conservative is intolerant.   T   F   U

    b. Many conservatives are not intolerant.   T   F   U

    c. A few conservatives are intolerant.   T   F   U

8. Children seldom enjoy playing with snakes.

    a. Frequently children enjoy playing with snakes.   T   F   U

    b. Children always enjoy playing with snakes.   T   F   U

    c. Children never enjoy playing with snakes.   T   F   U

9. Several minors were served liquor at the party.

    a. Few minors were served liquor at the party.   T   F   U

    b. Every minor was served liquor at the party.   T   F   U

    c. No minor was served liquor at the party.   T   F   U

10. No professor is on time for his classes.

    a. A few professors are not late for their classes.   T   F   U

    b. Those who are on time for their classes are always

        professors.   T   F   U

    c. Several of those who were on time for their

        classes were professors.   T   F   U

CHAPTER SIX

Further Immediate Inferences

"You can draw water out of a water-well," said the Hatter;
"so I should think you could draw treacle out of a treacle-well
—eh, stupid?"

Alice in Wonderland—LEWIS CARROLL

1. Obversion and Conversion

1.1 Obversion

It is sometimes useful to be able to say the same thing in a different way. Not only does this improve our style, but we understand something better when we can state it in different ways. The same proposition, the same meaning, may be stated affirmatively or negatively. The two sentences "Every well-educated student of history studies Greek" and "No well-educated student of history fails to study Greek" assert the same proposition. The term *those who fail to study Greek* can now be represented by $\bar{P}$ or non-P, so that the second proposition is Se$\bar{P}$. The two propositions SaP and Se$\bar{P}$ have the same subject; both are universal; they differ in quality, and their predicate terms are mutually exclusive; the one is the *complement* or *contradictory* of the other.

To obvert a given proposition, two steps are needed:
1. Change the quality of the given proposition.
2. Negate the predicate term.

Thus the obverse of SaP is Se$\bar{P}$; when obverted, SeP becomes Sa$\bar{P}$; SiP becomes So$\bar{P}$; SoP becomes Si$\bar{P}$.

Obversion:

Given	Obverse
SaP	Se$\bar{P}$
SeP	Sa$\bar{P}$
SiP	So$\bar{P}$
SoP	Si$\bar{P}$
Se$\bar{P}$	SaP
Sa$\bar{P}$	SeP
So$\bar{P}$	SiP
Si$\bar{P}$	SoP

Note that all four types of propositions, A, E, I, O, are obverted by following the same procedure; namely, by changing the quality of the given proposition and by changing the predicate of the given to its contradictory.

> "All sheep are woolly" is equivalent to
> "No sheep is nonwoolly."

> "No snakes are attractive" is equivalent to
> "All snakes are unattractive."

> "Some snakes are poisonous" is equivalent to
> "Some snakes are not nonpoisonous."

And finally "Some students are not Freshmen" (SoP) is obverted to "Some students are nonFreshmen (Si$\bar{P}$). Note that the *not* in "Some students are not Freshmen" modifies the verb, whereas in "Some students are nonFreshmen" the *non* is a part of the predicate term, so that the proposition is affirmative in quality. Note also that this makes no real difference, since both the meaning and the truth value of the two are the same.

1.2 Conversion

In addition to obversion, E and I propositions may be converted, so that SeP is equivalent to PeS and SiP is equivalent to PiS. "No dogs are cats" means the same as "No cats are dogs," and "Some Democrats are conservative" is equivalent to "Some conservatives are Democrats." *O propositions cannot be converted validly,* as is obvious from the fact that the true proposition "Some human beings are not women" when *illicitly converted* becomes the false proposition "Some women are not human beings."

An A proposition can be converted by limitation, when its terms designate and when there is no shift in the mode of existence designated. "All S is P" when converted becomes "Some P is S"; the converse of an A proposition is thus an I. The reason for this should be clear if you reflect on the nature of the distribution of the subject and predicate terms of A propositions. The A proposition has a distributed subject and an undistributed predicate. In conversion, the predicate becomes the subject, and what was undistributed in the original is now distributed. Such an inference is invalid, since this would be equivalent to jumping from a knowledge of *some* things (undistributed) to a supposed knowledge of *all* things (distributed term).

The subject term of the proposition "All circle-squarers are at U.R.I." mentions what is impossible; it has no actual designation and thus cannot be converted to mean that some people at U.R.I. are *actually* circle-squarers. However, as long as we remain in the realm of what is impossible, the converse "Some people at U.R.I. are circle-squarers" is as meaningful as "All circle-squarers are at U.R.I." There is no difficulty in converting "All sheep are woolly" to "Some woolly animals are sheep," since here both terms designate the same mode of actual existence.

In summary:

Given	Converse
SaP	PiS
SeP	PeS
SiP	PiS

O Propositions have no converse.

By combining and alternating obversion and conversion, we can draw further inferences. Given SaP, its *obverse* is SeP̄; the converse of SeP̄ is P̄eS, the *converted obverse* of the given; P̄eS can in turn be obverted to P̄aS̄, the *contrapositive* of the given; P̄aS̄ can then be converted by limitation to S̄iP̄, the *inverse* of the given, which when obverted becomes S̄oP, the *partial inverse* of the given. Since S̄oP has no converse, no further inferences can be drawn when we begin with obversion. However, by beginning again with the conversion of the given SaP, the *converse* PiS can then be obverted to PoS̄, the *obverted converse*. No further derivatives are possible, since the obverted converse PoS̄ is an O proposition and cannot be converted.

In summary:

	(1)	(2)	(3)	(4)	(5)	(6)	(7)
Given SaP:	SeP̄	P̄eS	P̄aS̄	S̄iP̄	S̄oP	PiS	PoS̄

where (1) is the obverse of the given,

     (2) is the converted obverse,

     (3) is the contrapositive,

     (4) is the inverse,

     (5) is the partial inverse,

     (6) is the converse,

     (7) is the obverted converse.

The seven derivative propositions are in turn comparable with their corresponding contradictories, contraries or subcontraries, and sub- or superimplicants. The given proposition is comparable with its contradictory SoP, its contrary SeP, and its subimplicant SiP; the obverse of the given SeP̄ is in turn comparable with its contradictory SiP̄, its contrary SaP̄, and its subimplicant SoP̄; the converted obverse is comparable with its contradictory P̄iS, its contrary P̄aS, and its subimplicant P̄oS; the contrapositive of the given, with its contradictory P̄oS̄, its contrary P̄eS̄, and its subimplicant P̄iS̄; the inverse S̄iP̄ compares with its contradictory S̄eP̄, its subcontrary S̄oP̄, and its superimplicant S̄aP̄; the obverted inverse S̄oP compares in turn with S̄aP, S̄iP, S̄eP; the converse, with PeS, PoS, PaS; and finally the obverted converse, with PaS̄, PiS̄, PeS̄.

The same process of alternation of obversion and conversion can

(1)

be applied to an E proposition. Given SeP, beginning with obver-

(2)

sion, its *obverse* SaP̄ can be converted to P̄iS, the *converted obverse,* which when obverted yields the *contrapositive* P̄oS̄. Since P̄oS̄ cannot be converted, no further inference can be drawn when our initial step was obversion; however, returning to SeP, its *converse* PeS can be obverted to PaS̄, the *obverted converse,* which when converted becomes S̄iP, the *partial inverse* of an E, which in the final step can be obverted to S̄oP̄, the *inverse* of the given. An E proposition thus has an *obverse* SaP̄, a *converted obverse* P̄iS, a *contrapositive* P̄oS̄, a *converse* PeS, an *obverted converse* PaS̄, a *partial inverse* S̄iP, and an *inverse* S̄oP̄. Each of these derivatives, of course, can be compared with its contrary, contradictory, subcontrary, and sub- or superimplicant.

An I proposition only has an *obverse* SoP̄, a *converse* PiS, and an *obverted converse* PoS̄, while an O proposition has an *obverse* SiP̄, a *converted* obverse P̄iS, and a *contrapositive* P̄oS̄, identical with that of an E proposition. Each of the derivatives of an I and an O is comparable with its contradictory, subcontrary, and superimplicant.

If you do not think this is noteworthy, let us put it into words. Starting with the proposition "Logic is always dull" (an A proposition), we can translate this into the following propositions:

1. Logic never fails to be dull.
2. Nothing that fails to be dull is logic.
3. Anything that fails to be dull is nonlogic.
4. Nonlogical subjects are sometimes other than dull.
5. Nonlogical subjects are seldom dull.
6. Dull subjects are sometimes of a logical sort.
7. Dull subjects seldom fail to be of a logical sort.

All these follow from the original, and if the given is true, they are all true. But please note that if the original proposition were *false,* then only those propositions agreeing with it in quantity (other universal propositions in this case) would be false. This is one of the peculiarities of immediate inference and is reflected in the relationships between universal propositions and the falsehood of particular propositions.

In summary:

	(1)	(2)	(3)	(4)	(5)	(6)	(7)
Given SeP:	SaP̄	P̄iS	P̄oS̄	PeS	PaS̄	S̄iP	S̄oP̄

where (1) is the obverse of the given,
(2) is the converted obverse,
(3) is the contrapositive,
(4) is the converse,

(5) is the obverted converse,
(6) is the partial inverse,
(7) is the inverse.

	(1)	(2)	(3)
Given SiP:	PiS	PoS̄	SoP̄

where (1) is the converse of the given,
(2) is the obverted converse,
(3) is the obverse.

	(1)	(2)	(3)
Given SoP:	SiP̄	P̄iS	P̄oS̄

where (1) is the obverse of the given,
(2) is the converted obverse,
(3) the contrapositive.

EXERCISES

Part I

Given that "Countries receiving U.S. aid are never poor" is true, what do you know about the following?

1.	Countries failing to receive U.S. aid are never rich.	T	F	U
2.	Few poor countries fail to receive U.S. aid	T	F	U
3.	No rich country receives U.S. aid.	T	F	U
4.	Few countries receiving U.S. aid are rich.	T	F	U
5.	Countries failing to receive U.S. aid are always rich.	T	F	U
6.	Every country which does not receive U.S. aid is poor.	T	F	U
7.	Several poor countries are countries which do not receive U.S. aid.	T	F	U
8.	At least one poor country does not receive U.S. aid.	T	F	U
9.	A few rich countries fail to receive U.S. aid.	T	F	U
10.	Every rich country receives U.S. aid.	T	F	U
11.	At least one country receiving U.S. aid is rich.	T	F	U
12.	Several countries which do not receive U.S. aid fail to be poor.	T	F	U
13.	Few countries failing to receive U.S. aid are poor.	T	F	U

14. No poor country fails to receive U.S. aid.   T   F   U
15. Every poor country receives U.S. aid.   T   F   U
16. Every rich country fails to receive U.S. aid.   T   F   U
17. At least one rich country does not receive U.S. aid.   T   F   U
18. Countries receiving U.S. aid are never rich.   T   F   U
19. No country that fails to receive U.S. aid is poor.   T   F   U
20. A few poor countries receive U.S. aid.   T   F   U

Part II

In each of the following assume that the first proposition is *true* and determine the truth value of *a, b, c,* and *d.*

1. It is obviously false that dictators always retire voluntarily.
    a. Many who retire voluntarily are other than dictators.   T   F   U
    b. Some who retire voluntarily are not dictators.   T   F   U
    c. A few dictators do not fail to retire voluntarily.   T   F   U
    d. People who retire voluntarily never fail to be dictators.   T   F   U
2. No organization except the government can spend more than it earns.   T   F   U
    a. Every organization other than the government cannot afford to spend more than it earns.   T   F   U
    b. Several organizations other than the government are not unable to spend more than they earn.   T   F   U
    c. The government alone can spend more than it earns.   T   F   U
    d. Organizations other than the government never are able to spend more than they earn.   T   F   U
3. Only the worthy deserve welfare support.
    a. Whoever is unworthy does not deserve to be supported by welfare.   T   F   U
    b. Many of the undeserving who are supported by welfare are not unworthy.   T   F   U
    c. Anyone failing to deserve welfare support is never unworthy.   T   F   U
    d. A few deserving welfare support are not unworthy.   T   F   U

4. All that shines is not sanitary.

    a. Many things that fail to shine are sanitary.   T F U

    b. Whatever shines is other than sanitary.   T F U

    c. Whatever is sanitary fails to shine.   T F U

    d. Many things that fail to shine are not other than
sanitary.   T F U

Part III

Given the first statement (*a*) as true, what can you infer about
b? Underline Valid, Invalid, or Undetermined and give your
reason by filling in the appropriate number and/or letter selected
from the key list.

Key list: A. Contradictory of   1. obverse of given

            B. Contrary of   2. converted obverse of given

            C. Subcontrary of   3. contrapositive of given

            D. Subimplicant of   4. inverse of given

            E. Superimplicant of 5. partial inverse of given

                                        6. converse of given

                                        7. obverted converse of given

1. Given: *a.* At cocktail parties heavy subjects are always treated
lightly.

    b. Whatever is not treated lightly is not discussed at cocktail
parties.

    Valid   Invalid   Undetermined   *Reason:*

2. Given: *a.* To know Baby Jane is to love her.

    b. A few people who do not love Baby Jane do not know her.

    Valid   Invalid   Undetermined   *Reason:*

3. Given: *a.* Blessed is the man that loves the poor.

    b. Only those that do not love the poor are other than blessed.

    Valid   Invalid   Undetermined   *Reason:*

4. Given: *a.* All students are not lazy.

    b. No student is lazy.

    Valid   Invalid   Undetermined   *Reason:*

5. Given: *a.* To be or not to be, that is the question.

    b. What is other than the question is not whether to be or not
to be.

    Valid   Invalid   Undetermined   *Reason:*

6. Given: *a.* I complain only when exercises are not easy to understand.
   b. Sometimes when exercises are easy to understand I still complain.
   Valid   Invalid   Undetermined   *Reason:*

7. Given: *a.* No nonwhite rabbit is a nonwearer of kid gloves.
   b. Only white rabbits wear kid gloves.
   Valid   Invalid   Undetermined   *Reason:*

8. Given: *a.* A few of those who are willing to tell their age are Tories.
   b. A few Tories refuse to tell their age.
   Valid   Invalid   Undetermined   *Reason:*

9. Given: *a.* Some who do not consult Dodos are not non-Eaglets.
   b. Eaglets never consult Dodos.
   Valid   Invalid   Undetermined   *Reason:*

10. Given: *a.* Some of those who do not steal eggs are not non-serpents.
    b. Some serpents do not steal eggs.
    Valid   Invalid   Undetermined   *Reason:*

11. Given: *a.* All those who are talented in answering doorbells are other than frogs.
    b. All frogs lack talent in answering doorbells.
    Valid   Invalid   Undetermined   *Reason:*

12. Given: *a.* Some who are not very confused are other than those who are many different sizes in a single day.
    b. Anyone who is many different sizes in a single day is very confused.
    Valid   Invalid   Undetermined   *Reason:*

13. Given: *a.* Some who put too much pepper in the soup are cooks.
    b. Some cooks are not those who do not put too much pepper in the soup.
    Valid   Invalid   Undetermined   *Reason:*

14. Given: *a.* Some non-March hares are not those who do not speak roughly to dormice.
    b. March hares never speak roughly to dormice.
    Valid   Invalid   Undetermined   *Reason:*

15. Given: *a.* Some of those who were able to put Humpty Dumpty together again were not the King's men.
    b. Some of the King's men were able to put Humpty Dumpty together again.
    Valid   Invalid   Undetermined   *Reason:*

16. Given: *a.* Few kings can stop a Bandersnatch.
    b. A few who are unable to stop a Bandersnatch are other than kings.
    Valid   Invalid   Undetermined   *Reason:*

17. Given: *a.* Some snarks are friendly.
    b. Some snarks are not friendly.
    Valid   Invalid   Undetermined   *Reason:*

18. Given: *a.* No one who hunted the snark was other than a maker of bonnets and hoods.
    b. No makers of bonnets and hoods hunted the snark.
    Valid   Invalid   Undetermined   *Reason:*

19. Given: *a.* All who are immensely skillful are billiard makers.
    b. Some billiard makers are immensely skillful.
    Valid   Invalid   Undetermined   *Reason:*

20. Given: *a.* Some noncommon snarks are not harmless.
    b. Common snarks are harmless.
    Valid   Invalid   Undetermined   *Reason:*

21. Given: *a.* All snarks are boogums.
    b. No snarks are nonboogums.
    Valid   Invalid   Undetermined   *Reason:*

22. Given: *a.* No Jubjub is a bird which is not desperate.
    b. All Jubjubs are desperate birds.
    Valid   Invalid   Undetermined   *Reason:*

23. Given: *a.* Some who wear hats made of brown paper are not eccentric old drapers.
    b. Some eccentric old drapers do not wear hats made of brown paper.
    Valid   Invalid   Undetermined   *Reason:*

24. Given: *a.* Only those who grow shorter and shorter are young men of Oports.
    b. No young men of Oports grow shorter and shorter.
    Valid   Invalid   Undetermined   *Reason:*

5. Given: *a.* Some of those who are able to talk are Jabberwocks.
   b. Some Jabberwocks are not unable to talk.
   Valid   Invalid   Undetermined   *Reason:*

Part IV

Using the key list of *Part III* and "Every criminal is reluctant to show remorse" as true, what can you infer about the following?

1. No one who is eager to show remorse is a criminal.
   Valid   Invalid   Undetermined   *Reason:*
2. A few noncriminals are among those who fail to be reluctant to show remorse.
   Valid   Invalid   Undetermined   *Reason:*
3. Many who are reluctant to show remorse are criminals.
   Valid   Invalid   Undetermined   *Reason:*
4. Every criminal is eager to show remorse.
   Valid   Invalid   Undetermined   *Reason:*
5. Some who are eager to show remorse are not noncriminals.
   Valid   Invalid   Undetermined   *Reason:*
6. A few noncriminals are reluctant to show remorse.
   Valid   Invalid   Undetermined   *Reason:*
7. A few who are reluctant to show remorse are noncriminals.
   Valid   Invalid   Undetermined   *Reason:*
8. Everyone who is not reluctant to show remorse is a criminal.
   Valid   Invalid   Undetermined   *Reason:*
9. No one who is not reluctant to show remorse is a noncriminal.
   Valid   Invalid   Undetermined   *Reason:*
0. A few who are eager to show remorse are other than criminals.
   Valid   Invalid   Undetermined   *Reason:*

CHAPTER SEVEN

Compound Propositions

"You know what to beautify is, I suppose?"
"Yes," said Alice doubtfully. . . .
"Well, then," the Gryphon went on, "if you don't know
what to uglify is, you are *a simpleton."*

Alice in Wonderland—LEWIS CARROLL

Our primary concern thus far has been with simple categorical propositions, with terms and their relations; however, in ordinary everyday speech two or more simple propositions are combined in different ways into compound propositions. Whereas the simple A, E, I, O propositions that we have studied make unqualified—that is, categorical—assertions, certain compound propositions are hypothetical: the truth of one component may in some way depend on the truth of another.

Apparently no connection is intended when someone asserts that "Sugar is sweet and you are sweet"; the conjunct *Sugar is sweet* is simply asserted; the conjunct *you are sweet* is also asserted, but that *Sugar is sweet* has nothing to do with your being *sweet* and vice versa; in fact, the term *sweet* is here used analogously.

For practical purposes we shall not be concerned with the establishment of causal relationships between the component parts of compound propositions, but shall confine ourselves to their minimal meaning.

Conjunction

Two or more propositions may be conjoined by the use of the word *and* or some equivalent. One might simply state, "George Washington was President," and use a second sentence to state Abraham Lincoln was President. Ordinarily, however, both propositions would be conjoined in a single compound statement: "Washington was President and Lincoln was President." Conjunctions are frequently expressed by words such as *and, both, in addition to, besides, moreover, also, likewise, as well as, together with, along with, too, furthermore, in conjunction with*. Let us use the letter P to stand for a single proposition and the letter Q to stand for a second proposition. We shall use the dot · as an abbreviation of *and*. If P is equivalent to the proposition "New York is a large city" and Q is equivalent to "Chicago is a large city," then $(P \cdot Q)$ is an abbreviation of the conjunction of the two propositions; namely, "New York is a large city" and "Chicago is a large city." Of course, in ordinary usage we probably would say something like "In addition to New York, Chicago is also a large city" or more simply "New York and Chicago are both large." In any case, our present task as logicians is to establish the minimal meaning asserted by $(P \cdot Q)$.

In the preceding example, the two simple propositions conjoined into the compound propositions $(P \cdot Q)$ were both true. Consider the conjunction of the two simple propositions $(P \cdot Q)$, but now let P be equivalent to the false statement "Goldwater was elected President in 1964" and let Q be equivalent to the true statement "Johnson was elected President in 1964." While it is true that Johnson was elected, the conjunction of a true proposition with a false proposition has the effect of falsifying the compound proposition. To assert that both Goldwater and Johnson were elected President in 1964 is obviously false. For a conjunction to be true, each and every component, each conjunct, must be true. When two statements are joined together, if one or both are false, the combination, the total statement, is false.

Consider the two statements P = "China is now at war with Russia" and Q = "England is now at war with France." Their conjunction $(P \cdot Q)$ is obviously false. Keep in mind that a statement

containing a negative is not necessarily false. The proposition "Chi**
is not now at war with Russia" is true, as is the proposition "Englar
is not now at war with France." Consequently, when P stands f
the proposition "China is now at war with Russia," *not* P, writt**
$\sim$P, will be true; and likewise when Q is equivalent to "Englar
is now at war with France," *not* Q, written $\sim$Q, will be true, ar
the conjunction ($\sim$P $\cdot$ $\sim$Q) is then a true compound propositio

Notice further that when a part of a conjunction is false and t**
rest is true, the order in which the parts are introduced makes **
difference with respect to the truth of the compound propositio**
The propositions "Goldwater was elected President in 1964" ar
"Johnson was elected President in 1964" are equivalent to "Johns(
was elected President in 1964 and Goldwater was elected Preside:
in 1964." (P $\cdot$ Q) is equivalent to (Q $\cdot$ P).

The precise meaning of conjunction can be summarized. By lettir
P stand for any simple proposition and by letting Q stand for a**
simple proposition, the conjunction (P and Q), abbreviate
(P $\cdot$ Q), is true if, and only if, both conjuncts are true; in all oth**
instances the conjunction is false. Between two propositions, the:
are only four possibilities: both are true; the first is false, and t**
second is true; the first is true, and the second is false; or both a
false. The possible truth value of two conjoined propositions can th**
be noted in detail:

The first possibility

$$\frac{P \cdot Q}{T \quad T},$$

where the T under P indicates that P is true and the T under Q ir
dicates that Q is true. Since the conjunction of two true propositior
is true, we can indicate this by placing a *t* under the sign of co**
junction, under the dot $\cdot$. The first case is now written

$$\frac{P \cdot Q}{T \, t \, T}.$$

The second possibility is

$$\frac{P \cdot Q}{F \quad T},$$

where the F under P indicates that P is false and the T under Q indicates that Q is true. The falsity of a conjunction of a false and a true proposition can be indicated by placing an *f* under the sign of conjunction:

$$\frac{P \cdot Q}{F\ f\ T}.$$

The third possibility is

$$\frac{P \cdot Q}{T\ \ \ F},$$

where the T under P indicates that P is true, while the F under Q indicates that Q is false. That the conjunction between a true and a false statement is false can be indicated by placing an *f* under the sign of conjunction:

$$\frac{P \cdot Q}{T\ f\ F}.$$

The fourth and final possibility is when both conjuncts are false,

$$\frac{P \cdot Q}{F\ \ \ F},$$

as is indicated by the F under both P and Q. The falsity of the conjunction of two false propositions can be indicated by placing an *f* under the sign of conjunction:

$$\frac{P \cdot Q}{F\ f\ F}.$$

The four possibilities are frequently combined into a single *truth table*.

$$\frac{P \cdot Q}{\begin{array}{c} T\ t\ T \\ F\ f\ T \\ T\ f\ F \\ F\ f\ F \end{array}}$$

The middle column, utilizing lower-case letters, indicates the truth value of the conjunction between two propositions. The first instance, where both P and Q are true, is to be noted carefully, for it is the sole instance where a conjunction is true. Thus, the meaning of conjunction can be remembered easily if we note that a conjunction is true when both conjuncts are true, and otherwise it is false; in abbreviated form,

$$\frac{P \cdot Q}{T \ t \ T}$$

is the important case to remember.

Compound propositions of the conjunctive variety are not limited to the conjoining of two propositions. Three or more may be combined. Suppose we utilize the letters P, Q, and R to stand for three separate propositions. Their conjunction can then be written as $(P \cdot Q \cdot R)$. Instead of four possible combinations, we now have eight.

Case	P · Q · R		
1	T	T	T
2	F	T	T
3	T	F	T
4	F	F	T
5	T	T	F
6	F	T	F
7	T	F	F
8	F	F	F

Since propositions which are conjoined must all be true in order for their conjunction to be true, Case 1,

$$\frac{P \cdot Q \cdot R}{T \quad T \quad T},$$

is the sole instance when the conjunction is true. We can indicate this by placing a t under the signs of conjunction:

$$\frac{P \cdot Q \cdot R}{T \ t \ T \ t \ T}.$$

The falsity of the other cases can be indicated by placing an f under the conjunction signs. The completed table will now appear as follows:

P	·	Q	·	R
T	t	T	t	T
F	f	T	f	T
T	f	F	f	T
F	f	F	f	T
T	f	T	f	F
F	f	T	f	F
T	f	F	f	F
F	f	F	f	F

Theoretically it is possible to construct tables for more than three propositions, but for four propositions we would need to list 16 possibilities; for 5 propositions, 32 possibilities; for 6 propositions, 64 possibilities. To work with so many possibilities is impractical and unnecessary, since a conjunction between $(P \cdot Q \cdot R \cdot S \cdot T \cdot V)$ will be true if, and only if, each and every proposition is true; in all other instances, where one or more propositions are false, the conjunction as a whole is false.

Compound propositions are by no means limited to conjunctions. Alternatives between two propositions are frequently expressed by the word *or*. The precise meaning of compound propositions stating alternatives requires our attention.

2. Alternation

The ambiguity of the word *or* frequently leads to confusion in our understanding of compound alternative propositions. The word *or* is used to refer to two different concepts. In its weak or inclusive usage, *or* asserts the truth of at least one alternative and allows that additional alternatives may also be true. In its strong or exclusive sense, *or* asserts the truth of a single alternative and denies the possible truth of additional alternatives.

2.1 Weak alternation

Suppose someone says "I shall go to New York or to Chicago." Does he intend to say that if he goes to New York, he will not go to Chicago, and if he goes to Chicago, he will not go to New York? Is it possible that he will go to New York and also go to Chicago?

Your answers depend on whether *or* is understood in an inclusive a weak, sense, or in an exclusive, a strong, sense. To use *or* exclusivel is to assert at least one alternative to be true, but not more than one When two alternatives are given and *or* is used exclusively, on alternative is alleged to be true and the other is asserted to be false

However, when two alternatives are given and *or* is used in it weak or inclusive sense, at least one alternative is asserted to b true and the other may also be true. To remove the ambiguity con nected with the word *or,* we shall introduce two symbols. When *o* is weak or inclusive, we shall use a lower-case v, and when it i strong or exclusive we shall use the same letter in italic, *v*. By usin P to stand for a single proposition and Q to stand for a singl proposition, a weak alternation between the two propositions ca then be expressed as (P v Q). Thus, (P v Q) asserts that either P i true or Q is true and possibly both are true.

Consider the proposition "Either you study hard or you fail th course." Suppose that we understand *or* in its weak or inclusiv sense. Let P be equivalent to the proposition "You study hard" an let Q be equivalent to "You fail the course." There are four possibl cases that can now arise. Unfortunately both alternatives can b true: you may study hard and still fail the course. Perhaps th teacher is too dull, or you are not smart. *Or* used in its weak sens does not exclude the possibility that P is true and Q is also true,

$$\frac{P \text{ v } Q}{T \quad T},$$

as is indicated by the T under P and the T under Q. To indicat that this is one possible case, we shall place a lower-case *t* under th v, the sign of weak alternation:

$$\frac{P \text{ v } Q}{T \text{ t } T}.$$

The second possibility is that you do not study hard and do fail th course,

$$\frac{P \text{ v } Q}{F \quad T},$$

where the F under P indicates that it is false that you studied hard and the T under the Q indicates that it is true that you failed th

ourse. To show that this is one of the instances allowed by our origi-
al statement, we shall again place a lower-case *t* under the sign of
eak alternation:

$$\frac{P \vee Q}{F \ t \ T}.$$

A third possibility is a happier one; namely, you do study hard,
nd you do not fail the course:

$$\frac{P \vee Q}{T \quad F}.$$

o indicate that is also a possible meaning allowed by our original
ssertion, we shall again place a *t* under the sign of weak alternation:

$$\frac{P \vee Q}{T \ t \ F}.$$

The original proposition, "Either you study hard or you fail the
ourse," allows for three ways in which the proposition can be true:
hen both alternatives are true; when the first is false, and the sec-
nd is true; and when the first is true, and the second is false.

The sole remaining possibility, namely, that both alternatives are
lse, is excluded. The meaning of weak alternation is that at least
ne alternative must be true. Both may be, but one must be. To
ate that either you study hard or you fail the course means that
is not possible for you to fail to study hard and to still pass the
ourse. To indicate that our original statement does not allow both
lternatives to be false, we shall place a lower-case *f* under the sign
f weak alternation:

$$\frac{P \vee Q}{F \ f \ F}.$$

ur original assertion $(P \vee Q)$ thus excludes any case where both
lternatives are false.

To assert $(P \vee Q)$ is to deny that P is false and Q is false. The
ur possible cases can now be summarized in a truth table.

Case	P $\vee$ Q
1	T t T
2	F t T
3	T t F
4	F f F

As we have noted, Case 4 is the sole possibility that is excluded b our original assertion. We will do well to remember

$$\frac{P \vee Q}{F \; f \; F}$$

since it is the single instance that is incompatible with the truth o a weak alternative proposition.

Weak alternation is not limited to two alternatives. Three or mor may be given. Frequently, two alternatives are presented as if the were the only ones or as if they were mutually exclusive. It is, for ex ample, not necessary to choose between being Red and dead. It possible to be both Red and dead. Most of us wish to remain aliv and free. However, as in the case of conjunction, when three altei natives are given, there are eight possibilities. We need only remem ber that a compound proposition composed of weak alternatives false if, and only if, every alternative is false. It makes no differenc how many alternatives are given: if one is true, the alternation as whole is true; otherwise, when every alternative is false, the con pound proposition is false.

2.2   Strong alternation

The word *or* when used in its strong sense intends to assert tha one and only one alternative is true. When the class is over, eithe you immediately go back to the dorm or you do not. The logica principle of excluded middle, "Either P is true or P is not true, utilizes *or* in its strong sense. *Or* is always strong or exclusive whe the one alternative is the denial or contradictory of the other.

Strong alternation shares with weak alternation the meaning tha one alternative is true; but whereas the weak usage of *or* include the possibility that more than one alternative may be true, th stronger usage of *or* excludes the possibility that more than on alternative is true.

Unless there is a context to the contrary that clearly indicates tha *or* is to be understood in its strong or exclusive sense, we shall in terpret it as weak. Suppose, however, that one were to say, "I sha go either to New York or to Chicago, and I can't possibly do both. Here *or* is clearly exclusive. By letting P represent "I shall go to Ne York" and Q represent "I shall go to Chicago," the strong alterna

on can now be written (P v Q), where v expresses the notion that
her P is true or Q is true and both cannot be true. In other
ords, if P is true, Q is false, and if Q is false, P is true, but it is
possible for P to be false and for Q to be false. The original state-
ent (P v Q) rules out the possibility of my going to New York and
Chicago. By placing a T under P, a T under Q, and an f under
e sign of strong alternation,

$$\frac{P \, v \, Q}{T \, f \, T},$$

can express a part of the meaning of strong alternation. The sec-
d possibility, that I do not go to New York, but do go to Chicago,

$$\frac{P \, v \, Q}{F \quad T},$$

compatible with the original proposition and can be indicated by
acing a t under the sign of strong alternation,

$$\frac{P \, v \, Q}{F \, t \, T}.$$

ie third possibility, where I go to New York and do not go to Chi-
go,

$$\frac{P \, v \, Q}{T \quad F},$$

also within the intention of the original statement, as can be shown
placing a t under the sign of strong alternation:

$$\frac{P \, v \, Q}{T \, t \, F}.$$

ie fourth possibility, that I go neither to New York nor to Chicago,

$$\frac{P \, v \, Q}{F \quad F},$$

incompatible with the original statement, as can be shown by plac-
g an f under the sign of strong alternation:

$$\frac{P \, v \, Q}{F \, f \, F}.$$

In summary, the four possible cases can be noted in a table:

Case	P v Q
1	T f T
2	F t T
3	T t F
4	F f F

Note that the preceding table for (P v Q) differs from that (P v Q) in that when the alternation is weak, the first possibil⸱ (where both alternatives are true) is compatible with the meani⸱ of P v Q, whereas it is incompatible when the alternation is stror⸱

Or in its strong sense may also be used with more than two alte⸱ natives. Here we must remember that of all the possible cases, the⸱ are two ways in which a strong alternation is false: first, when no⸱ of the alternatives are true, and secondly, when more than o⸱ alternative is true. The other possible cases are true.

3. Conditional Propositions

We have seen how simple propositions are combined into cor⸱ pound propositions by conjunction and weak and strong altern⸱ tion. At times, two simple propositions are connected by asserti⸱ that the one invariably follows the other, that a certain conditi⸱ will be followed by a certain consequent. For example, one mig⸱ wish to assert that if you study hard, you will pass the course, wit⸱ out implying that if you do not study hard, you will fail the cour⸱ On the other hand, one might wish to assert that if you study har⸱ you will pass the course, and if you do not study hard, you will n⸱ pass the course. In the first instance—if you study hard, you w⸱ pass the course—studying hard is held to be sufficient to insure ac⸱ demic success, but the possibility of gaining such success witho⸱ hard study is allowed. The second case, asserts two condition⸱ namely, that on the condition that you study hard, you will pass, ar⸱ if you pass, you must study hard.

3.1 Single conditionals

When a single condition is held to be sufficient to occasion a ce⸱ tain consequent, we shall utilize the sign ⊃ to express it. By letti⸱

be equivalent to *you study hard* and Q equivalent to *you pass the course*, (P ⊃ Q) means "If you study hard, then you pass the course." The sign ⊃ stands for if—then.

The relationship between the antecedent of the conditional proposition, indicated by P in the preceding example, and the consequent of the conditional, indicated by Q, is such that given P as true, the consequent Q must also be true. The truth of P is sufficient ground to warrant the conclusion that Q is also true. However, it does not follow that P must be true whenever Q is true. The truth of P is not necessary to insure that Q is true. It may be possible to pass the course without studying hard.

Consider another example. Suppose we accept as true the proposition "If you have acute appendicitis, then you must have your appendix removed."

Let P = you have acute appendicitis.

Let Q = you must have your appendix removed.

Our original assertion can now be written (P ⊃ Q).

What is here intended? Again there are four possibilities. The first possible case is indicated by placing a T under both P and Q:

$$\frac{P \supset Q}{T \quad T}.$$

In this unhappy circumstance, you do have acute appendicitis and you do have your appendix removed. That this instance is compatible with our original assertion of (P ⊃ Q) can be indicated by placing a *t* under the if—then sign:

$$\frac{P \supset Q}{T \; t \; T}.$$

A second possibility is indicated by placing an F under P and a T under Q:

$$\frac{P \supset Q}{F \quad T}.$$

Here you do not have acute appendicitis, but you still have your appendix removed. Our original assertion did not preclude the possibility of having your appendix removed for some other reason. To indicate that this instance is compatible with the meaning of (P ⊃ Q), we shall place a *t* under the sign of if—then:

$$\frac{P \supset Q}{F \quad t \quad T}.$$

What our original statement excludes is the possibility of your hav
ing acute appendicitis and not having your appendix removed. The
third case, where the antecedent P is true and the consequent Q i
false,

$$\frac{P \supset Q}{T \quad \quad F},$$

is incompatible with the intended meaning of (P ⊃ Q), as can be
indicated by placing an *f* under the implication sign:

$$\frac{P \supset Q}{T \quad f \quad F}.$$

The fourth and final possibility, where you do not have acute
appendicitis and you do not have your appendix removed,

$$\frac{P \supset Q}{F \quad \quad F},$$

is perfectly compatible with the meaning of (P ⊃ Q), as can be
shown by placing a *t* under the implication sign:

$$\frac{P \supset Q}{F \quad t \quad F}.$$

The four cases can be summarized in a table:

Case	P ⊃ Q
1	T t T
2	F t T
3	T f F
4	F t F

Note carefully that Case 3 alone is false; all other instances are
true. The meaning of a simple conditional statement can be easily
remembered by noting what it excludes, by noting that a single con
ditional is false when the antecedent is true and the consequent i
false:

$$\frac{P \supset Q}{T \quad f \quad F}.$$

3.2 Biconditionals

Certain compound propositions assert two conditional statements. Consider the sentence "You will pass the course if, and only if, you study hard." The expression *if, and only if* intends to set forth two things: the first is that if you are to pass the course, you study hard; the second, that if you do study hard, you will pass the course. In other words, if you do not study hard you will not pass, and if you do study hard you will. To study hard is equivalent to passing, and not studying hard is equivalent to failing.

Consider the sentence "The third world war can be avoided if, and only if, we achieve total disarmament." Notice that the desired result, the consequence of meeting a certain condition, is the avoidance of the third world war. The achievement of total disarmament is here held to be necessary and sufficient to result in the avoidance of the third world war. Let P stand for *We achieve total disarmament*. Let Q be equivalent to *the third world war can be avoided*.

The first *if* is separated by commas from the antecedent, *we achieve total disarmament*. The consequent, *the third world war can be avoided*, is stated at the beginning of the sentence. The first proposition asserted by the sentence is $(P \supset Q)$; namely, if we achieve total disarmament, then the third world war can be avoided. The meaning of the sentence is not yet fully given. A second proposition is intended by the expression *only if*. The sentence also asserts the proposition "Only if we achieve total disarmament can the third world war be avoided." In other words, if we do not achieve total disarmament, the third world war cannot be avoided $(\sim P \supset \sim Q)$, which can be transposed to its equivalent "If the third world war can be avoided, then we do achieve total disarmament" $(Q \supset P)$.[1] Biconditional statements can be written as two conditionals $(P \supset Q)(Q \supset P)$, but it is preferable to introduce a new sign, since a biconditional proposition asserts an equivalence. In the preceding example, the achievement of total disarmament is asserted to be equivalent to the avoidance of the third world war.

[1] That $(\sim P \supset \sim Q)$ is equivalent to its transposed form $(Q \supset P)$ should be obvious when we remember that an A proposition SaP is equivalent to its full contrapositive $\overline{P}a\overline{S}$. The reasoning here is analogous.

In other words, either we do disarm and avoid the war, or we d
not disarm and we have the war. To assert the relation of equiva
lence we shall introduce the sign ≡. That P is equivalent to Q
(P ≡ Q) means that when P is true, Q is also true, and when
is false, Q is also false.

Consider another sentence: "The Great Society is achieved if, and
only if, poverty is abolished."

Let P = Poverty is abolished.

Let Q = The Great Society is achieved.

The sentence asserts (P ⊃ Q) and (Q ⊃ P); namely, if poverty i
abolished, the Great Society is achieved, and if the Great Society i
achieved, then poverty is abolished. The abolishment of poverty i
thus asserted to be equivalent to the Great Society. The two condi
tional propositions (P ⊃ Q) and (Q ⊃ P) can thus be expressed b
a single notation (P ≡ Q). Here again there are four possibilities
The first is the case where we are successful in abolishing poverty and
where the result is in fact the Great Society: P and Q are both
true,

$$\frac{P \equiv Q}{T \quad T}.$$

That this meaning is compatible with the intended meaning of th
original can be noted by placing a t under the sign of equivalence,

$$\frac{P \equiv Q}{T \quad t \quad T}.$$

A second possibility is that we fail to abolish poverty and the Grea
Society comes to be anyway. In this case P is false, while Q is true

$$\frac{P \equiv Q}{F \quad T}.$$

Here the equivalence of P and Q is clearly denied. Our original state
ment denied that Q could be true when P is false, since it asserted
that the Great Society is achieved if, and only if, poverty is abolished
that if we achieve the Great Society, then poverty is abolished, which
rules out the possibility of having the Great Society without having
abolished poverty. To indicate that this instance is incompatible with
the meaning of the original proposition we shall place an f under the
sign of equivalence,

$$\frac{P \equiv Q}{F \; f \; T}.$$

A third possibility is that we do abolish poverty and still do not achieve the Great Society:

$$\frac{P \equiv Q}{T \quad F}.$$

This, too, is ruled out by the meaning of the original, for we were told that the Great Society would follow the abolishment of poverty, so if P is true, Q cannot be false. By placing an f under the sign of equivalence, we can indicate that this third possibility is incompatible with the original:

$$\frac{P \equiv Q}{T \; f \; F}.$$

The fourth possibility is that we do not abolish poverty and we do not attain the Great Society,

$$\frac{P \equiv Q}{F \quad F}.$$

Our original assertion did not rule out the possibility of not attaining the Great Society as long as we do not succeed in abolishing poverty. It simply asserted that if we did abolish poverty then we would attain the Great Society, and, if the latter is attained, poverty is abolished. Two simple propositions are equivalent in truth value when both are true or both are false. $(Q \supset P)$ excludes the possibility of Q's being true when P is false, and $(P \supset Q)$ excludes the possibility of P's being true when Q is false, but the possibility of P's being false when Q is false is compatible with

$$\frac{Q \supset P}{F \; t \; F}$$

and with

$$\frac{P \supset Q}{F \; t \; F}.$$

The compatibility of the falsity of P and Q with the original proposition can be shown by placing a t under the sign of equivalence:

$$\frac{P \equiv Q}{F \quad t \quad F} \ .$$

The meaning of equivalence can be summarized in the following table:

Case	$P \equiv Q$
1	T t T
2	F f T
3	T f F
4	F t F

Notice that when the antecedent and the consequent of a biconditional proposition are either both true or both false (Cases 1 and 4), the biconditional is true; in all other instances (Cases 2 and 3), it is false.

4. Interdefinability of Compound Propositions

The meaning of one type of compound proposition can be expressed by another type of proposition. Let us summarize the truth tables that we have developed in the course of explicating the meaning of conjunction, weak and strong alternation, single conditionals, and biconditional propositions.

Case	Conjunction (Table I) $(P \cdot Q)$	Weak Alternation (Table II) $(P \vee Q)$	Strong Alternation (Table III) $(P \underline{v} Q)$	Single Conditional (Table IV) $(P \supset Q)$	Biconditional (Table V) $(P \equiv Q)$
1	T t T	T t T	T f T	T t T	T t T
2	F f T	F t T	F t T	F t T	F f T
3	T f F	T t F	T t F	T f F	T f F
4	F f F	F f F	F f F	F t F	F t F

Let us begin by noticing again that the conjunction of two propositions affirms both that P is true and that Q is true (Table I, Case 1) and denies either that P is false or that Q is false (Table I, Cases 2 and 3), as well as denying the possibility of both being false (Table I, Case 4). A conjunction is equivalent to the negation of a weak alternation. For example, to state that both Russia and China are Communist countries $(P \cdot Q)$, where P = Russia is a

Communist country and Q = China is a Communist country, is the same as saying "It is false that either Russia or China is not a Communist country" $\sim(\sim P \vee \sim Q)$. In other words, you cannot possibly agree that China is not a Communist country if you admit that Russia is $\sim(P \supset \sim Q)$. Both are Communist countries:

$$(P \cdot Q) \equiv \sim(\sim P \vee \sim Q) \equiv \sim(P \supset \sim Q)$$

The meaning of weak alternation (Table II) can readily be expressed in a conjunction. To say that either P is true or Q is true is to deny that both are false (Table I, Case 4)

$$(P \vee Q) \equiv \sim(\sim P \cdot \sim Q).$$

To express weak alternation as a simple conditional, note that if P is false, Q is true (Table II, Case 2) $(\sim P \supset Q)$. To assert that you will go either to New York or to Chicago, and possibly to both, means that it is false that you will go neither to New York nor to Chicago. If you do not go to New York, then you will go to Chicago.

Consider further the single conditional $(P \supset Q)$. From Table IV, Case 3, note that $(P \supset Q)$ is equivalent to denying that P is true when Q is false $(P \supset Q) \equiv \sim(P \cdot \sim Q)$. To assert that if you marry you will be happy is equivalent to saying that it is false that you marry and are unhappy. In other words, either you do not get married or you are happy $(\sim P \vee Q)$. The following are thus equivalent:

$$(P \supset Q) \equiv \sim(P \cdot \sim Q) \equiv (\sim P \vee Q).$$

From Table III, Cases 1 and 4, we can see that a strong alternation $(P \, v \, Q)$ is equivalent to the denial that P and Q are both false and to the denial that they are both true. To state that you will go to New York or to Chicago, and not both, means that it is false that you go neither to New York nor to Chicago, and it is also false that you go to New York and to Chicago:

$$(P \, v \, Q) \equiv \sim(\sim P \cdot \sim Q) \cdot \sim(P \cdot Q).$$

If you do not go to New York, then you do go to Chicago $(\sim P \supset Q)$, Case 2, and, of course, if you go to New York, then you do not go to Chicago, Case 3 $(P \supset \sim Q)$.

From Table V, we see that biconditional propositions assert that if P is true, Q is true, and if Q is true, P is true (Case 1). In other words, from Cases 1 and 4, we can see that either P is true and Q is true or P is false and Q is false.

To know how to express the same meaning in different kinds of propositions increases our ability to express ourselves and increases our understanding. In the handling of evidence in the form of arguments, it enables us to recognize and substitute equivalent expressions. The following equivalences will subsequently prove useful and should be noted carefully.

1. $\sim(P \cdot Q) \equiv (\sim P \vee \sim Q)$
2. $\sim(P \vee Q) \equiv (\sim P \cdot \sim Q)$
3. $(P \supset Q) \equiv (\sim P \vee Q)$
4. $(P \supset Q) \equiv \sim(P \cdot \sim Q)$
5. $(P \equiv Q) \equiv (P \cdot Q) \vee (\sim P \cdot \sim Q)$
6. $(P \equiv Q) \equiv (P \supset Q) \cdot (Q \supset P)$

Our ability to state the meaning of one proposition in terms of another enables us to draw inferences. For example, given the falsity of $(P \supset Q)$, we can affirm the truth of $\sim(P \supset Q)$. By utilizing the equivalence in No. 3 above, $\sim(P \supset Q)$ is equivalent to $\sim(\sim P \vee Q)$, which in turn is equivalent to $(P \cdot \sim Q)$, as in No. 2 above. To deny the truth of the proposition "If you work in the summer, then you have a lot of money in the fall," I need simply to state, although you did work in the summer, you still do not have money in the fall: $\sim(P \supset Q) \equiv (P \cdot \sim Q)$.

5. Translation of Simple Categorical Propositions into Compound Propositions

Simple categorical propositions can be translated into compound propositions. A, E, I, O propositions assert a relation between two terms. "All S is P" asserts that for anything whatsoever, if it is a member of class S, then it is also a member of P. SaP can be conveniently interpreted to mean for every x, if x is an S then x is a P, which may be written (x) $(Sx \supset Px)$. This abbreviation indicates that any individual that falls within the extension of S is one and the same with some of the individuals included in the extension of P.

It is impossible to tell whether the expression "x is an S" is true or false, since x here refers to a *variable*. The expression is thus a *propo-*

itional function. Consider the statement "All heavy smokers are in danger of lung cancer," where S = *heavy smokers* and P = *those in danger of lung cancer.* S and P here refer to classes which unfortunately have many members. The expressions *x is a heavy smoker* and *x is in danger of lung cancer* are not concrete; we do not know what *x* refers to; that is, *x* is a variable: it can stand for anything. We shall use letters *x, y, z* to refer to variables and we shall use lower-case *a, b, c, d,* and so on to refer to concrete individuals. To translate SaP into a compound proposition, we must select an individual member within the extension of S. By selecting an instance—a concrete case—a simple categorical proposition is translated into a compound hypothetical proposition. Since "All S is P," any single member of S is P. By substituting an individual—for example, John, *j,* a *constant*—in place of the variable *x,* we can now infer that "If John is a heavy smoker then John is in danger of lung cancer," that is, (Sj ⊃ Pj).

The expression (x) (Sx ⊃ Px) now becomes a compound proposition by selecting an individual member of S. Since we do not know categorically whether the individual selected really is a member of S, the mode of our intention can no longer express certainty; it must now be hypothetical. At times we may wish to assert an implicative relation, but we may be content merely to assert that such and such happens to be the case in abstraction from causal connections. Unless a contrary indication is given, we shall not concern ourselves with causal connections. The inference (x) (Sx ⊃ Px), therefore (Sj ⊃ Pj), where j is an individual, utilizes the principle of the Universal Instantiation, abbreviated UI; that is, "For every *x,* if phi is a predicate of *x,* then phi must be a predicate of every individual instance, or concrete case of *x.*"

If for every *x, x* is a phi, then if *a* is an instance of *x,* then *a* is phi.

$$(x)\phi x \therefore \phi\, a \text{ (by UI)}$$

Universal affirmative and negative propositions of the A and E type are thus transformed into compound hypotheticals by substituting propositions for the subject and predicate terms.

$$SaP \equiv (x)\ (Sx \supset Px) \equiv (Sj \supset Pj)\,(by\ UI)$$
$$SeP \equiv (x)\ (Sx \supset \sim Px) \equiv (Sj \supset \sim Pj)\,(by\ UI)$$

I- and O-type propositions may be translated into compound propositions of the conjunctive type, but here greater caution must be exercised. The statement "Some S is P" asserts that there is an x, $(\exists x)$, which is a member of S and which is also a member of P; that is, $(\exists x)(Sx \cdot Px)$. Here we may substitute an individual instance in place of the variable x, but we must *be careful not to use the same individual more than once* in a given context.

$$(\exists x)(Sx \cdot Px) \therefore (Sa \cdot Pa),$$

where a is the name of an individual within the extension of the class S that is one and the same individual designated by the term P. This principle of Existential Instantation, EI, $(\exists x) \phi x \therefore \phi a$, where a is *an individual not previously referred to in the context,* enables us to translate simple categoricals into compound categoricals. When more than one particular proposition is referred to in a single context, the translation will require more than one individual name. For example, consider the two simple propositions:

1. "Some animals that eat grass are horses" $(\exists x)(Gx \cdot Hx)$.
2. "Some animals that eat grass are cows" $(\exists x)(Gx \cdot Cx)$.

To translate (1) $(\exists x)(Gx \cdot Hx)$ (2) $(\exists x)(Gx \cdot Cx)$ into $(Ga \cdot Ha)$ and $(Ga \cdot Ca)$ would lead to the conclusion that the same individual a is both a horse and a cow. Since the class of animals that eats grass has more than one member, our translation of $(\exists x)(Gx \cdot Hx)$ and $(\exists x)(Gx \cdot Cx)$ should have heeded the restriction that the same individual cannot be used more than once in a context. We need to refer to more than one individual, a and b. The translation then becomes: $(\exists x)(Gx \cdot Hx) \therefore (Ga \cdot Ha) \lor (Gb \cdot Hb)$. That there is an x such that x eats grass and x is a horse allows us to infer that a eats grass and a is a horse, or b eats grass and b is a horse. That there is an x such that x eats grass and x is a cow allows us to infer that a eats grass and a is a cow or b eats grass and b is a cow; that is, $(\exists x)(Gx \cdot Cx) \therefore (Ga \cdot Ca) \lor (Gb \cdot Cb)$.

EXERCISES

Part I

1. Construct a truth table to determine whether the following propositions are equivalent.

a. $(P \lor Q) \equiv \sim(\sim P \cdot \sim Q)$
b. $\sim(P \cdot Q) \equiv (\sim P \lor \sim Q)$
c. $(P \supset Q) \equiv (\sim P \lor Q)$
d. $(P \supset Q) \equiv \sim(P \cdot \sim Q)$
e. $(P \lor Q) \equiv (P \supset \sim Q)(Q \supset \sim P)$
f. $(P \equiv Q) \equiv (P \supset Q)(Q \supset P)$
g. $(P \equiv Q) \equiv (P \cdot Q) \lor (\sim P \cdot \sim Q)$
h. $(P \cdot Q) \supset R \equiv (P \supset Q) \supset R$
i. $(P \cdot Q) \supset R \equiv P \supset (Q \supset R)$
j. $(P \supset Q) \equiv (Q \supset P)$
k. $(P \supset Q) \equiv (\sim P \supset \sim Q)$
l. $(P \supset Q) \equiv (\sim Q \supset \sim P)$
m. $(P \supset Q) \equiv (\sim P \supset Q)$
n. $(P \lor Q) \equiv (\sim P \supset Q)$
o. $P \lor (Q \cdot R) \equiv (P \cdot Q) \lor (P \cdot R)$
p. $P \lor (Q \cdot R) \equiv (P \lor Q) \cdot (P \lor R)$

2. Assuming that A, B, C are true statements and X, Y, Z are false statements, which of the following compound statements are true.

a. $(A \cdot B) \cdot Z$
b. $(A \cdot B) \supset Y$
c. $\{[(A \cdot B) \supset C] \supset [(A \cdot B) \cdot Z]\}$
d. $(A \lor B) \equiv (C \lor Z)$
e. $\sim\{[(A \cdot B) \supset C] \supset [(A \cdot B) \supset Z]\}$
f. $(X \lor Z) \supset (A \cdot B)$
g. $(X \lor A) \supset (C \cdot B)$
h. $(A \cdot B \cdot C) \supset Z \supset (X \cdot Y)$
i. $\sim\{[(A \cdot B) \lor Z] \supset (X \cdot C)\}$

Part II

. Translate each of the following conjunctions into alternatives and simple conditional propositions.

a. Washington and Lincoln were both Presidents.
b. Neither Jefferson nor Washington was assassinated.
c. Besides being dishonest, cheating destroys the academic community.
d. In addition to becoming suicidal, LSD users suffer auditory hallucinations.

    e. The college year was divided into three parts and the student
        were compelled to attend every session.

    f. The couples wriggled to the watusi and gyrated to the jerk.

    g. Both the free speech movement and the filthy speech move-
        ment have lost their popularity on certain campuses.

    h. The Houses of Congress appropriated the requested funds
        and they expressed their approval of the President's policy.

    i. Totalitarian countries make a mistake about what a democ-
        racy will do and regard us as decadent.

    j. It is impossible to have "free sex" without destroying the basic
        structure of the family.

    k. The world is teetering on the brink of a nuclear war, and dis-
        armament is the only solution.

2. Translate each of the following alternatives into conjunctions
   and simple conditional propositions.

    a. On the majority of campuses the students seem either unin-
        terested or scornful of the sexual freedom movement.

    b. The choice must be made between being Red and dead.

    c. Either we must repeal the nuclear age or the human race must
        learn to live with tremendous destructive power.

    d. We must either disarm unilaterally or fight a nuclear war.

    e. Either peace is the only desire of men and nations or it is
        necessarily first in their hierarchy of values.

    f. Either we are hypocritical in our profession of equality or we
        must be willing to treat everyone fairly.

    g. Either a student studies hard or he does not get the most out
        of his educational experience.

    h. Either more highways will be constructed or we shall continue
        to have traffic problems.

    i. Either adequate economic safeguards will be found or there
        will be a recession.

    j. Either you make the right decision now or you will always be
        unhappy.

3. Translate the following simple conditionals into conjunctions and
   alternations:

    a. If the United States maintains insuperable power and manages that power with intelligence and prudence, mankind will be neither Red nor dead.

b. If anyone resorts to nuclear war, the resulting destruction will be entirely disproportionate to any rational goal.

c. If in a nuclear age a nation is promoting morality, it must be willing to pay a high price.

d. If we want peace with justice, then we must be willing to engage in warfare.

e. If we wish to enjoy pleasure rationally, then we must be temperate in our actions.

f. If premarital intercourse is morally permissible, University health service should be authorized to prescribe contraceptives to any student desiring them.

g. If the government is successful in its war on poverty, unemployment will be virtually eliminated.

h. We can survive as a nation only if we act wisely.

i. Conservation programs will work only if the public is cooperative.

j. Logic courses are easy only if a student studies hard.

4. Translate the following equivalences into alternative and simple conditional propositions.

a. To be just is equivalent to being virtuous.

b. To be a Euclidean triangle is equivalent to being a three-sided plane figure with three internal angles equal to 180°.

c. Being temperate is equivalent to being in control of one's emotions.

d. To be human is equivalent to being a rational animal.

e. To be insane is equivalent to being legally incompetent.

5. Translate the simple propositions at the end of Chapter IV into compound propositions.

REVIEW EXERCISES

Part I

Determine the truth or falsity of the following:

1. The word *fact* is never ambiguous.   T   F

2. Essentially the scientific method is simply the application of deductive and inductive logic to our experience.   T   F
3. Concepts and words are identical.   T   F
4. Sensation alone is sufficient for knowledge.   T   F
5. To call a man a sentient being and an ox a sentient being utilizes the expression *sentient being* in an analogical sense.   T   F
6. *The Second World War* is a singular term.   T   F
7. A term is used collectively when reference is made to each member falling within the extension of the subject.   T   F
8. A concept has a single meaning, and yet it applies to many particular things or instances.   T   F
9. The ways we can speak about a subject, in terms of species, genus, differences, properties, or accidents, are known as the categories.   T   F
10. A real definition asserts the intensional meaning of a connotative definition as the predicate of a proposition.   T   F

Part II

1. List at least five directives which are useful in the formulation of intensional or connotative definitions.
2. List at least five categories and give an example of each.
3. Enumerate the predicables.
4. What is meant by the univocal, equivocal, and analogical use of terms? Illustrate each.
5. Formulate two principles governing a good division. Illustrate.

Part III

Translate the following sentences into standard logical forms.

1. Not a few regard Communist China as an aggressive power that has to be stopped.
2. A few dissenters say that China is behaving like any other great power.
3. China's policies are an exaggerated response to a sense of insecurity.
4. Irrational is every effort to check Chinese expansionism.

5. China is an aggressive power.
6. Few, if any, historians underestimate the great sequences of Chinese history.
7. Historical analogies are always dangerous.
8. Marxist-Leninist slogans never justify wanton aggression.
9. Chinese emperors frequently sought to bring about revolution in Tanzania.
10. Policy makers in Washington never fail to study history.

Part IV

Given the first proposition as *true,* what can you determine about each of the following?

1. At least certain underdeveloped nations will eventually become developed.
   a. At least a few underdeveloped nations will not become developed.   T F U
   b. Eventually every underdeveloped nation will become developed.   T F U
   c. Underdeveloped nations never will become developed.   T F U
2. Countries always seek to annex neighboring countries.
   a. A few countries seek to annex neighboring countries.   T F U
   b. Not every country seeks to annex neighboring countries.   T F U
   c. Never does a country seek to annex its neighboring country.   T F U
3. All governments are not neutral.
   a. Few governments are neutral.   T F U
   b. Every government is neutral.   T F U
   c. No government is neutral.   T F U
4. Communists never interfere in the internal affairs of other nations.
   a. Few Communists interfere in the internal affairs of other nations.   T F U
   b. A few Communists interfere in the internal affairs of other nations.   T F U

    c. Communists always interfere in the internal affairs of other nations.   T F U

5. Only a wealthy nation is a military power.
    a. Several military powers are wealthy nations.   T F U
    b. Every wealthy nation is a military power.   T F U
    c. Every military power is a wealthy nation.   T F U

Part V

Given the first statement as *false,* what can you infer about the second?

1. *a.* Only a nation oblivious to its geopolitical position dares challenge the military potential of China.
   b. No nation that dares challenge the military potential of China is oblivious to its geopolitical position.   T F U
2. *a.* A few radicals want the U.S. to contain Communist China without the help of China's neighbors.
   b. At least some radicals do not want the U.S. to contain Communist China without the help of China's neighbors.   T F U
3. *a.* Whoever wishes to contain China must go to war with China.
   b. No one who wishes to contain China must go to war with China.   T F U
4. *a.* The nuclear power of the U.S. successfully contained the Soviet Union.
   b. The nuclear power of the U.S. did not successfully contain the Soviet Union   T F U
5. *a.* All students are not geniuses.
   b. Every student is a genius.   T F U

Part VI

A. In each of the following sets of propositions, assuming that the first is *true,* what do you know about the second?
   1. *a.* Americans never fail to worry about the draft.
     b. Few Americans fail to worry about the draft.   T F U

2. *a.* Many youngsters regard the draft as a remote
threat.
   b. Some youngsters do not regard the draft as a
remote threat.   T F U
3. *a.* The draft has become the most urgent problem for practically every American male.
   b. The draft can never become the most urgent
problem for practically every American male. T F U
4. *a.* A few members of the post-World War II generation fail to be affluent.
   b. Members of the post-World War II generation
never fail to be affluent.   T F U
5. *a.* Vietniks frequently burn their draft cards.
   b. Vietniks always burn their draft cards. T F U

B. In each of the following sets of propositions, assuming that the
first is *false,* what do you know about the second?
1. *a.* Nearly every student today is more interested in the future
of man than in the national interest.
   b. Few, if any, of today's students are more interested in man's future than in the national
interest.   T F U
2. *a.* An unlimited war fails to demand the full
strength of the U.S.
   b. Unlimited wars never fail to demand the full
strength of the U.S.   T F U
3. *a.* Only local people know local problems.
   b. No one who knows local problems is local. T F U
4. *a.* Most draft officials deny that the system is
undemocratic.
   b. Draft officials seldom deny that the system is
undemocratic.   T F U
5. *a.* For many, going into the Army is not their
ideal.
   b. To go into the Army is the ideal of everyone. T F U

Part VII

Assuming that the first proposition is *true,* what can you determine about each of the following?

1. Whoever makes the noise sets the tone.
   a. Everyone who is silent sets the tone.   T   F   U
   b. A few that fail to make the noise are not tone set-
      ters.   T   F   U
   c. Whoever fails to set the tone fails to make the
      noise.   T   F   U
   d. Few tone setters are other than the noise makers.   T   F   U
   e. No tone setter is a noise maker.   T   F   U
   f. Noise makers always fail to set the tone.   T   F   U
   g. Those failing to set the tone are never noise mak-
      ers.   T   F   U
   h. Many of the silent fail to set the tone.   T   F   U
2. Adults never lost their cool.
   a. Few persons other than adults fail to lose their
      cool.   T   F   U
   b. Everyone who fails to lose his cool is a nonadult.   T   F   U
   c. No one who fails to lose his cool is an adult.   T   F   U
   d. Whoever loses his cool is other than an adult.   T   F   U
   e. No nonadult loses his cool.   T   F   U
   f. Every nonadult is a person who fails to lose his
      cool.   T   F   U
3. Only a few Kookies were removed from the gallery.
   a. A few Kookies were not among those who were not
      removed from the gallery.   T   F   U
   b. A few of those removed from the gallery were not
      other than Kookies.   T   F   U
   c. Several of those removed from the gallery were
      not Kookies.   T   F   U
   d. Kookies never fail to be removed from the gallery.   T   F   U
4. Few, if any, drug addicts can stop taking drugs.
   a. Many who cannot stop taking drugs are not other
      than drug addicts.   T   F   U
   b. Several persons who cannot stop taking drugs are
      drug addicts.   T   F   U
   c. No one who cannot stop taking drugs is a drug
      addict.   T   F   U
   d. No drug addict can stop taking drugs.   T   F   U

Part VIII

Assuming that the first proposition is *false,* what do you know about each of the following?

1. Whatever satisfies human desires is true.
    a. Nothing failing to satisfy human desires is true.   T F U
    b. Whatever fails to satisfy human desires is true.   T F U
    c. Several things which do not satisfy human desires
    are true.   T F U
    d. Several things which satisfy human desires are
    true.   T F U
2. Whoever is valiant is courageous.
    a. Everyone who fails to be valiant is other than
    courageous.   T F U
    b. Many who fail to be valiant are not those who
    fail to be courageous.   T F U
    c. Those who lack being valiant are never lacking
    in courage.   T F U
    d. No one who is valiant fails to be courageous.   T F U
3. Nobody in the State Department is disloyal.
    a. Some people who are not in the State Depart-
    ment are not loyal.   T F U
    b. Everyone who is not in the State Department is
    loyal.   T F U
    c. No one who is outside the State Department is
    loyal.   T F U
    d. A few of those outside the State Department are
    loyal.   T F U
4. Only atheists are Communists.
    a. Whoever is not an atheist is other than a Com-
    munist.   T F U
    b. Anyone who is not a Communist fails to be an
    atheist.   T F U
    c. No one who fails to be an atheist is a Communist.   T F U
    d. Every atheist is a Communist.   T F U
5. Whoever favors medicare is a Socialist.
    a. No one who is not a Socialist favors medicare.   T F U

b. Some persons who are not Socialists do not fail
to favor medicare. T F U

c. No one who favors medicare is a Socialist. T F U

d. A few who favor medicare are Socialists. T F U

CHAPTER EIGHT

Categorical Syllogisms

*"Well, in our country," said Alice, . . . "you'd generally get
to somewhere else—if you ran very fast for a long time. . . ."*
*"A slow sort of country!" said the Queen. "Now, here, you
see, it takes all the running you can do, to keep in the same
place. If you want to get somewhere else, you must run at least
twice as fast as that!"*

Through the Looking Glass—LEWIS CARROLL

1. Formal Validity

When we argue, we usually try to defend or give reasons why we
hold such and such to be so and so. The way we argue depends in
part on our skill, on the subject under consideration, and on the
number of reasons we offer in support of what we wish to assert. A
discussion of the Supreme Court, for example, might lead to the
conclusion that whatever the Supreme Court decides is just. When
challenged to defend this point of view, a party to the dispute
might simply offer two reasons; namely, that whatever the Supreme
Court decides is constitutional and whatever is constitutional is just.
A second party to the dispute might admit the validity of the reasoning, but challenge the reasons by arguing in a more complicated
way. He might say, "If what is constitutional is just, then either the
Constitution is a perfect document or justice is simply whatever is
legal in the United States; and since no human document is perfect,
if what is constitutional is just, then justice is simply whatever is

legal in the United States, and to hold to the latter is to open the door to tyranny instead of freedom."

Different ways of reasoning give rise to different argument forms. Our discussion of the *form* of such arguments is not concerned with the *truth* or *falsity* of the propositions involved. We are here interested only in the validity of the reasoning. Of course, when an argument is sound, its premises will be true and its reasoning valid. The conclusion will then be necessarily true. It is impossible to draw a false conclusion from factually true premises by a valid reasoning process. But it *is* possible for the conclusion of an argument to be true when the premises are false and the reasoning is invalid. Indeed, the conclusion may also be true when some or all of the premises are false and the reasoning is valid. The conclusion may even be true when the reasoning is invalid and the premises are true. In addition, a false conclusion may be drawn from premises, no matter whether true or false, if the reasoning is fallacious; and even when the reasoning is correct, a false premise may also lead to a false conclusion.

It will make our task much simpler if we limit our study to the validity of the form of the reasoning involved and do not here concern ourselves with either the truth or falsity of the premises or the truth or falsity of the conclusion.

2. The Structure of the Categorical Syllogism

The first type of argument—the categorical syllogism—is made up of three categorical propositions. Two of these offer the reasons, the premises, from which the third categorical, the conclusion, is drawn.

The conclusion, as well as the premises, of a categorical syllogism may be any combination of A, E, I, or O propositions. The term appearing as the predicate of the conclusion is known as the *major term* of the argument; the term appearing as the subject of the conclusion is the *minor term* of the argument.

Consider the basic structure of one of the arguments:

1. Whatever is constitutional is just.
2. Whatever is decided by the Supreme Court is constitutional.
3. Therefore, whatever is decided by the Supreme Court is just.

The conclusion is an A proposition; its predicate term P can be written as *whatever is just,* and its subject term S is *decisions reached by the Supreme Court.* S is then the minor term of the argument, and P is the major term of the argument. You will note that S, the minor term, also appears in the second premise, and P, the major term, appears in the first premise. The premise in which the major term appears is the *major premise;* the premise in which the minor term appears is the *minor premise.* When we write a categorical syllogism in its standard logical form, we follow this order: first, the major premise, then the minor premise, then the conclusion.

Thus far we have said nothing about the term *whatever is con- stitutional.* This appears in both premises, but it does not occur in the conclusion. We shall call such a term M, the *middle term.*

A categorical syllogism then consists of three, and only three, terms —the major, the minor, and the middle term—each of which occurs twice, and of three, and only three, categorical propositions. The major term always occurs as the predicate of the conclusion, but it may be either the subject or the predicate of the major premise. Likewise, the minor term is always the subject of the conclusion, but it may appear as either the subject or the predicate of the minor premise. The middle term occurs in both premises, never in the conclusion; but the middle term may be either the subject of a premise or the predicate. Four basic *figures* or variations are thus possible. While the conclusion is always the same, the middle term may appear as the subject of the major premise and the predicate of the minor,

$$M \quad P$$
$$S \quad M$$
$$\overline{S \quad P}, \text{ Figure I};$$

as the predicate of both premises,

$$P \quad M$$
$$S \quad M$$
$$\overline{S \quad P}, \text{ Figure II};$$

as the subject of both premises,

$$M \quad P$$
$$M \quad S$$
$$\overline{S \quad P}, \text{ Figure III};$$

and as the predicate of the major premise and the subject of the minor premise,

$$
\begin{array}{cc}
\text{P} & \text{M} \\
\text{M} & \text{S} \\
\hline
\text{S} & \text{P, Figure IV.}
\end{array}
$$

Not every syllogistic form which we obtain by inserting A, E, I, or O propositions into these figures will be valid, however. According to traditional rules an argument will be valid in the first figure only in the following cases:

Major premise	MaP	MaP	MaP	MeP	MeP	MeP
Minor premise	SaM	SaM	SiM	SaM	SaM	SiM
Conclusion	SaP	SiP	SiP	SeP	SoP	SoP
	(1)	(2)	(3)	(4)	(5)	(6)

3. The Moods of the Syllogism

The variation in the quality and quantity of the categorical proposition of a syllogism is known as the *mood* of the syllogism. In referring to the mood, we begin with the major premise, then the minor, and then the conclusion. The mood of (6)

$$
\begin{array}{c}
\text{MeP} \\
\text{SiM} \\
\hline
\text{SoP}
\end{array}
$$

is thus EIO.

The valid moods in the first figure can therefore be summarized as:

1. AAA		4. EAE
2. AAI		5. EAO
3. AII		6. EIO

Other moods are possible, but they will not result in a valid argument, for reasons that we shall see.

The following is a complete list of valid moods in all four figures:

	(1)	(2)	(3)	(4)	(5)	(6)
Figure I	MaP	MaP	MaP	MeP	MeP	MeP
	SaM	SaM	SiM	SaM	SaM	SiM
	SaP	SiP	SiP	SeP	SoP	SoP

(7)	(8)	(9)	(10)	(11)	(12)
PaM	PaM	PaM	PeM	PeM	PeM
SeM	SeM	SoM	SaM	SaM	SiM
SeP	SoP	SoP	SeP	SoP	SoP

ure II

(13)	(14)	(15)	(16)	(17)	(18)
MaP	MaP	MeP	MeP	MiP	MoP
MaS	MiS	MaS	MiS	MaS	MaS
SiP	SiP	SoP	SoP	SiP	SoP

ure III

(19)	(20)	(21)	(22)	(23)	(24)
PaM	PaM	PaM	PeM	PeM	PiM
MaS	MeS	MeS	MaS	MiS	MaS
SiP	SeP	SoP	SoP	SoP	SiP

ure IV

ese valid moods need not be committed to memory, but certain tures of the various figures are noteworthy.

By inspection you will find that the different valid moods are ited to:

a. AAA	d. AEE	g. EAE	j. IAI
b. AAI	e. AEO	h. EAO	k. OAO
c. AII	f. AOO	i. EIO	

Moods EIO and EAO occur in all four figures. Figure I shares AE with Figure II; it shares AAI with Figures III and IV and II with Figure III. Mood AAA is valid only when it occurs in the st figure.

The other figures also have certain noteworthy features. You will that the conclusion of a valid argument in the second figure is ways negative and that it is the only figure in which AOO has a lid occurrence. The second figure shares AEO and AEE with the urth figure. The third figure never has a universal conclusion; its nclusion is always particular. The mood OAO does not occur sewhere, but IAI is shared with the fourth figure. The fourth figure es not contain any moods that do not occur elsewhere; thus some gicians prefer to dispense with it altogether.

The ambitious student may wish to remember most of the valid oods in each figure by means of certain code names. The mood AA in the first figure can easily be recalled by the word ARBARA, since the vowel A occurs three times. Similarly the ood EAE in the first figure can be remembered by the word ELARENT, since EAE are the only vowels. DARII and FERIO can help recall AII and EIO in the first figure. The following a list of helpful code names. With the exceptions of BARBAR CELARENT, DARII, and FERIO, which can easily be committ to memory, it is rather impractical and unnecessary to memori the others. But they can serve as a useful reference.

FIGURE I	FIGURE II	FIGURE III	FIGURE IV
BARBARA	CESARE	DARATI	FRESISON
CELARENT	CAMESTRES	DATISI	BRAMANT
DARII	FESTINO	DISAMIS	CAMENES
FERIO	BAROCO	FERISON	FESAPO
		FELAPTON	DIMARIS
		BOCARDO	

You will note that the moods AAI and EAO in the first figure a actually redundant and constitute a weakened form. Since fro the premises MaP and SaM the conclusion SaP could have be drawn, and from MeP and SaM we could have concluded Se Such weakened conclusions are valid according to the rules we sh formulate, but they cannot be readily tested by every technique.

In the second figure EAO and AEO are also weakened, where in the third figure the premises AA in DARAPTI and EA FELAPTON are more than we need to reach the conclusion. T. same conclusions can be attained in DATISI and FERISON. Lik wise in the fourth figure the conclusion of BRAMANTIP can I attained in DIMARIS and that of FESAPO can be attained FRESISON. Syllogisms containing strengthened premises—name DARAPTI, FELATON, BRAMANTIP, and FESAPO and tl weakened moods AAI, EAO, in the first figure, EAO and AEO the second, and AEO in the fourth—are to be *tested solely* *means of the four axioms of a valid syllogism.* The other tests a simply inapplicable.

4. *Determining the Validity of Syllogisms*

We have listed the valid moods in each figure, but what mak them valid and why are they alone valid?

Let us draw a Venn diagram of AAA in the first figure. Sin

e are now dealing with three terms, we shall need three circles. For
)nvenience we shall number the different segments.

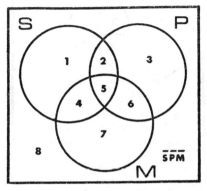

FIGURE 9.

If we now take as our syllogism, "All menacing things are petri-
ying. All spiders are menacing. Thus, all spiders are petrifying,"
magine that the circle S contains everything denoted by the term
piders, P contains whatever is petrifying, and M whatever is a
nenace. Area 1 would then have spiders, but nothing that is either
nenacing or petrifying, so we may write it as (SP̄M̄); Area 2 has
piders which are petrifying, but not menacing (SPM̄); Area 3 con-
ains things which are petrifying, but not menacing, and which are
ther than spiders (S̄PM̄); Area 4 contains menacing spiders which
lo not petrify (SP̄M); Area 5 is filled with spiders which both
nenace and petrify (SPM); Area 6 contains things other than
piders which are both menacing and petrifying (S̄PM); and Area
` holds what is menacing but is neither a spider nor petrifying
`S̄P̄M); while Area 8 encloses whatever is neither a spider nor
)etrifying nor a menace (S̄P̄M̄), but which falls within our realm of
liscourse, that is, living things.

Let us accept the premise that "All menacing things are petri-
`ying," MaP. When we draw this on our diagram, we eliminate
Areas 4 and 7, as in Figure 10.

Now let us also accept the minor premise, "All spiders are menac-
ng." By adding that to our first diagram, we now obtain the dia-
;ram below. The proposition "All spiders are menacing" is equiva-

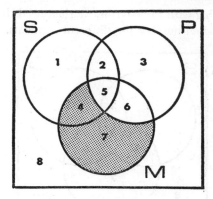

Figure 10.

lent to "No spiders are nonmenacing," which means that Area 1 and 2 are empty of membership. All the spiders that are left are to be found in Area 5. Areas 1, 2, 4, and 7 have been shaded out to indicate they are empty, and Areas 3 and 6 do not contain any spiders at all.

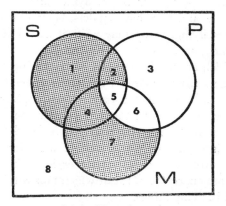

AAA (first figure)
Figure 11.

We do not need any further diagram; the conclusion "All spiders are petrifying" can be seen from Area 5.

The argument:

All menacing things are petrifying
All spiders are menacing
∴ All spiders are petrifying

thus valid. That is, the conclusion can be inferred from the
remises, so that if you accept the latter, you must also accept the
ormer.

It is evident, then, that any argument of the form

MaP
SaM
∴ SaP

a valid argument. The validity of this figure and mood can read-
y be seen from the diagram.

FIGURE 12.

Let us keep the same mood AAA and change the figure to be the
econd, as in the following argument: "Whatever the legislature
ecides is legal, because only what is just is legal, and what the legis-
ature decides is just." Here S contains "Whatever the legislature
ecides," P contains "What is legal," M contains "What is just."

When we diagram the proposition "only what is just is legal,"
aM, we deny that Areas 2 and 3 have members. Whatever is legal
just, so that just and legal things must be somewhere in Areas 5
nd 6, as this diagram shows.

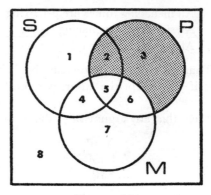

FIGURE 13.

When we add the minor premise SaM to this diagram we the
shade Area 1, since this must also be empty.

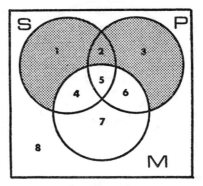

AAA (second figure)
FIGURE 14.

The conclusion SaP cannot be seen on the diagram, for there ma
still be decisions of the legislature in Area 4 which are not include
among what is just. We have no information about this area's bein
empty. Thus the argument AAA in the second figure can be see
(from the diagram) not to lead validly to the conclusion SaP.

A categorical syllogism is a mediate inference. The conclusion
drawn about the minor and major term on the basis of the relation
ship that each sustains to a third or middle term. However, th

conclusion cannot be valid unless either the minor or the major term is related to every member of the middle term. *The middle term must be distributed at least once;* otherwise the conclusion does not follow, and it will not appear on the Venn diagram. We have just seen an example which failed to obey this rule.

A diagram of the mood AEE in the second figure results in shading Areas 2 and 3 when the major premise PaM is placed on it and in shading 4 and 5 when the minor premise SeM is diagramed. The conclusion SeP can be seen on the diagram, since Areas 2 and 5 are clearly seen to be empty after the premises are diagramed.

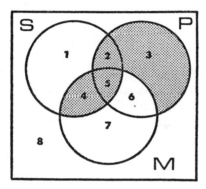

AEE (second figure)
FIGURE 15.

But when in the diagram we retain the mood AEE and change the figure to the first, we cannot find our conclusion on the diagram, because the major premise MaP shades Areas 4 and 7 and the minor premise SeM shades Area 5, but the conclusion denies that Area 2 has any members.

The basic reason why AEE in the first figure is invalid is that the conclusion SeP refers to every member of S and every member of P. Both terms are distributed; but when reference was made to the major term in the major premise MaP, the major term was undistributed. A valid deductive inference about every member of a class cannot be drawn on the basis of a reference to some members of that class. In other words, *no term may be distributed in the conclusion which was undistributed in the premises.*

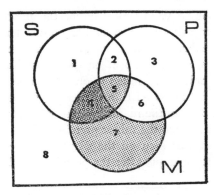

AEE (first figure)
Figure 16.

The mood EAE is valid in both the first and second figures, as seen in the accompanying diagram. The major premise denies membership to Areas 5 and 6, and the minor premise denies membership to Areas 1 and 2, and therefore "No S's are P."

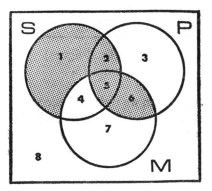

EAE (first and second figures)
Figure 17.

But when we change the mood to EAA, the conclusion SaP cannot be read on the diagram, for there is still at least one S in Area 4 which is not in P. If a premise is negative, the conclusion must also be negative; and conversely, when the conclusion is negative, a premise must be negative. *A negative conclusion cannot be drawn from two affirmative premises, and an affirmative conclusion cannot be drawn when any premise is negative.* Note the diagram of AAE, first figure. The premises MaP and SaM in the first figure are both affirmative; the negative conclusion SeP is clearly invalid.

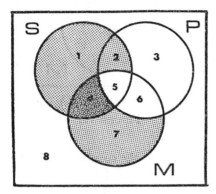

AAE (first figure)
FIGURE 18.

The next two diagrams will indicate further that *two negative premises do not yield a valid conclusion of any sort.*

Let us look first at the mood EEE in any figure. Here MeP shades Areas 5 and 6 and SeM shades Area 4, but the conclusion SeP requires that Area 2 be shaded when in fact it is not. The mood EEA would also be invalid.

Likewise in the next diagram no conclusion can be drawn from the premises E and O. The information from E enables us to shade Areas 5 and 6. The information from O enables us only to place an *x* either on the line between Areas 1 and 2 or in Area 7. It does not affect the *x* between Areas 4 and 7. Obviously we cannot conclude SaP because Areas 1 and 4 are not shaded, and we cannot conclude SeP since Area 2 is unshaded.

In summary, then, a syllogism is invalid when any of the following occurs:

1. The middle term is undistributed. It must be distributed at least once.

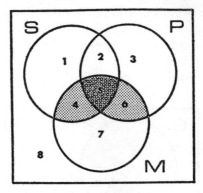

EEE (any figure)
Figure 19.

2. A term is distributed in the conclusion and undistributed in the premises.

3. An affirmative conclusion is drawn from a negative premise or a negative conclusion is drawn from two affirmative premises.

4. A conclusion is drawn from two negative premises.

In all other instances a syllogistic argument is valid. Remember however, that an argument which does not contain three, and only three, terms and three, and only three, propositions is not a syllogism.

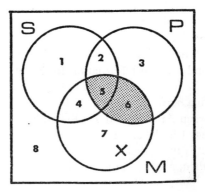

EO (any figure)
Figure 20.

An inspection of the diagrams of all the valid syllogisms will indicate that in each case the following rules are obeyed.

1. *The middle term is distributed at least once.*

2. *No term is distributed in the conclusion which is undistributed in a premise.*

3. *Whenever a premise is negative, the conclusion is negative, and vice versa.*

4. *A valid conclusion is never drawn from two negative premises.*

Whenever the middle term is undistributed, the fallacy committed is known as an *undistributed middle.* When the major term is distributed in the conclusion and undistributed in the premise as in AEE, first figure, the fallacy committed is known as an *illicit major;* when the minor term is distributed in the conclusion and is undistributed in the premise as in AAA, third figure, the fallacy is known as an *illicit minor.* The violation of the principle that a negative conclusion requires a negative premise is known as the fallacy of *a negative conclusion without a negative premise,* and the violation of the principle that a negative premise requires a negative conclusion is known as the fallacy of *a negative premise without a negative conclusion.* The drawing of a conclusion from two negative premises is known as the fallacy of *exclusive premises.* The introduction of more or less than three terms is known as the fallacy of the *pseudo-syllogism.*

EXERCISES

Reduce the following arguments to standard logical form. Name the major, minor, and middle term. State the figure and mood. Determine whether the argument is valid or invalid by applying the rules of a categorical syllogism. If invalid, name the fallacy committed.

1. University professors always have graduate degrees, since they are reasonably intelligent, and anyone who has a graduate degree is reasonably intelligent.

2. Financial depressions are never desired by business leaders, since such depressions are never beneficial to society as a whole, and only what is desired by the leaders of the community is beneficial to society as a whole.

3. Conservatives always cling obscurely to the past, so they never accept change graciously, since no one who clings obscurely to the past accepts change graciously.

4. Only liberals feel there is nothing to fear from the Russians, and since whoever feels there is nothing to fear from the Russians opposes U.S. policy in Vietnam, it follows that every liberal opposes U.S. policy in Vietnam.

5. All Americans are not opposed to armed intervention, since many Americans are unafraid of the risk of atomic war, and no one unafraid of running the risk of atomic war is opposed to armed intervention.

6. Few advocates of fair housing are insincere, since they all have a sense of justice, and no one with a sense of justice is insincere.

7. Every congressman is a politician, since only politicians are statesmen, and at least some congressmen are statesmen.

8. At least a few progressives are realists, and progressives are always reformers, so at least some reformers are realists.

9. Every economist is economy-minded, so whoever is economy-minded favors price control, since whoever favors price control is an economist.

10. Some chickens are not able to fly, since they are always fenced in, and some things that are able to fly are not fenced in.

11. Since every student is reasonably intelligent, and only those responsible for their behavior are reasonably intelligent, it follows that only those responsible for their behavior are students.

12. Only those in high income brackets are wealthy, because only those who contribute to employment are in high income brackets, and whoever is wealthy contributes to employment.

13. Since the expansion of war is always inevitable, and whatever is inevitable never leads to disaster, the expansion of war never leads to disaster.

14. Since only Communists violate the legal political structure, and no responsible citizen is guilty of such violation, it follows that responsible citizens are never Communists.

15. Witch doctors always believe in voodoo, since only the superstitious believe in voodoo, and whoever is superstitious has such a belief.

16. Few women are unemployed, since many women are economically self-sufficient, and the unemployed are never economically self-sufficient.

17. At least a few politicians are honest, since all of them are ambitious, and at least some ambitious people are honest.

18. Some animals are not mammals, since all bipeds are mammals, and some bipeds are animals.

19. Whoever is sincere is a fanatic, and some sincere people are religious, so some of the religious are fanatics.

20. Labor unions never exploit the worker, since whoever exploits the worker is selfish, and labor unions are never selfish.

21. Since athletes never smoke, they obviously favor the prevention of cancer, because whoever favors the prevention of cancer never smokes.

22. Since daffodil pickers never smoke, and smokers are always prone to cancer, daffodil pickers never are prone to cancer.

23. Dead cancer victims requiring coffins always fit nicely into flip-top boxes designed for smokers, because only dead cancer victims requiring coffins are smokers, and every smoker fits nicely into flip-top boxes designed for smokers.

24. Pornography never poisons the mind, since whatever poisons the mind is to be condemned by censorship, and pornography is not to be condemned by censorship.

25. Since any man that does not wish to smell like a man any more wishes to smell like clover hay, and few that rush to buy foo-foo juice in a department store wish to smell like clover hay, it follows that a few men that do not wish to smell like a man any more are not those who rush to buy foo-foo juice in a department store.

26. Education is always inseparable from religious assumptions, since it always deals with ultimate values, and whatever deals with ultimate values is inseparable from religious assumptions.

27. Since only those who have access to public funds are public institutions, and whoever has access to public funds is entitled to the complete and absolute control of all education, public institutions are always entitled to the complete and absolute control of all education.

28. Since a few men of wit are fond of flattery, and whoever is fond of flattery eats the food of fools, a few men of wit eat the food of fools.

29. No Berlin-bound convoy submits to a head count, since no Berlin-bound convoy lowers its tail gate, and no one who lowers his tail gate submits to a head count.

30. Every ancient Indian document is written in Sanskrit, and most of the Upanishads are ancient Indian documents, so at least several of the Upanishads were not written in Sanskrit.

31. Whatever the Supreme Court decides is just, because whatever it decides is constitutional, and only what is just is constitutional.

32. Whatever is legal is what the legislature decides, because only what is just is decided by the legislature, and whatever is legal is just.

33. Whatever is legal is what the legislature decides, because whatever is just is what the legislature decides, and only what is legal is just.

34. Every flunkey needs a footman, since anyone who needs a footman is fagged, and whatever is fagged is a flunkey.

35. Since a few divorces are acceptable to the majority of voters, and only what is an asset to a political career is acceptable to the majority of voters, some divorces are an asset to a political career.

36. Since abductions are always shameful, and only what is shameful is depraved, it follows that at least some abductions are depraved.

37. A few fraternity parties are dull, since only fraternity parties are chaperoned, and chaperoned parties are always dull.

38. A misdemeanor is never a crime, since only crimes are felonies, and a misdemeanor is never a felony.

39. No cotton picker is a chicken plucker, because all chicken pluckers are finger lickers, and no cotton picker is a finger licker.

40. Because only the partially conditioned are responsible, and some human beings are partially conditioned, it follows that some human beings are responsible.

41. Nothing that creeps is very friendly, so few snails are friendly, since snails always creep.

42. Many college courses are not useful, because only college courses

require real intellectual effort, and there are things that require real intellectual effort other than college courses.

43. Only what fails to fade away dies, so, since old soldiers never fail to fade away, they never die.

44. At least a few arguments on this exam are valid, because only when it is valid does an argument obey the rules, and there are arguments on this exam which obey the rules.

45. Many logicians are mad, because most mad people like logic, and only logicians like logic.

46. Since only what is destructive is tragic, and wrecked marriages are destructive, they are tragic.

47. Every oyster is a vegetarian, since to have no teeth is to be a vegetarian, and to have no teeth is to be an oyster.

48. Whatever has pretty legs swims in a bikini, so, since worms do not have pretty legs, they never swim in a bikini.

CHAPTER NINE

Additional Tests of Categorical Syllogisms

"There's no use trying," [*Alice*] *said: "one* can't *believe impossible things."*

"I daresay you haven't had much practice," said the Queen. "When I was your age, I always did it for half-an-hour a day. Why, sometimes I've believed as many as six impossible things before breakfast."

Through the Looking Glass—LEWIS CARROLL

The rules of the categorical syllogism studied in the preceding chapter are sufficient to test the validity of every categorical syllogism. Nothing more is needed for practical purposes. Additional tests can be applied within certain limits.[1]

1. Venn Diagrams of Valid Arguments

1.1 Venn Diagrams in the First Figure

The detailed application of Venn diagrams is shown in the following.

To test the validity of BARBARA in Figure I, Step I translates the premise into equations.

Step I. Premises written in equation form: (*a*) MaP is equivalent to $M\bar{P} = O$; (*b*) the minor premise SaM becomes $S\bar{M} = O$.

[1] The Venn diagram technique is not applicable to a particular conclusion drawn from two universal premises.

Step II. Visualize the major premise by drawing it on your diagram.

a. Since $M\bar{P} = O$, shade that part of circle M which is outside the circle P, the result will be:

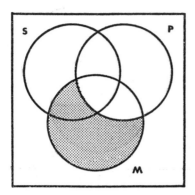

FIGURE 21.

Your diagram now indicates that all M's are P's.

b. Now visualize your minor premise $S\bar{M} = O$ by shading the area of circle S which is outside of M, thereby indicating that "No S is $\bar{M}$" or "All S is M." Your diagram now looks as follows:

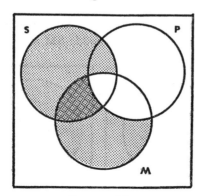

FIGURE 22.

CAUTION: Exception. When both premises are universal, begin with the major premise; but if the major premise is particular, begin with the minor premise.

Step III. Try to read the conclusion "All S is P" on the diagram. If the conclusion is readily evident, the argument is valid; otherwise it is invalid.

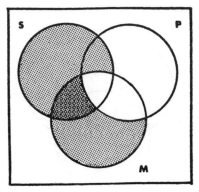

FIGURE 23.

In the diagram of BARBARA the shaded areas indicate that "All S is P." $S\bar{P} = O$.

The diagrams of the remaining valid arguments in Figure I are derived as follows.

CELARENT

Step I. *a.* Translation of major MeP into equation $MP = O$.
   b. Translation of minor SaM: $S\bar{M} = O$.

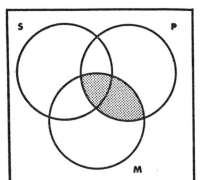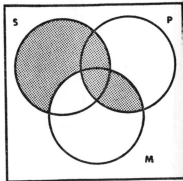

FIGURE 24.   FIGURE 25.

Step II. a. MP = O.   *b.* MP = O combined with SM̄ = O.

Step III. From the completed diagram in Step II*b* we can see that "No S is P."

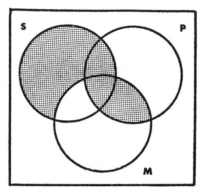

FIGURE 26.

DARII

Step I. *a.* Translation of major MaP ≡ MP̄ = O.

b. Translation of minor SiM ≡ SM ≠ O.

Step II. a. MP̄ = O.   *b.* MP̄ = O combined with SM ≠ O.

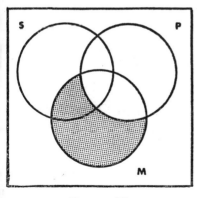

FIGURE 27.

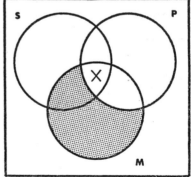

FIGURE 28.

Step III. It is evident from the above *x* that "Some S is P."

FERIO

> *Step I.* *a.* Translation of major MeP ≡ MP = O.
> *b.* Translation of minor SiM ≡ SM ≠ O.

> *Step II. a.* MP = O.   *b.* Combine MP = O with SM ≠ O.

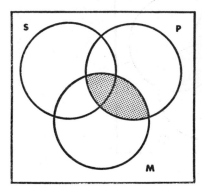

FIGURE 29.   FIGURE 30.

Step III. It is evident from the *x* in the above diagram that "Some S is not P."

1.2   Venn diagrams in the second figure

CESARE

> *Step I.* *a.* Translation of major PeM ≡ PM = O.
> *b.* Translation of minor SaM ≡ SM̄ = O.

> *Step II. a.* PM = O.   *b.* PM = O combined with SM̄ = O.

Step III. This enable us to read that "No S is P" (Figure 32).

Note. The diagram of CESARE is identical with that of CELARENT.

CAMESTRES

> *Step I.* *a.* Translation of major PaM ≡ PM̄ = O.
> *b.* Translation of minor SeM ≡ SM = O.

> *Step II. a.* PM̄ = O.   *b.* PM̄ = O combined with SM = O.

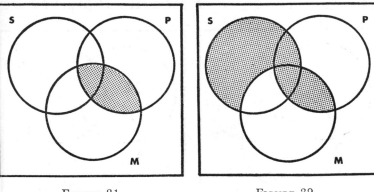

FIGURE 31.   FIGURE 32.

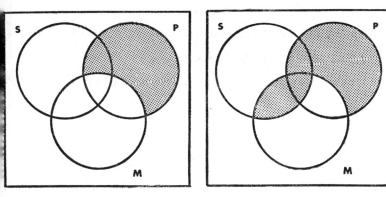

FIGURE 33.   FIGURE 34.

Step III. The conclusion "No S is P" is evident, since "All S is P̄."

FESTINO

   Step I.   *a.* Translation of major PeM ≡ PM = O.
          b. Translation of minor SiM ≡ SM ≠ O.
   Steps II, III. Result in a diagram identical with FERIO of Figure I.

BAROCO

   Step I.   *a.* Translation of major PaM ≡ PM̄ = O.
          b. Translation of minor SoM ≡ SM̄ ≠ O.

Step II. a. PM̄ = O.   *b.* PM̄ = O combined with SM̄ ≠ O.

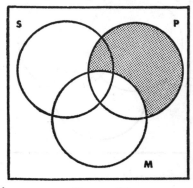

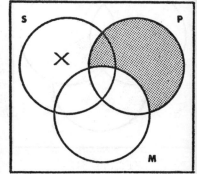

Figure 35.   Figure 36.

Step III. The *x* in the diagram indicates that "Some S is not P."

1.3   *Venn diagrams in the third figure*

We shall not utilize Venn diagrams to test DARAPTI or FELAPTON.

DATISI

Step I. a. Translation of major MaP ≡ MP̄ = O.
       b. Translation of minor MiS ≡ MS ≠ O.

Step II. a. MP̄ = O.   *b.* MP̄ = O combined with MS ≠ O.

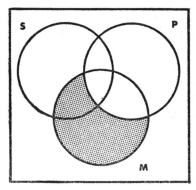

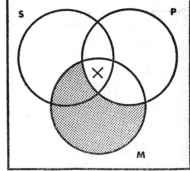

Figure 37.   Figure 38.

Step III. The *x* indicates that "Some S is P."

Note. The diagram of DATISI is identical with that of DARII.

DISAMIS

Step I.   *a.* Translation of major MiP $\equiv$ MP $\neq$ O.

         b. Translation of minor MaS $\equiv$ M$\bar{\text{S}}$ = O.

Step II. Note reverse order of *a* and *b* diagrams: minor first, since the major is particular.

    b. M$\bar{\text{S}}$ = O.   *a.* M$\bar{\text{S}}$ = O combined with MP $\neq$ O.

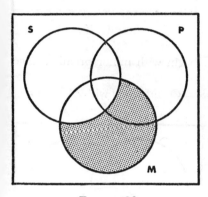
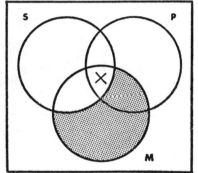

FIGURE 39.   FIGURE 40.

Step III. The *x* in the above diagram indicates that "Some S is P."

FERISON

Step I.   *a.* Translation of major MeP $\equiv$ MP = O.

         b. Translation of minor MiS $\equiv$ MS $\neq$ O.

Step II.

a. MP = O.   *b.* MP = O combined with MS $\neq$ O.

Note identical diagrams with FERIO and FESTINO.

Step III. "Some S is not P" is indicated by the *x*.

BOCARDO

Step I.   *a.* Translation of major MoP $\equiv$ M$\bar{\text{P}}$ $\neq$ O.

         b. Translation of minor MaS $\equiv$ M$\bar{\text{S}}$ = O.

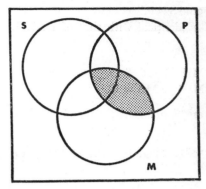

FIGURE 41.   FIGURE 42.

Step II. Note reversal of order: begin with minor premise, since major premise is particular.

  b. M$\bar{S}$ = O.   *a.* M$\bar{S}$ = O combined with M$\bar{P}$ ≠ O.

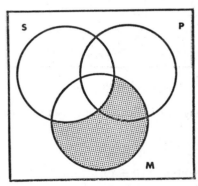
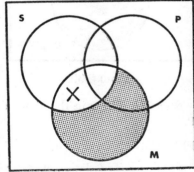

FIGURE 43.   FIGURE 44.

Step III. Read the conclusion "Some S is not P" indicated by the *x* in the preceding diagram.

1.4   Venn Diagrams in the Fourth Figure

FRESISON

  Step I. *a.* Translation of major PeM to PM = O.
            b. Translation of minor MiS to MS ≠ O.

Step II. a. PM = O.   *b.* PM = O combined with MS $\neq$ O.

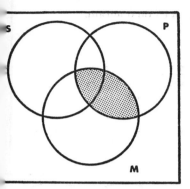

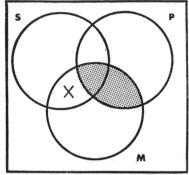

FIGURE 45.   FIGURE 46.

Step III. Read conclusion "Some S is not P," as indicated by *x* on ¡gram.

᾽MENES

Step I. a. Translation of major PaM ≡ P$\bar{\text{M}}$ = O.
          b. Translation of minor MeS ≡ MS = O.

Step II. a. P$\bar{\text{M}}$ = O.   *b.* P$\bar{\text{M}}$ = O combined with MS = O.

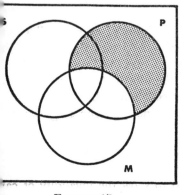

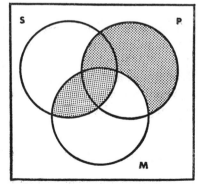

FIGURE 47.   FIGURE 48.

Note. Diagram of **CAMENES** is identical with that of **CAME TRES.**

Step III. Read conclusion "No S is P" on diagram.

DIMARIS

> *Step I.*   *a.* Translation of major PiM $\equiv$ PM $\neq$ O.
>   *b.* Translation of minor MaS $\equiv$ M$\bar{\text{S}}$ = O.

> *Step II.* Note reversal of Steps *a* and *b*.

>   *b.* M$\bar{\text{S}}$ = O.   *a.* M$\bar{\text{S}}$ = O combined with PM $\neq$

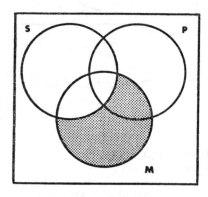
                                        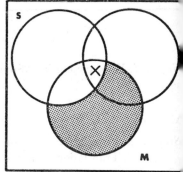

        Figure 49.   Figure 50.

The preceding diagrams show the validity of every possible categorical syllogism with the exception of AAI and EAO in the first figure, EAO and AEO in the second figure, AAI and EAO in the third figure, and AAI and EAO in the fourth. Arguments with two universal premises and a particular conclusion should be tested applying the rules of the syllogism, and not by Venn diagrams.

2. *The Possible Moods of the Syllogism*

Venn diagrams may also be used to show the invalidity of categorical syllogisms. However, as previously seen, the rules of the syllogism eliminate most moods very readily. The following table indicate the sixty-four possible moods of the categorical syllogism.

TABLE I.

1	2	3	4
A A A	A I A	A E A	A O A
A A E	A I E	A E E	A O E
A A I	A I I	A E I	A O I
A A O	A I O	A E O	A O O

TABLE II.

1	2	3	4
E A A	E E A	E O A	E I A
E A E	E E E	E O I	E I E
E A I	E E I	E O E	E I I
E A O	E E O	E O O	E I O

TABLE III.

1	2	3	4
I A A	I E A	I I A	I O A
I A E	I E E	I I E	I O E
I A I	I E I	I I I	I O I
I A O	I E O	I I O	I O O

TABLE IV.

1	2	3	4
O A A	O E A	O I A	O O A
O A E	O E E	O I E	O O E
O A I	O E I	O I I	O O I
O A O	O E O	O I O	O O O

Since each of these moods can occur in the four figures, there are thus 256 possible moods. Our treatment of categorical syllogisms in the preceding chapter disclosed that relatively few are valid.

Table I discloses four possible combinations of premises when the major premise is universal and affirmative:

AA   AI   AE   AO

From the preceding Venn diagrams we have seen that each of them can serve as the premises of valid argument: AA in BAR-BARA, AI in DARII, AE in CAMESTRES, and AO in BAROCO.

In Column 1, AAE and AAO draw a negative conclusion from affirmative premises and so cannot possibly be valid. In Column 2, the moods AIE and AIO are invalid for the same reason. The mood AIA commits the fallacy of illicit minor and violates the principle that whenever a premise is particular, the conclusion must be particular. In Column 3, AEA and AEI illegitimately draw an affirmative conclusion from a negative premise.

Thus, moods AAA, AAI, AII, AEE, AEO, AOO, alone are valid in Table I.

In Table II, Column 1, EA and EI are the only possible combinations of premises. EA occurs in CELARENT and EI in FERIO, FESTINO, FERISON, and FRESISON.

In Columns 1 and 4, EAA, EAI, EIA, EII, draw affirmative conclusions when a premise is negative, and EIE draws a universal conclusion from a particular premise. The arguments in Columns 2 and 3 are clearly invalid since both premises are negative.

EAE, EAO, EIO, are clearly the only valid moods remaining.

In Table III, Column I, IAA draws a universal conclusion from a particular premise and IAE and IAO draw a negative conclusion from affirmative premises, so that IAI is the only possible mood. In Column 2, IEA and IEI draw affirmative conclusions from a negative premise, while IEE and IEO commit the fallacy of illicit major. The moods in Columns 3 and 4 in Tables III and IV are eliminated, since a valid conclusion cannot be drawn when both premises are particular. In Table IV, Column 1, OAO, BOCARDO, is the only valid mood, since OAA and OAI draw an affirmative conclusion from a negative premise, while OAE draws a universal conclusion from a particular premise. The moods in Table IV, Column 2, have two negative premises. By way of summary:

AA	EA	IA	OA
AE	EI		
AI			
AO			

are the sole valid pairs of premises and

AAA	EAE	IAI	OAO
AEE	EIO		
AII			
AOO			

together with their weakened forms, AAI, AEO, and EAO, the sole valid moods. A categorical syllogism formulated with any other premises or in any other mood is bound to be invalid.

It should now be evident that most errors occur when a mood valid in one figure is employed in a figure where it is invalid. The

Venn diagrams on pages 176–191 are to illustrate the most frequent errors.

Familiarity with the most common errors should enable the student to avoid them. Our concern, however, is not simply to detect the errors of others, but to gain some facility in the construction of arguments. The categorical syllogism is a practical reasoning device only after much practice and thorough mastery.

3. Reduction of Arguments to the First Figure

By assuming the validity of BARBARA, CELARENT, DARII, and FERIO,[2] an additional test of the validity of arguments in the second, third, and fourth can be gained by the reduction of every categorical syllogism to the first figure. In most cases this reduction is quite straightforward.

CESARE in the second figure:

$$\frac{\begin{array}{l} PeM \equiv MeP \\ SaM \end{array}}{SeP}$$

and FESTINO

$$\frac{\begin{array}{l} PeM \equiv MeP \\ SiM \end{array}}{SoP}$$

are readily reduced by simple conversion of the major premise. CESARE thus becomes CELARENT, and FESTINO becomes FERIO.

CAMESTRES

$$\frac{\begin{array}{l} PaM \\ SeM \end{array}}{SeP}$$

requires greater ingenuity. The argument must first be rewritten with the premises transposed:

$$\frac{\begin{array}{l} SeM \equiv MeS \\ PaM \quad PaM \end{array}}{SeP \equiv PeS} .$$

Text continues on page 192.

[2] The assumption of the validity of arguments in the first figure is based on the axiom that what is true of the universal is true of the particular and what is not true of a universal is not true of a particular.

VENN DIAGRAMS AS TESTS OF INVALIDITY

MOOD AAA

(is shown in diagrams on this and following three pages)

Translation of premises:

$$M \text{ a } P \equiv M\bar{P} = 0$$
$$\underline{S \text{ a } M \equiv S\bar{M} = 0}$$
$$S \text{ a } P$$

Step 1

Step 2

Arrow indicates that All S is P.

Diag. I. Valid   Step 3

Translation of premises:

P a M ≡ PM̄ = O
S a M ≡ SM̄ = O
─────────────
S a P

Step 1

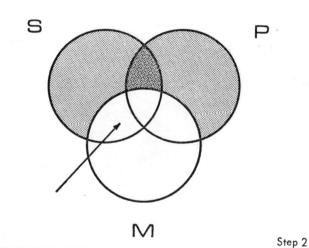

S

P

M

Step 2

Unshaded area indicated by arrow does not
permit conclusion: All S is P.

Diag. II. Invalid   Step 3

Translation of premises:

$$M \ a \ P \equiv M\bar{P} = O$$
$$M \ a \ S \equiv M\bar{S} = O$$
$$\overline{S \ a \ P}$$

Step 1

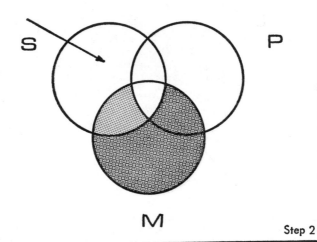

Step 2

Unshaded area indicated by arrow does not
permit conclusion: All·S is P. (Illicit minor)

Diag. III.   Step 3

Translation of premises:

$$P \ a \ M \ \equiv \ P\bar{M} \ = \ 0$$
$$\underline{M \ a \ S} \ \equiv \ M\bar{S} \ = \ 0$$
$$S \ a \ P$$

Step 1

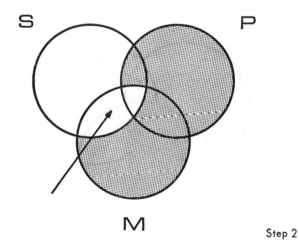

Step 2

Unshaded area indicated by arrow does not permit conclusion: All S is P.

Diag. IV. Invalid   Step 3

MOOD AEE

(in all four diagrams on this and following three pages)

Translation of premises:

$$M \ a \ P \equiv M\overline{P} = 0$$
$$\underline{S \ e \ M \equiv SM = 0}$$
$$S \ e \ P$$

Step 1

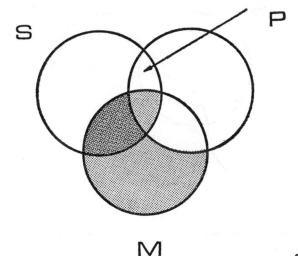

S   P

M

Step 2

Conclusion, No S is P cannot be read from diagram. Area indicated by arrow shows un-shaded area, while the conclusion drawn is that No S remains which is identical with P. (Illicit major)

Diag. I. Invalid   Step 3

Translation of premises:

$$P \ a \ M \equiv P\overline{M} = O$$
$$\underline{S \ e \ M \equiv SM = O}$$
$$S \ e \ P$$

Step 1

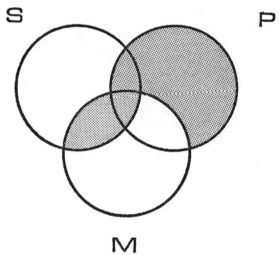

S

P

M

Step 2

Conclusion, No S is P is evident from diagram.

Diag. II. Valid CAMESTRES   Step 3

Translation of premises:

$$M \ a \ P \equiv M\overline{P} = O$$
$$M \ e \ S \equiv MS = O$$
$$\overline{S \ e \ P}$$

Step 1

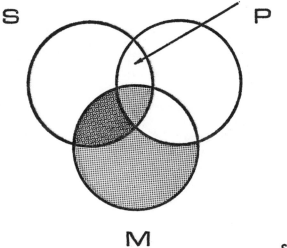

S   P

M

Step 2

Reasoning and diagram identical with
Diag. I of this group. (Illicit minor)

Diag. III. Invalid   Step 3

Translation of premises:

$$P \ a \ M \equiv P\bar{M} = O$$
$$\frac{M \ e \ S \equiv MS = O}{S \ e \ P}$$

Step 1

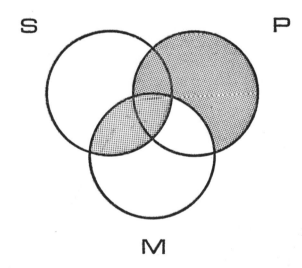

S   P

M

Step 2

Reasoning and diagram identical with Diag. II.

Diag. IV. Valid CAMENES   Step 3

MOOD IAI

(in all four diagrams on this and following three pages)

Translation of premises:

$$M \ i \ P \equiv MP \neq 0$$
$$\underline{S \ a \ M \equiv S\bar{M} = 0}$$
$$S \ i \ P$$

Step 1

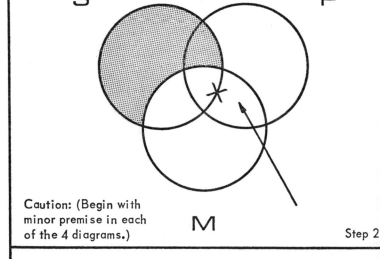

Caution: (Begin with
minor premise in each
of the 4 diagrams.)

Step 2

The x is on the line between the two areas indicated by
the arrow. The major premise does not indicate that it belongs in the area SP. Thus the conclusion that some S is
P cannot be drawn from the diagram.

Diag. I. Invalid   Step 3

Translation of premises:

$$P \ i \ M \equiv MP \neq 0$$
$$\frac{S \ a \ M \equiv S\bar{M} = 0}{S \ i \ P}$$

Step 1

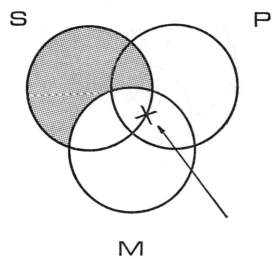

S   P

M

Step 2

Diagram identical with Diag. 1 of this
group. Reasoning the same.

Diag. II. Invalid   Step 3

Translation of premises:

$$M \text{ i } P \equiv MP \neq O$$
$$\underline{M \text{ a } S \equiv M\bar{S} = O}$$
$$S \text{ i } P$$

Step 1

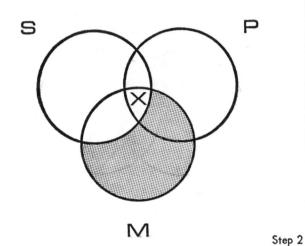

Step 2

The x in diagram indicates that Some S is P.

Diag. III. Valid   Step 3

Translation of premises:

$$P \ i \ M \equiv PM \neq O$$
$$M \ a \ S \equiv M\overline{S} = O$$
$$\overline{S \ i \ P}$$

Step 1

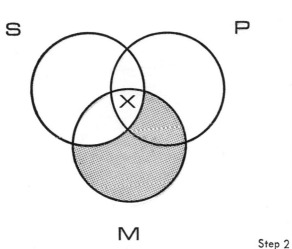

S

P

M

Step 2

Same reasoning as Diag. III of this group.

Diag. IV. Valid   Step 3

MOOD OAO

(in all four diagrams on this and following three pages)

Translation of premises:

$$M \; o \; P \equiv M\bar{P} \neq 0$$
$$\underline{S \; a \; M \equiv S\bar{M} = 0}$$
$$S \; o \; P$$

Step 1

S   P

×

Caution: Begin with
minor in all four fig-
ures.

M

Step 2

The major premise does not clearly indicate whether
the x belongs in M$\bar{S}$ or in M$\bar{P}$, consequently, the x must
be placed on the line. The conclusion Some S is not P
cannot be drawn since there is no x in S$\bar{P}$. (Undistributed middle)

Diag. I. Invalid   Step 3

Translation of premises:

$$P \circ M \equiv P\overline{M} \neq O$$
$$S \, a \, M \equiv S\overline{M} = O$$

$$\overline{S \circ P}$$

Step 1

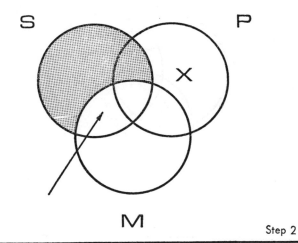

Step 2

The absence of an x in the area indicated by the arrow does not permit the conclusion to be drawn that Some S is not P. (Illicit major)

Diag. II. Invalid   Step 3

Translation of premises:

$$M \circ P \equiv M\overline{P} \neq O$$
$$\underline{M \mathrel{a} S \equiv M\overline{S} = O}$$
$$S \circ P$$

Step 1

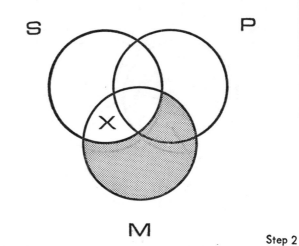

Step 2

The x on the diagram indicates that
Some S is not P.

Diag. III. Valid BOCARDO   Step 3

Translation of premises:

$$P \; o \; M \equiv P\bar{M} \neq 0$$
$$\underline{M \; a \; S \equiv M\bar{S} = 0}$$
$$S \; o \; P$$

Step 1

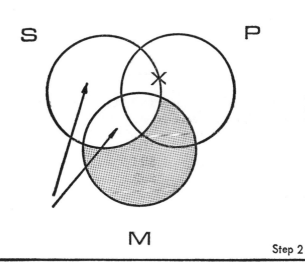

S   P

M

Step 2

The absence of an x in either of the two areas
indicated by the arrows does not warrant the conclusion Some S is not P. (Illicit minor)

Diag. IV. Invalid   Step 3

Continued from page 175.

By converting the conclusion and the major premise, CAMESTRES
is identical with CELARENT. It is, of course, always possible to
reduce CELARENT to the more readily recognizable BARBARA
by obverting both the major premise and the conclusion:

$$\frac{\begin{array}{l}\text{MeP}\\\text{SaM}\end{array}}{\text{SeP}}$$

is equivalent to

$$\frac{\begin{array}{l}\text{Ma}\bar{\text{P}}\\\text{SaM}\end{array}}{\text{Sa}\bar{\text{P}}}.$$

FERIO can also be reduced to DARII by obverting both the
major premise and the conclusion:

$$\frac{\begin{array}{l}\text{MeP}\\\text{SiM}\end{array}}{\text{SoP}}$$

is equivalent to

$$\frac{\begin{array}{l}\text{Ma}\bar{\text{P}}\\\text{SiM}\end{array}}{\text{Si}\bar{\text{P}}}.$$

BAROCO can be reduced to FERIO.
Step I. Obvert the major PAM $\equiv$ Pe$\bar{\text{M}}$.

Step II. Convert Pe$\bar{\text{M}}$ $\equiv$ $\bar{\text{M}}$eP.

Step III. Obvert the minor SoM $\equiv$ Si$\bar{\text{M}}$.
The argument is now in the first-figure form:

$$\frac{\begin{array}{l}\bar{\text{M}}\text{eP}\\\text{Si}\bar{\text{M}}\end{array}}{\text{SoP}}.$$

An alternative reduction of BAROCO can be accomplished by:

Step I. Substitute the full contrapositive for the major premise: $PaM \equiv \bar{M}a\bar{P}$.

Step II. Obvert the minor premise: $SoM \equiv Si\bar{M}$.

Step III. Obvert the conclusion $SoP \equiv Si\bar{P}$.

Step IV. Rewritten in first figure, BAROCO is equivalent to DARII:

$$PaM \equiv \bar{M}a\bar{P}$$
$$\frac{SoM \equiv Si\bar{M}}{SoP \equiv Si\bar{P}} .$$

DARAPTI is reducible to DARII by converting the strengthened minor premise MaS to its weakened form SiM:

$$MaP$$
$$\frac{MaS \text{ converts to } SiM}{SiP} .$$

DATISI reduces to DARII by converting the minor premise:

$$MaP \qquad MaP$$
$$\frac{MiS \equiv SiM}{SiP \qquad SiP} .$$

DISAMIS reduces to DARII:
Step I. Transpose premises and convert major premise:

$$MiP \qquad MaS$$
$$\frac{MaS \qquad PiM}{SiP \qquad SiP} .$$

Step II. Convert conclusion:

$$MaS$$
$$\frac{PiM}{PiS} .$$

FERISON reduces to FERIO by converting the minor premise:

$$MeP \qquad\qquad MeP$$
$$\frac{MiS \equiv SiM; \text{ thus } SiM}{SoP \qquad\qquad SoP} .$$

BOCARDO reduces to DARII:

Step I. Transpose premises:

$$\frac{\begin{array}{l}\text{MoP}\\\text{MaS}\end{array}}{\text{SoP}} \qquad \frac{\begin{array}{l}\text{MaS}\\\text{MoP}\end{array}}{\text{SoP}}.$$

Step II. Obvert MoP and the conclusion SoP, thus:

$$\frac{\begin{array}{l}\text{MaS}\\\text{Mi}\bar{\text{P}}\end{array}}{\text{Si}\bar{\text{P}}}.$$

Step III. Convert Mi$\bar{\text{P}}$ and Si$\bar{\text{P}}$.

Step IV. Rewrite in first figure:

$$\frac{\begin{array}{l}\text{MaS}\\\bar{\text{P}}\text{iM}\end{array}}{\bar{\text{P}}\text{iS}}.$$

FRESISON

$$\frac{\begin{array}{l}\text{PeM}\\\text{MiS}\end{array}}{\text{SoP}}$$

becomes FERIO by the simple conversion of both the major and minor premises.

BRAMANTIP

$$\frac{\begin{array}{l}\text{PaM}\\\text{MaS}\end{array}}{\text{SiP}}$$

becomes the weakened argument AAI.

Step I. Transpose premises:

$$\frac{\begin{array}{l}\text{MaS}\\\text{PaM}\end{array}}{\text{SiP}}.$$

Step II. Convert conclusion to PiS.

Step III. Rewrite:

$$\frac{\begin{array}{l} \text{MaS} \\ \text{PaM} \end{array}}{\text{PiS}}.$$

CAMENES becomes **CELARENT**:

$$\frac{\begin{array}{l} \text{PaM} \\ \text{MeS} \end{array}}{\text{SeP}}.$$

Step I. Transpose premises to:

$$\frac{\begin{array}{l} \text{MeS} \\ \text{PaM} \end{array}}{\text{SeP}}.$$

Step II. Convert conclusion SeP to PeS.

Step III. Rewrite:

$$\frac{\begin{array}{l} \text{MeS} \\ \text{PaM} \end{array}}{\text{PeS}}.$$

FESAPO becomes weakened argument **FERIO**:

$$\frac{\begin{array}{l} \text{PeM} \equiv \text{MeP} \\ \text{MaS} \equiv \text{SiM} \end{array}}{\text{SoP}}.$$

Step I. Convert major PeM to MeP.

Step II. Convert minor MaS to SiM.

Step III. Rewrite:

$$\frac{\begin{array}{l} \text{MeP} \\ \text{SiM} \end{array}}{\text{SoP}}.$$

DIMARIS becomes **DARII**:

Step I. Transpose premises:

PiM   MaS
MaS   PiM .
SiP   PiS

Step II. Convert conclusion SiP to PiS.

Step III. Rewrite:

MaS
PiM .
PiS

Practice in the conversion of syllogisms to the first figure provid
a greater degree of facility in the construction of syllogistic arg
ments and enables the student to recognize an argument as valid
reducing it to a familiar form. It provides an additional test
validity, since an argument that cannot be reduced to BARBAR,
CELARENT, DARII, or FERIO cannot possibly be a valid arg
ment.

4. Indirect Demonstration of Validity

An additional demonstration of the validity of syllogistic argume
tation can be gained indirectly. Remember that the conclusion of
valid argument necessarily follows from its premises. Suppose
consider an argument in BARBARA. Let us take as the maj
premise "Everyone who has a Ph.D. studies hard" and as the min
premise "Every Professor has a Ph.D." The conclusion necessari
follows that "Every Professor studies hard." In symbolic form:

M = Those who have a Ph.D.   MaP
P = Those that study hard.   SaM
S = Professors.   ∴ SaP .

Now, let us imagine that someone were to deny the conclusic
SaP "Every Professor studies hard." For the sake of the argumer
let us assume that the proposition "Every Professor studies hard"
false. Its contradictory SoP, "Some Professors do not study hard,"
then true. Assuming that such is the case and admitting the origin
major premise MaP, "Everyone who has a Ph.D. studies hard
together with the denial of the original conclusion SoP, we ca
formulate the argument:

$$MaP$$
$$SoP\ .$$
$$\overline{\qquad\qquad}$$
$$\therefore SoM$$

...e conclusion SoM, "Some Professors do not have a Ph.D.," can ...n be drawn. This new conclusion SoM contradicts the original ...nor premises of our argument. For we have already assumed ...M; namely, that every Professor has a Ph.D. What we have shown ...that the denial of SaP, that is, the assumption of SoP, together ...th the original premises leads to the absurdity of maintaining a ...ntradiction: SaM and SoM. Such a contradiction is impossible, so ...P cannot be true, and we are forced to admit SaP.

...This technique permits us to test the validity of syllogistic argu- ...ents, for when the argument is valid, the denial of the conclusion, ...mbined with the major premise, will lead to a valid conclusion ...hich contradicts the original minor premise.

Briefly stated in summary form:

...ARBARA

...iven:

1. MaP.
2. SaM / ∴ SaP.
3. SoP assuming the denial of the original conclusion.
4. ∴ SoM by combining 1 and 3 (BAROCO).
5. (SaM) · (SoM)   2, 4, absurd.
6. ∴ ∼ (SoP) Assumption in Step 3 is impossible, since it leads to ...surdity.
7. ∴ SaP denial of SoP in Step 6 is equivalent to affirming SaP.

The following is an indirect demonstration of frequently occurring ...lid forms of the syllogism: CELARENT, DARII, FERIO, ...ESARE, CAMESTRES, BAROCO, DISAMIS, and BOCARDO.

...ELARENT

...iven:

1. MeP.
2. SaM / ∴   SeP.

3. SiP	Assumption.
4. ∴ SoM	1, 3, FESTINO.
5. (SaM) · (SoM)	2, 4, absurd.
6. ~(SiP)	Impossible.
7. ∴ SeP	Denial of SiP in Step 6.

FERIO

Given:

1. MeP.	
2. SiM / ∴	SoP.
3. SaP	Assumption.
4. ∴ SeM	1, 3, CESARE.
5. (SeM) · (SiM)	4, 2, absurd.
6. ~(SaP)	Impossible.
7. ∴ SoP	Denial of SaP in Step 6.

CAMESTRES

Given:

1. PaM.	
2. SeM ∴	SeP.
3. SiP	Assumption.
4. SiM	1, 3 (DARII).
5. (SeM) · (SiM)	2, 4, absurd.
6. ~(SiP)	Impossible.
7. ∴ SeP	Denial of SiP in Step 6.

DARII

Given:

1. MaP.	
2. SiM / ∴	SiP.
3. SeP	Assumption.
4. ∴ SeM	1, 3, CAMESTRES.
5. (SeM) · (SiM)	4, 2, absurd.
6. ~(SeP)	Impossible.
7. ∴ SiP	Denial of SeP in Step 6.

CESARE

Given:

1.	PeM.	
2.	SaM / $\therefore$	SeP.
3.	SiP	Assumption.
4.	$\therefore$ SoM	1, 3, FERIO.
5.	(SaM) $\cdot$ (SoM)	2, 4, absurd.
6.	$\sim$(SiP)	Impossible.
7.	$\therefore$ SeP	Denial of SiP in Step 6.

BAROCO

Given:

1.	PaM.	
2.	SoM / $\therefore$	SoP.
3.	SaP	Assumption.
4.	SaM	1, 3, BARBARA.
5.	(SoM) $\cdot$ (SaM)	2, 4, absurd
6.	$\sim$(SaP)	Impossible
7.	$\therefore$ SoP	Denial of SaP in Step 6.

DISAMIS

Given:

1.	MiP.	
2.	MaS / $\therefore$	SiP.
3.	SeP	Assumption.
4.	MoS	3, 1, FESTINO.
5.	(MaS) $\cdot$ (MoS)	2,4, absurd.
6.	$\sim$(SeP)	Impossible.
7.	$\therefore$ Sip	Denial of SeP in Step 6.

BOCARDO

Given:

1.	MoP.	
2.	MaS / $\therefore$	SoP.
3.	SaP	Assumption.
4.	MoS	3, 1, BAROCO.

5. $(MaS) \cdot (MoS)$ 2, 4, absurd.
6. $\sim(SaP)$ Impossible.
7. $\therefore$ SoP   Denial of SaP in Step 6.

5. Antilogisms

A further test of validity—the method of the antilogism—is applicable to most categorical syllogisms. The testing procedure is as follows.

Step I. Substitute the contradictory of the original conclusion.

Step II. Translate the premises and the contradictory of the original conclusion into equivalent equations.

Step III. Check the argument to determine its validity by applying the following rules:

Rule 1. A valid antilogism contains two equations and one inequation.

Rule 2. In a valid antilogism the two equations have one term in common, used once negatively and once affirmatively.

Rule 3. In a valid antilogism the terms occurring in the inequation occur in a manner identical with their occurrence in the equations.

Let us apply this procedure to BARBARA.

Step I.

1. MaP
2. SaM .
$\therefore$ 3. SoP

Step II.

1. $M\bar{P} = O$
2. $S\bar{M} = O$.
$\therefore$ 3. $S\bar{P} \neq O$

Step III. Determination of validity. Application of rules:

Rule 1. The argument as formulated in Step II contains two equations (1 and 2) and one inequation (3).

Rule 2. The two equations have one term in common, used once negatively ($\bar{M}$ in 2) and once affirmatively (M in 1).

Rule 3. The terms occurring in the inequation $S\bar{P}$ occur in a manner identical with their occurrence in the equations

(S in 3 is identical with S in 2, and $\bar{P}$ in 3 is identical with $\bar{P}$ in 1).

Conclusion: Argument is valid.

Let us apply the same procedure to the argument **AEE** in the first figure.

Step I.

MaP	Substitution of contradictory	MaP
SeM	of original conclusion	SeM
SeP		SiP

Step II. Translation into equations:

$$1.\ M\bar{P} = O$$
$$2.\ SM = O$$
$$3.\ SP \neq O$$

Step III. Determination of validity by application of rules. Complies with Rule 1 since:

Rule 1. Argument has 2 equations and 1 inequation.

Rule 2. Violates Rule 2, since the term common to the equation M fails to occur once negatively and once affirmatively.

Rule 3. Violates Rule 3, since P in the inequation in 3 does not occur in a manner identical with its occurrence in the equation 1.

∴ Invalid: violates Rules 2 and 3.

Valid Antilogisms in the First Figure

	BARBARA	CELARENT	DARII	FERIO
Step I. Substitute contradictory of original conclusion.	MaP SaM $SaP \to SoP$	MeP SaM $SeP \to SiP$	MaP SiM $SiP \to SeP$	MeP SiM $SoP \to SaP$
Step II. Translation into equations.	$M\bar{P} = O$ $S\bar{M} = O$ $S\bar{P} \neq O$	$MP = O$ $S\bar{M} = O$ $SP \neq O$	$M\bar{P} = O$ $SM \neq O$ $SP = O$	$MP = O$ $SM \neq O$ $S\bar{P} = O$
Step III. Determination of validity by rules.	Valid. Conforms to Rules 1, 2, 3.	Valid. Conforms to Rules 1, 2, 3.	Valid. Conforms to Rules 1, 2, 3.	Valid. Conforms to Rules 1, 2, 3.

Valid Antilogisms in the Second Figure

	CESARE	CAMESTRES	FESTINO	BAROCO
Step I. Substitute contradictory of original conclusion.	PeM SaM $SeP \rightarrow SiP$	PaM SeM $SeP \rightarrow SiP$	PeM SiM $SoP \rightarrow SaP$	PaM SoM $SoP \rightarrow SaP$
Step II. Translation into equations.	$P\overline{M} = O$ $S\overline{M} = O$ $SP \neq O$	$P\overline{M} = O$ $SM = O$ $SP \neq O$	$PM = O$ $SM \neq O$ $S\overline{P} = O$	$P\overline{M} = O$ $S\overline{M} \neq O$ $S\overline{P} = O$
Step III. Determination of validity by rules.	Valid. Conforms to Rules 1, 2, 3.	Valid. Conforms to Rules 1, 2, 3.	Valid. Conforms to Rules 1, 2, 3.	Valid. Conforms to Rules 1, 2, 3.

Valid Antilogisms in the Third Figure

	DATISI	DISAMIS	FERISON	BOCARDO
Step I. Substitute contradictory of original conclusion.	MaP MiS $SiP \rightarrow SeP$	MiP MaS $SiP \rightarrow SeP$	MeP MiS $SoP \rightarrow SaP$	MoP MaS $SoP \rightarrow SaP$
Step II. Translation into equations.	$M\overline{P} = O$ $MS \neq O$ $SP = O$	$MP \neq O$ $M\overline{S} = O$ $SP = O$	$MP = O$ $MS \neq O$ $S\overline{P} = O$	$M\overline{P} \neq O$ $M\overline{S} = O$ $S\overline{P} = O$
Step III. Determination of validity by rules.	Valid by Rules 1, 2, 3.	Valid by Rules 1, 2, 3.	Valid by Rules 1, 2, 3.	Valid by Rules 1, 2, 3.

Valid Antilogisms in the Fourth Figure

	FERISON	CAMENES	DIMARIS
Step I. Substitute contradictory of original conclusion.	PeM MiS $SoP \rightarrow SaP$	PaM MeS $SeP \rightarrow SiP$	PiM MaS $SiP \rightarrow SeP$
Step II. Translation into equations.	$PM = O$ $MS \neq O$ $S\overline{P} = O$	$P\overline{M} = O$ $MS = O$ $SP \neq O$	$PM \neq O$ $M\overline{S} = O$ $SP = O$
Step III. Determination of validity by rules.	Valid by Rules 1, 2, 3.	Valid by Rules 1, 2, 3.	Valid by Rules 1, 2, 3.

6. Common Fallacies Detected by Antilogisms

Mood AAA in Second, Third, and Fourth Figures

Step I. Substitution of denial of conclusion.	PaM SaM $SaP \rightarrow SoP$	MaP MaS $SaP \rightarrow SoP$	PaM MaS $SaP \rightarrow SoP$

Step II. Translation into equations.	$P\overline{M} = O$ $S\overline{M} = O$ $S\overline{P} \neq O$	$M\overline{P} = O$ $M\overline{S} = O$ $S\overline{P} \neq O$	$P\overline{M} = O$ $M\overline{S} = O$ $S\overline{P} \neq O$
Step III. Determination of validity by rules.	Invalid. Violates Rules 2, 3.	Invalid. Violates Rules 2, 3.	Invalid. Violates Rule 3.

Mood AOO in First, Third, and Fourth Figures

Step I. Substitution of denial of conclusion.	MaP SoM SoP → SaP	MaP MoS SoP → SaP	PaM MoS SoP → SaP
Step II. Translation into equations.	$M\overline{P} = O$ $S\overline{M} \neq O$ $S\overline{P} = O$	$M\overline{P} = O$ $M\overline{S} \neq O$ $S\overline{P} = O$	$P\overline{M} = O$ $M\overline{S} \neq O$ $S\overline{P} = O$
Step III. Determination of validity by rules.	Invalid. Violates Rules 2, 3.	Invalid. Violates Rules 2, 3.	Invalid. Violates Rule 3.

Mood OAO in First, Second, and Fourth Figures

Step I. Substitution of denial of conclusion.	MoP SaM SoP → SaP	PoM SaM SoP → SaP	PoM MaS SoP → SaP
Step II. Translation into equations.	$M\overline{P} \neq O$ $S\overline{M} = O$ $S\overline{P} = O$	$P\overline{M} \neq O$ $S\overline{M} = O$ $S\overline{P} = O$	$P\overline{M} \neq O$ $M\overline{S} = O$ $S\overline{P} = O$
Step III. Determination of validity by rules.	Invalid. Violates Rules 2, 3.	Invalid. Violates Rules 2, 3.	Invalid. Violates Rule 3.

Mood IAI in First and Second Figures

Step I. Substitution of denial of conclusion.	MiP SaM SiP → SeP	PiM SaM SiP → SeP
Step II. Translation into equations.	$MP \neq O$ $S\overline{M} = O$ $SP = O$	$PM \neq O$ $S\overline{M} = O$ $SP = O$
Step III. Determination of validity by rules.	Invalid. Violates Rules 2, 3.	Invalid. Violates Rules 2, 3.

Mood EAE in Third and Fourth Figures

Step I. Substitution of denial of conclusion.	MeP MaS SeP → SiP	PeM MaS SeP → SiP
Step II. Translation into equations.	$M\underline{P} = O$ $M\overline{S} = O$ $SP \neq O$	$PM = O$ $M\overline{S} = O$ $SP \neq O$
Step III. Determination of validity by rules.	Invalid. Violates Rules 2, 3.	Invalid. Violates Rules 2, 3.

Mood AII in Second and Fourth Figures

Step I. Substitution of denial of conclusion.	PaM SiM SiP → SeP	PaM MiS SiP → SeP
Step II. Translation into equations.	$P\overline{M} = O$ $\underline{SM} \neq O$ $SP = O$	$P\overline{M} = O$ $\underline{MS} \neq O$ $SP = O$
Step III. Determination of validity by rules.	Invalid. Violates Rules 2, 3.	Invalid. Violates Rules 2, 3.

Mood AEE in First and Third Figures

Step I. Substitution of denial of conclusion.	MaP SeM SeP → SiP	MaP MeS SeP → SiP
Step II. Translation into equations.	$M\overline{P} = O$ $\underline{SM} = O$ $SP \neq O$	$M\overline{P} = O$ $\underline{MS} = O$ $SP \neq O$
Step III. Determination of validity by rules.	Invalid. Violates Rules 2, 3.	Invalid. Violates Rules 2, 3.

Summary. In this chapter we have explored the structure of a categorical syllogism in some detail. Additional tests of validity have been thoroughly analyzed: the method of Venn diagrams, of reduction to the first figure, of indirect proof, and of antilogism.

EXERCISES

. *a.* What valid conclusions can be drawn in each of the four figures, when the following are used as premises?

> AA
> AE
> EA
> AI
> IA
> OA
> AO
> EI

b. Can you find any additional premises that can yield a valid conclusion in any of the four figures?

c. What fallacies invariably follow when both premises are particular?

d. Can a valid conclusion be drawn in the second figure with two affirmative premises? Give your reasons.

e. Can a universal conclusion be drawn in the third figure? Give your reasons.

f. What mood or moods, if any, are valid in all four figures?

2. Construct five valid syllogisms for each code name BARBARA, CELARENT, etc.

3. Test the validity of the syllogisms in the preceding chapter by Venn diagrams and the method of antilogisms. (Remember that weakened arguments and arguments with strengthened premises cannot be subjected to these tests.)

CHAPTER TEN

Enthymemes and Sorites

"What sort of things do you *remember best?" Alice ventured to ask.*

"Oh, things that happened the week after next," the Queen replied in a careless tone.

Through the Looking Glass—LEWIS CARROLL

1. Enthymemes

The syllogistic arguments previously analyzed seldom occur in ordinary discourse. However, syllogistic arguments are often implied, even though one of the premises or the conclusion may be unexpressed. When the major premise is omitted, the argument is an enthymeme of the first order; when the minor premise is omitted, it is a second-order enthymeme; and when the conclusion is omitted, it is of the third order.

To solve an enthymeme of the first order, for example,

$$
\frac{(\quad)}{\therefore \overline{\text{SaP,}}}{\text{SaM}}
$$

it is necessary to introduce the suppressed (that is, omitted) major premise MaP; to solve a second-order enthymeme of the form

$$
\frac{\text{PaM}}{(\underline{\quad})}{\therefore \overline{\text{SeP,}}}
$$

it is necessary to supply the minor premise SeM or MeS; and to solve a third-order enthymeme of the form

$$PaM$$
$$\underline{SoM}$$
$$(\quad\underline{\quad}\quad),$$

we must insert the only valid conclusion that can be drawn, which is SoP.

Whenever it is possible, the premise that is to be introduced should be one that would make the argument valid. However, in some arguments of the first and second order it may not be possible to supply any premise that would make the argument valid, since a rule has already been violated.

For example, no premise can be supplied to make the following arguments valid:

$$MaP \qquad\qquad\qquad (\quad)$$
$$\underline{(\quad\underline{\quad}\quad)} \qquad\qquad \underline{McS}$$
$$SeP \qquad\qquad\qquad SiP$$

Each has already broken a rule: can you spot which requirement each violated? Likewise, in the third order no conclusion can be found to make the following arguments valid.

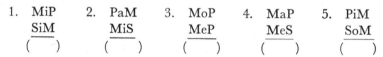

1. MiP   2. PaM   3. MoP   4. MaP   5. PiM
    $\underline{SiM}$ $\underline{MiS}$ $\underline{MeP}$ $\underline{MeS}$ $\underline{SoM}$
    (   )   (   )   (   )   (   )   (   )

The first two cases commit the fallacy of undistributed middle; the third, that of exclusive premises; the fourth and fifth, illicit major.

Careful study and practice with enthymemes is of practical value. For example, suppose in a bull session someone were to argue, "God does not exist; seeing is believing, isn't it?" The conclusion *God does not exist* is stated. The minor term S ≡ God, the major term P ≡ What exists. The conclusion is thus of the form SeP. The expression *seeing is believing* answers the question "Why?" What is the reason for asserting the conclusion SeP? God does not exist, because God is not seen. The middle term of the argument M ≡ What can be perceived. The minor premise is thus SeM. The major premise is suppressed. There are two possibilities. Either we must assume whatever is capable of being perceived exists, MaP, or whatever exists is capable of being perceived, PaM. If we assume

> 1. MaP
> 2. SeM / ∴ SeP,

the argument is invalid (illicit major), although in principle few would deny the truth of MaP. If we assume

> 1. PaM
> 2. SeM / ∴ SeP,

the argument is valid; the point at issue, however, is whether the major premise is true.

The senses are capable of perceiving what is physical. Whether or not all existence is physical is precisely what separates theists from nontheists. It is not the task of the logician as logician to take sides on such philosophical issues. Our problem is simply to bring suppressed premises to the foreground. Their truth must be debated elsewhere.

The critical student will constantly be searching for suppressed premises. Let us analyze a few examples. Whenever possible, we shall supply a premise that makes the argument valid. However, in our first example it is not possible to supply a premise which will make the argument valid.

Example 1: In an enlightened democracy, where the people are sovereign, only what is unacceptable to the local citizenry ought to be prohibited, so obviously we must conclude that the use of Federal troops ought always to be prohibited.

Shorn of its rhetoric, Example 1 contains the following second-order enthymeme:

Major premise:	PaM	S = The use of Federal troops.
Minor (suppressed):	( )	P = What ought always to be prohibited.
Conclusion:	SaP	M = What is unacceptable to the local citizenry.

Since the conclusion is affirmative, the missing minor cannot be negative. And since the conclusion is universal, the missing minor cannot be particular. The suppressed minor is either SaM, The use of Federal troops is always unacceptable to the local citizenry, or MaS, What is always unacceptable to the local citizenry is the use of Federal troops.

The completed argument is either

$$\begin{array}{r} \text{PaM} \\ \text{SaM} \\ \hline \text{invalid (undistributed middle)} \therefore \overline{\text{SaP}} \end{array}$$

or

$$\begin{array}{l} \text{PaM} \\ \underline{\text{MaS}} \\ \therefore \overline{\text{SaP}} \text{ invalid (illicit minor)}. \end{array}$$

Example 2: The American dream supports the premise that every citizen has rights guaranteed by the Constitution. Consequently, every citizen ought to have an equal opportunity to realize his capacity to be a full human personality.

Analysis: First-order enthymeme.

Missing major: ( )   S = Citizens.

$$\begin{array}{r} \underline{\text{SaM}} \\ \therefore \text{SaP} \end{array}$$

P = Those who ought to have an equal opportunity to realize their capacity to be full human personalities.

M = Those who have rights guaranteed by the Constitution.

Completed argument: BARBARA

$$\begin{array}{l} \text{MaP} \\ \underline{\text{SaM}} \\ \therefore \text{SaP} \end{array}$$

Missing premise: Whoever has rights guaranteed by the Constitution ought to have equal opportunity to realize his capacity to be a full human personality.

Example 3: Not every person that commits an act of violence is legally responsible, since the insane are never legally responsible.

Analysis: Second-order enthymeme.

	MeP	S = Persons who commit an act of violence.
Missing minor:	( )	P = Legally responsible.
	∴ SoP	M = Insane.

Missing minor: SiM.

Some persons who commit an act of violence are insane.

Valid   MeP
        SiM
        ‾‾‾‾
        SoP   FERIO

Example 4: Since we must admit that whatever is beneficial to society as a whole is necessary, and at least certain taxes are beneficial, need we say more?

Analysis: Third-order enthymeme.

	MaP	S = Taxes.
	SiM	P = What is necessary.
Conclusion suppressed:	( )	M = What is beneficial to society as a whole.

Conclusion: SiP = Some taxes are necessary   MaP
                                          SiM
                                          ‾‾‾‾
                                          SiP   DARII

Example 5: Racial discrimination is never tolerable in American democracy, since it is always unjust.

Analysis: First-order enthymeme.

Suppressed major:	( )	S = Racial discrimination.
	SaM	P = Tolerable in American democracy.
	SeP	M = What is unjust.

Missing premise: MeP   Nothing unjust is tolerable in American democracy.

Completed argument: MeP
                     SaM
                     ‾‾‾‾
                     SeP   Valid: CELARENT

Example 6: Few, if any, human acts are completely mechanical, so at least some of them are not predetermined.

Analysis: First-order enthymeme.

	( )	S = Human acts.
Missing major:	SoM	P = Predetermined.
	∴ SoP	M = Completely mechanical.

Observation: The missing premises must be affirmative, since one premise is already negative. It must also be universal, since two particulars do not yield a valid conclusion. If it were MaP, the argument would contain an illicit major. To be valid it must be PaM: Whatever is predetermined is completely mechanical.

Fully stated, the argument is: PaM

  SoM
  ‾‾‾‾
  SoP Valid: BAROCO

Example 7: There are cases of slander that are not adequately covered by law, so some cases that ought to be censored are not adequately covered by law.

Analysis: Second-order enthymeme.

	MoP	S = Cases that ought to be cen-
Missing minor:		sored.
	(___)	P = Adequately covered by law.
	SoP	M = Cases of slander.

Observation: To be valid, the minor must be universal and affirmative. To distribute the middle term, it must be MaS.
∴ Missing minor: All cases of slander ought to be censored.

Argument fully stated: MoP

  MaS
  ‾‾‾‾
  ∴ SoP Valid: BOCARDO

Example 8: Since every dishonest person cheats, we can conclude that some cheats are students.

Analysis: First-order enthymeme.

Suppressed major: (   )   S = Cheats.
$$\frac{MaS}{SiP}$$ P = Students.
M = Dishonest persons.

Missing premise: There are dishonest students or some students are dishonest.

PiM
Completed argument: $\frac{MaS}{SiP}$ Valid: DIMARIS

2. *Sorites*

Third-order enthymemes may be combined into syllogistic chains without introducing any new logical principles. Such compound syllogistic arguments are known as sorites.

Let us analyze the following: "Everyone knows that the recent revolutions in South America are Castro Communism, which is Russian Marxism. Don't let anyone fool you, Russian Marxism is still dialectical materialism. And the latter is a decaying ideology, and as such it constitutes a danger to world peace. The conclusion should be obvious."

What conclusion? Our first step is to examine the passage carefully and note the propositions it contains.

Step I.   *a.* The recent revolutions in South America are Castro Communism.
   b. Castro Communism is Russian Marxism.
   c. Russian Marxism is dialectical materialism.
   d. Dialectical materialism is a decaying ideology.
   e. A decaying ideology is a danger to world peace.

Step II.   Translate the propositions in Step I into symbolic form.

   a. RaC   R = Recent revolutions in South America.
   b. CaM   C = Castro Communism.
   c. MaD   M = Russian Marxism.
   d. DaI   D = Dialectical materialism.
   e. IaP   I = Decaying ideology.
          P = Danger to world peace.

Notice that the terms C, M, D, and I occur twice, while R and P occur only once.

Step III. Supply the missing links (for convenience we can state the minor premise first).

1.	RaC	2a.	RaM
2.	CaM	3.	MaD
∴2a.	RaM	∴3a.	RaD
3a.	RaD	4a.	RaI
4.	DaI	5.	IaP
∴4a.	RaI	∴	RaP

With practice the conclusion "The recent revolutions in South America constitute a danger to world peace" can be drawn immediately. One of the simplest ways of handling sorites is to translate the premises into equations. The propositions in Step II then become:

$$1.\ R\bar{C} = O$$
$$2.\ C\bar{M} = O$$
$$3.\ M\bar{D} = O$$
$$4.\ D\bar{I} = O$$
$$5.\ I\bar{P} = O$$

The conclusion $R\bar{P} = O$ can be read immediately, since as previously noted R and $\bar{P}$ are the only terms which do not occur twice. The method of antilogism can be applied to be certain that a valid conclusion has been drawn. Remember that a negative premise entails a negative conclusion and that a particular premise requires a particular conclusion.

Three requirements must be met for Sorites to be valid:

1. One proposition must be an inequation, the others equations.
2. The term common to two equations must be negative in one and affirmative in the other.
3. The terms occurring in the inequation occur in a manner identical with their occurrence in the equations.

Let us apply this test to the following: "Right-wing extremists always fail to accept cultural change, and whoever does that is reactionary. And obviously no reactionary can be effective in society. Need I say more?"

Step I.   Write out propositions.

      a. All right-wing extremists are those who fail to accept cultural change.

      b. All those who fail to accept cultural change are reactionaries.

      c. No reactionary can be effective in society.

Step II.   Symbolize the propositions in Step I.

a. EaC	$E\bar{C} = O$	E =	Right-wing extremists.
		C =	Those who fail to accept cultural change.
b. CaR	$C\bar{R} = O$		
		R =	Reactionaries.
c. ReS	$RS = O$	S =	Those who can be effective in society.

Step III. Find the conclusion by supplying the missing premises or by a short cut: Note that E and S occur only once. The conclusion must be constructed in terms E and S. Since one premise was negative, the conclusion must be negative.[1] We can conclude EeS:

[1] We shall not draw weakened conclusions nor use strengthened premises.

No right-wing extremist can be effective in society.

$$
\begin{array}{ll}
1. & E\bar{C} = O \\
2. & C\bar{R} = O \\
3. & \underline{RS = O} \\
\therefore & ES = O
\end{array}
$$

By applying the method of antilogism, we can test the conclusion drawn:

$$
\begin{array}{ll}
1. & E\bar{C} = O \\
2. & C\bar{R} = O \\
3. & \underline{RS = O} \\
\therefore & ES \neq O
\end{array}
$$

The argument meets the test. $ES \neq O$ is an inequation; Premises 1, 2, 3, are equations. C and $\bar{C}$, R and $\bar{R}$, occur once negatively and once affirmatively in the equations, and E and S in the inequation occur in an identical manner in the equation.

EXERCISES

Part I

The following are first-, second-, or third-order enthymemes. Circle "major," "minor," or "conclusion" to show the part that is missing and then *write it out*. Whenever possible, construct a valid argument. If it is impossible to make the argument valid, indicate the fallacy that has been committed.

Note: The conclusion is in italics whenever it is given.

1. Every large landowner is wealthy, so *some farmers are not wealthy.*
   Write out:
   Missing: Major   Minor   Conclusion
            Valid?   Fallacy?

2. Every patriot is willing to die for his country, and traitors are never willing to die for their country.
   Write out:
   Missing: Major   Minor   Conclusion
            Valid?   Fallacy?

3. *Few religious people doubt the existence of God,* because at least some of them possess strong faith.
   Write out:
   Missing: Major   Minor   Conclusion
            Valid?   Fallacy?

4. Since every dog is tame, *no snails are tame.*
   Write out:
   Missing: Major   Minor   Conclusion
            Valid?   Fallacy?

5. Loyal Americans are always extremely patriotic, so *Birchers are always loyal Americans.*
   Write out:
   Missing: Major   Minor   Conclusion
            Valid?   Fallacy?

6. Only extremists are fascists, so *no congressmen are fascists.*
   Write out:
   Missing: Major   Minor   Conclusion
               Valid?   Fallacy?

7. Highly civilized nations always control their crime rate, so *underdeveloped countries never control their crime rate.*
   Write out:
   Missing: Major   Minor   Conclusion
               Valid?   Fallacy?

8. Pineapples are sweet, and some sweet things are liked by children.
   Write out:
   Missing: Major   Minor   Conclusion
               Valid?   Fallacy?

9. Nothing intelligible puzzles me, but logic puzzles me.
   Write out:
   Missing: Major   Minor   Conclusion
               Valid?   Fallacy?

10. No children are accustomed to smoke cigars, so, *children are never disobedient.*
    Write out:
    Missing: Major   Minor   Conclusion
                Valid?   Fallacy?

11. *Some people always grumble at the weather,* since misfits always grumble about the weather.
    Write out:
    Missing: Major   Minor   Conclusion
                Valid?   Fallacy?

Part II

Find the conclusion to the following sorites.[2]

1. No potatoes of mine, that are new, have been boiled;
   All my potatoes in this dish are fit to eat;
   No unboiled potatoes of mine are fit to eat.

2. No ducks waltz;
   No officers ever decline to waltz;
   All my poultry are ducks.

[2] This exercise was taken from Lewis Carroll, *Symbolic Logic* (New York, Dover Publications, 1958).

3. There are no pencils of mine in this box;
   No sugarplums of mine are cigars;
   The whole of my property, that is not in this box, consists of cigars.

4. All ducks in this village that are branded "B" belong to Mrs. Bond;
   Ducks in this village never wear lace collars, unless they are branded "B";
   Mrs. Bond has no gray ducks in this village.

5. Nobody who really appreciates Beethoven fails to keep silence while the Moonlight Sonata is being played;
   Guinea pigs are hopelessly ignorant of music;
   No one who is hopelessly ignorant of music ever keeps silence while the Moonlight Sonata is being played.

6. The only articles of food that my doctor allows me are such as are not very rich;
   Nothing that agrees with me is unsuitable for supper;
   Wedding cake is always very rich;
   My doctor allows me all articles of food that are suitable for supper.

7. Promise-breakers are untrustworthy;
   Wine-drinkers are very communicative;
   A man who keeps his promises is honest;
   No teetotalers are pawnbrokers;
   One can always trust a very communicative person.

8. No shark ever doubts that it is well fitted out;
   A fish that cannot dance a minuet is contemptible;
   No fish is quite certain that it is well fitted out unless it has three rows of teeth;
   All fishes, except sharks, are kind to children;
   No heavy fish can dance a minuet;
   A fish with three rows of teeth is not to be despised.

9. I trust every animal that belongs to me;
   Dogs gnaw bones;
   I admit no animals into my study, unless they will beg when told to do so;
   All the animals in the yard are mine;
   I admit every animal that I trust into my study;

The only animals that are really willing to beg when told to do so are dogs.

10. The only animals in this house are cats;

Every animal is suitable for a pet, that loves to gaze at the moon;

When I detest an animal, I avoid it;

No animals are carnivorous, unless they prowl at night;

No cat fails to kill mice;

No animals ever take to me, except what are in this house;

Kangaroos are not suitable for pets;

None but carnivora kill mice;

I detest animals that do not take to me;

Animals that prowl at night always love to gaze at the moon.

CHAPTER ELEVEN

Arguments Involving Compound Propositions

"Always speak the truth—think before you speak—and write it down afterwards."

Through the Looking Glass—LEWIS CARROLL

1. Conditional Arguments

The categorical syllogism is a simple form of argument; it is useful for certain purposes, but frequently we find it necessary to employ some more complicated type of inference. The categorical syllogism consists of three, and only three, categorical propositions, containing three, and only three, properly arranged terms. It would be misleading and awkward, to say the least, to try to use a categorical syllogism when the premises of an argument consist of conditional, conjunctive, or alternative propositions.

Assume the truth of the following statement: "If you pass the final exam, you will pass the course." What can you conclude if you do not pass the course? Did you fail the final exam? Suppose that you pass the course: can you conclude that you passed the final? And if you do not pass the final exam, can you conclude that you will not pass the course? Is it possible to fail the course although you did pass the final exam?

Let us suppose that we change the given statement to "You will pass the course if, and only if, you pass the final exam." How will this affect your answers to the preceding questions? Because of the careless use of conditional statements in our ordinary conversation, we sometimes say "if . . . then" when we mean "if, and only if."

Consider our illustration once again. Let us suppose a professor were to announce to his class, "If you pass the final exam, then you pass the course." Would he mean to say that if you do not pass the final exam you will fail, even though you entered the final with a straight A for the term? This is hardly likely. What will happen if you do not pass the final is simply not certain. Even if you do find out later that you passed the course, you still do not necessarily know whether you passed the final exam. The original statement tells you two things with certainty: it is impossible for you to pass the final exam and fail the course, and you may also conclude that if you failed the course, you also failed the final exam. In other words, either you do not pass the final exam or you will pass the course.

Let us use the letter P to stand for the antecedent of the original conditional statement *you will pass the final exam,* and let us use Q to stand for the consequent of the original statement *you will pass the course.* $(P \supset Q)$ means "If P then Q." Using this symbolism, together with $\sim$ as a sign of negation, the previously discussed cases can be written:

A. 1. $P \supset Q$ Major Premise
    2. $\underline{P}$ Minor Premise
    $\therefore$ Q   Conclusion

B. 1. $P \supset Q$ Major Premise
    2. $\underline{\sim Q}$ Minor Premise
    $\therefore$ $\sim P$ Conclusion

C. 1. $P \supset Q$ Major Premise
    2. $\underline{\sim P}$ Minor Premise
    $\therefore$ $\sim Q$ Conclusion

D. 1. $P \supset Q$ Major Premise
    2. $\underline{\quad\quad Q}$ Minor Premise
    $\therefore$ P   Conclusion

Any argument of the form A,

$$\frac{\begin{array}{l} P \supset Q \\ P \end{array}}{\therefore Q},$$

is valid, and we shall refer to it as Modus Ponens, MP for short. Any argument of the form B,

$$\frac{\begin{array}{l} P \supset Q \\ \sim Q \end{array}}{\therefore \sim P},$$

is also valid, and we shall refer to it as Modus Tollens, abbreviated MT. The argument form listed under C commits the fallacy of denying the antecedent, DA, and under D of affirming the consequent, AC.

Going back to our original example, the arguments

1. If you pass the final, you pass the course: Major Premise
2. You pass the final   Minor Premise
∴ You pass the course   Conclusion

and

1. If you pass the final, you pass the course: Major Premise
2. You did not pass the course   Minor Premise
∴ You did not pass the final   Conclusion

are clearly valid, being examples of Modus Ponens (MP) and Modus Tollens (MT), respectively.

It is, however, equally evident that the argument:

1. If you pass the final, you pass the course
2. You did not pass the final
∴ You did not pass the course

commits the fallacy of denying the antecedent, DA, and

1. If you pass the final, you pass the course
2. You pass the course
∴ You pass the final

commits the fallacy of affirming the consequent, AC.

2. Biconditional Arguments

The situation is different, however, in the case where the major premise states "You pass the course if, and only if, you pass the final." Passing the course and passing the final are equivalent. There are four valid forms that a biconditional argument can take.

$a.$ $P \equiv Q$	$b.$ $P \equiv Q$	$c.$ $P \equiv Q$	$d.$ $P \equiv Q$
P	$\sim Q$	$\sim P$	Q
$\therefore$ Q	$\therefore$ $\sim P$	$\therefore$ $\sim Q$	$\therefore$ P

However, to argue

$e.$ $P \equiv Q$	$f.$ $P \equiv Q$
$\sim P$	$\sim Q$
$\therefore$ Q	$\therefore$ P

is to commit the *biconditional fallacy*.

3. Hypothetical Arguments

The hypothetical argument form

$$
\begin{array}{ll}
1. & P \supset Q \\
2. & \underline{Q \supset R} \\
\therefore & P \supset R
\end{array}
$$

is closely related to a first-figure categorical syllogism, except that the premises are transposed in such a way that the minor premise is written first and, in the case of hypothetical syllogisms, the propositions involved are conditional statements. Note the similarity, however, between a valid Hypothetical Syllogism (HS)

$$
\begin{array}{ll}
1. & P \supset Q \\
2. & \underline{Q \supset R} \\
\therefore & P \supset R
\end{array}
$$

and a first-figure categorical with transposed premises

$$
\begin{array}{ll}
1. & SaM \\
2. & \underline{MaP} \\
\therefore & SaP
\end{array}
$$

Also note that the fallacy of the undistributed middle, committed in the second figure (with transposed premises), corresponds to the fallacy of illicit hypothetical:

Categorical	*Illicit Hypothetical Syllogism*

SaM

<u>PaM</u>   Undistributed Middle

∴ SaP

P ⊃ Q

<u>R ⊃ Q</u>

∴ P ⊃ R

The fallacy of an *Illicit Hypothetical* is not to be confused with the valid argument

    1. (P ⊃ Q)

    2. (∼R ⊃ ∼Q) / ∴ (P ⊃ R)

where (P ⊃ Q) and (∼R ⊃ ∼Q) are premises from which the conclusion (P ⊃ R) is drawn.

For the argument

    1. (P ⊃ Q)

    2. (∼R ⊃ ∼Q) / ∴ (P ⊃ R)

simply has not yet been reduced to standard hypothetical form. The second premise (∼R ⊃ ∼Q) can be transposed or contraposed to its equivalent, 3. (Q ⊃ R). Written out in full, from

    1. (P ⊃ Q)

    2. (∼R ⊃ ∼Q)

we derive 3. (Q ⊃ R), from (∼R ⊃ ∼Q) by contraposition, which now permits us to combine 1. (P ⊃ Q) with 3. (Q ⊃ R) to reach the conclusion (P ⊃ R) by means of a hypothetical syllogism. Stated more succinctly:

    1. (P ⊃ R)   Premise.

    2. (∼R ⊃ ∼Q) Premise.

    3. (Q ⊃ R) from 2 by contraposition (Contra.).

    ∴ (P ⊃ R) from 1, 3, by Hypothetical Syllogism (HS).

Corresponding to sorites consisting of chains of categorical syllogisms, hypothetical syllogisms may be combined into a hypothetical chain of varying length.

Given the following ten conditional hypothetical propositions, for example, the conclusion can be found by rearranging their order and drawing the suppressed conclusions, which then serve as a link in the chain. Or, more simply from the premises:

Given:	Rewritten:	
1. H ⊃ I	5. P ⊃ Q	
2. X ⊃ A	10. Q ⊃ R	
3. T ⊃ Z	∴ P ⊃ R	5. P ⊃ Q
4. R ⊃ S	4. R ⊃ S	10. Q ⊃ R
5. P ⊃ Q	∴ P ⊃ S	4. R ⊃ S
6. I ⊃ K	9. S ⊃ T	9. S ⊃ T
7. A ⊃ H	∴ P ⊃ T	3. T ⊃ Z
8. Z ⊃ X	3. T ⊃ Z	8. Z ⊃ X
9. S ⊃ T	∴ P ⊃ Z	2. X ⊃ A
10. Q ⊃ R	8. Z ⊃ X	7. A ⊃ H
	∴ P ⊃ X	1. H ⊃ I
	2. X ⊃ A	6. I ⊃ K
	∴ P ⊃ A	
	7. A ⊃ H	
	∴ P ⊃ H	
	1. H ⊃ I	
	∴ P ⊃ I	
	6. I ⊃ K	
	∴ P ⊃ K	

we can infer (P ⊃ K) immediately simply by recognizing a *Multiple Hypothetical Argument*.

4. Weak Alternative Arguments

Assume the following premise: "You must study harder or you will fail the course." Can we infer that you will pass the course if you study harder? And if you fail the course, does it mean you did not study harder? Suppose you do not study harder; will you then fail the course? And what if you pass the course: does this mean you did study harder? Are you sure of your answers?

The difficulty hinges on the word *or*. The premise "You must study harder or you will fail the course" uses *or* in an inclusive sense, for it is possible for you to study harder and still not pass the course. By using the symbol v to indicate weak alternation and by using P to stand for *you must study harder* and Q to stand for *you will fail the course,* we can construct the following alternative syllogisms.

Case 1. P v Q   Case 2. P v Q   Case 3. P v Q   Case 4. P v Q
　　　　　　~P　　　　　　　　~Q　　　　　　　　P　　　　　　　　　Q
　　　　∴ Q　　　　　　　∴ P　　　　　　∴ ~Q　　　　　　∴ ~P

The removal of the ambiguity connected with the word *or* now makes it easy to decide what can necessarily be inferred in each of the preceding cases. It is not possible to infer with necessity that you will pass the course if you study harder (Case 3), nor is it necessary to conclude that you did not study harder, even though you failed the course (Case 4). It is necessary, however, to conclude that you will fail the course if you do not study harder (Case 1), and if you pass the course, this does mean that you did study harder (Case 2).

Weak alternative propositions assert that P or Q must be true and that possibly both are true. Consequently, if one alternant is known to be false, the other must be true. Any argument of the form

　　　　　　1. P v Q
　　　　　　2. ~P
　　　　　∴ Q

or

　　　　　　1. P v Q
　　　　　　2. ~Q
　　　　　∴ P

is thus valid. Cases 3 and 4

　　　　1. P v Q　　　　1. P v Q
　　　　2. P　　　　　　2. Q
　　∴ ~Q　　　　　∴ ~P

commit the *fallacy of affirming one alternant and denying the other.*

To affirm both alternants

Case 5.	1. P v Q	Case 6.	1. P v Q
	2. P		2. Q
	∴ Q		∴ P

is to commit the *fallacy of affirming both alternants*.

To deny both alternants

Case 7.	1. P v Q	Case 8.	1. P v Q
	2. ~P		2. ~Q
	∴ ~Q		∴ ~P

is to commit the *fallacy of denying both alternants*.

5. Strong Alternative Arguments

Alternative syllogistic arguments may also contain the word *or* used in its strong, exclusive sense, *v*, meaning one or the other, and not both.

Consider the premise "Either the patient will fully recover from his injuries or he will die of them."

Let P = The patient will fully recover from his injuries.

Let Q = The patient will die of his injuries.

Case 1.	1. P *v* Q	Case 3.	1. P *v* Q
	2. ~P		2. P
	∴ Q		∴ ~Q

Case 2.	1. P *v* Q	Case 4.	1. P *v* Q
	2. ~Q		2. Q
	∴ P		∴ ~P

Since *or* is used in its exclusive sense, all four cases are valid. In practice we shall interpret *or* in its inclusive sense, except where the strong or exclusive sense is unavoidable. For instance, whenever one alternant is the contradictory of the other, *or* is used in its strong sense; for example, either the patient is still alive or he is not.

A strong or exclusive alternative syllogism is invalid if, and only if, both alternants are affirmed or both are denied.

Case 5. P v Q   Case 6. P v Q   Case 7. P v Q   Case 8. P v Q
        P   Q   ~P   ~Q
    ∴ Q   ∴ P   ∴ ~Q   ∴ ~P

Disjunctive Arguments

Arguments can be expressed in disjunctive propositions, where the major premise is of the form ~(P · Q).[1]

Assume the following proposition: "It is impossible for you to be drafted and to graduate with your class."

Let D = You are drafted.
Let G = You graduate with your class.
This premise states: ~(D · G).
Consider the following cases:

Case 1. 1. ~(D · G)   Case 3. 1. ~(D · G)
         2. D   2. ~D
         ∴ ~G   ∴ G

Case 2. 1. ~(D · G)   Case 4. 1. ~(D · G)
         2. G   2. ~G
         ∴ ~D   ∴ D

Cases 1 and 2 are clearly valid, since the major premise rules out the possibility of being drafted and of still graduating. Consequently, if you are drafted, it must be false that you graduate; and conversely, if you graduate, it is false that you are drafted.

Cases 3 and 4 are invalid. The major premise does not rule out the possibility that you are not drafted and you still do not graduate, nor does it imply that the only reason you do not graduate is because you are drafted. "It is impossible for you to be drafted and to graduate" is equivalent to an inclusive alternation: Either you are not drafted and/or you do not graduate. It is impossible for you to be drafted and to graduate. If you are drafted, you do not graduate. If you graduate, you are not drafted.

[1] For practical purposes, we shall not consider whether it is necessarily the case that it is false that P and Q are both true.

7. The Interchangeability of Argument Forms

The interdefinability of compound propositions make it po
sible to express the same argument in different forms: $(P \supset Q$
is equivalent to $(\sim P \vee Q)$, and $(\sim P \vee Q)$ is equivalent t
$\sim(P \cdot \sim Q)$.

The following argument forms are thus equivalent and may b
used interchangeably.

	Valid Alternative	*Valid Disjunctive*
Modus Ponens	*Syllogism*	*Syllogism*
1. $P \supset Q$	1. $\sim P \vee Q$	1. $\sim(P \cdot \sim Q)$
2. P	2. P	2. P
$\therefore Q$	$\therefore Q$	$\therefore Q$
Modus Tollens	*Valid Alternative* *Syllogism*	*Valid Disjunctive* *Syllogism*
1. $P \supset Q$	1. $\sim P \vee Q$	1. $\sim(P \cdot \sim Q)$
2. $\sim Q$	2. $\sim Q$	2. $\sim Q$
$\therefore \sim P$	$\therefore \sim P$	$\therefore \sim P$

A biconditional proposition $P \equiv Q$ is equivalent to

$$(P \cdot Q) \vee (\sim P \cdot \sim Q)$$

and to two conditional propositions $(P \supset Q) \cdot (Q \supset P)$. Th
latter is equivalent to two alternatives $(\sim P \vee Q) \cdot (\sim Q \vee P$
which in turn are equivalent to two disjunctions

$$\sim(P \cdot \sim Q) \cdot \sim(Q \cdot \sim P).$$

Consider the proposition "A person is completely happy if, an
only if, he fully realizes his potential as a human being."

Let P = To be completely happy.

Let Q = To realize fully one's potential as a human being.

The proposition

$$(P \equiv Q) \equiv (P \cdot Q) \vee (\sim P \cdot \sim Q) \equiv (P \supset Q)(Q \supset P) \equiv$$
$$(\sim P \vee Q) \cdot (\sim Q \vee P) \equiv \sim(P \cdot \sim Q) \cdot \sim(Q \cdot \sim P).$$

Consider P ≡ Q; namely, to be completely happy is fully to realize oneself as a human being. This means that either you are completely happy and have fully realized your potential as a human being or you are not completely happy and have not fully realized your potential as a human being (P · Q) v (∼P · ∼Q).

In other words, if you are completely happy, then you have fully realized your potential as a human being, and if you have fully realized your potential as a human being, then you are completely happy. This means that either you are not completely happy or you have fully realized your human potential, and either you have not fully realized your human potential or you are completely happy (∼P v Q) · (∼Q v P). Or still again: It is impossible that you are completely happy and have not fully realized your potential and it is impossible that you have fully realized your potential and are not completely happy ∼(P · ∼Q) · ∼(Q · ∼P).

The interchangeability of the preceding equivalences is evident from the following valid argument forms.

Valid Biconditionals

1. P ≡ Q	1. P ≡ Q	1. P ≡ Q	1. P ≡ Q
2. P	2. Q	2. ∼P	2. ∼Q
∴ Q	∴ P	∴ ∼Q	∴ ∼P

Valid Exclusive Alternatives

1. (P · Q) v (∼P · ∼Q)	1. (P · Q) v (∼P · ∼Q)
2. P	2. Q
∴ Q	∴ P

1. (P · Q) v (∼P · ∼Q)	1. (P · Q) v (∼P · ∼Q)
2. ∼P	2. ∼Q
∴ ∼Q	∴ ∼P

Note: The denial of one conjunct implies that the compound proposition as a whole is false.

Valid Conditionals

1. (P ⊃ Q) · (Q ⊃ P)	1. (P ⊃ Q) · (Q ⊃ P)
2. P	2. Q
∴ Q Modus Ponens	∴ P Modus Ponens

1. $(P \supset Q) \cdot (Q \supset P)$
2. $\sim P$
∴ $\sim Q$ Modus Tollens

1. $(P \supset Q) \cdot (Q \supset P)$
2. $\sim Q$
∴ $\sim P$ Modus Tollens

Valid Inclusive Alternatives

1. $(\sim P \lor Q) \cdot (\sim Q \lor P)$
2. P
∴ Q

1. $(\sim P \lor Q) \cdot (\sim Q \lor P)$
2. Q
∴ P

1. $(\sim P \lor Q) \cdot (\sim Q \lor P)$
2. $\sim P$
∴ $\sim Q$

1. $(\sim P \lor Q) \cdot (\sim Q \lor P)$
2. $\sim Q$
∴ $\sim P$

Valid Disjunctives

1. $\sim(P \cdot \sim Q) \cdot \sim(Q \cdot \sim P)$
2. P
∴ Q

1. $\sim(P \cdot \sim Q) \cdot \sim(Q \cdot \sim P)$
2. $\sim Q$
∴ P

1. $\sim(P \cdot \sim Q) \cdot \sim(Q \cdot \sim P)$
2. $\sim P$
∴ $\sim Q$

1. $\sim(P \cdot \sim Q) \cdot \sim(Q \cdot \sim P)$
2. $\sim Q$
∴ $\sim P$

8. Dilemmas

The dilemma does not introduce any basically new logical prin‑
ciples; it combines what has already been introduced. For example
if you knew that $(A \supset B)$ and $(C \supset D)$ and you knew A is tru
and C is true, you could then conclude by Modus Ponens that B i
true and D is true.

Likewise, if by Modus Tollens, you knew $(A \supset B)$ and $(C \supset D$
and $(\sim B$ and $\sim D)$, you could conclude $(\sim A$ and $\sim C)$. Suppose
however, you were given:

> Major premise: $(A \supset B) \cdot (C \supset D)$
> Minor premise: $(A \lor C)$
> The conclusion *must* be: ∴$(B \lor D)$.

Such an argument is known as a *Constructive Dilemma* (CD).
Likewise, if you were given:

Major premise: $(A \supset B) \cdot (C \supset D)$
Minor premise: $(\sim B \text{ v} \sim D)$
The conclusion *must* be: $(\sim A \text{ v} \sim C)$.

Such an argument is known as a *Destructive Dilemma* (DD).

The force of a dilemma can be escaped by denying the inescapability of the minor premise when the disjunction is weak, or by denying one or both of the conditionals in the major premise, or by constructing a counterdilemma. In the first instance, you try to escape between the horns and make an effort to show that A and C are not the only alternatives, since it is possible to choose instead between E and F. You might then argue:

Major premise: 1. $(E \supset \sim B) \cdot (F \supset \sim D)$
Minor premise: 2. $(E \text{ v } F)$
Conclusion: ∴ $(\sim B \text{ v} \sim D)$

or in the case of a destructive dilemma you might contend that

Major premise: 1. $(\sim A \supset \sim E) \cdot (\sim C \supset \sim F)$
Minor premise: 2. $(E \text{ v } F)$
Conclusion: ∴ $(A \text{ v } C)$

In the second instance, you might try to take the dilemma by the horns and admit the validity of the minor alternative premise, but deny one or both of the conditionals in the major. You might then argue in the case of the previous constructive dilemma:

Major premise: 1. $(A \supset \sim B) \cdot (C \supset \sim D)$
Minor premise: 2. $(A \text{ v } C)$
                 ∴ $(\sim B \text{ v} \sim D)$

and in the case of the original destructive dilemma

Major premise: 1. $(\sim A \supset B) \cdot (\sim C \supset D)$
Minor premise: 2. $(\sim B \text{ v} \sim D)$
                 ∴ $(A \text{ v } C)$

The third way of escaping the force of a dilemma is to construct a counterdilemma. To rebut the original constructive dilemma, one might argue:

Major premise: 1. $(A \supset \sim D) \cdot (C \supset \sim B)$
Minor premise: 2. $(A \lor C)$
∴ $(\sim D \lor \sim B)$

To rebut the original destructive dilemma:

Major premise: 1. $(\sim C \supset B) \cdot (\sim A \supset D)$
Minor premise: 2. $(\sim B \lor \sim D)$
∴ $(C \lor A)$

The following examples illustrate the techniques described.

8.1   Illustrations of rebuttal

Rebuttal of simple constructive dilemma: "If we continue to stockpile nuclear weapons, the result will be an atomic holocaust, but to cease this activity implies a willingness to surrender our national sovereignty. There is no other alternative except to continue or to discontinue the stockpiling of nuclear weapons. So we shall either have an atomic holocaust or we must be willing to surrender our national sovereignty."

On the contrary: "The continuation of the stockpiling of nuclear weapons implies that we are unwilling to surrender our national sovereignty, and if we do discontinue our stockpiling of nuclear weapons we shall not need to fight an atomic war. It is evident that we shall either continue or discontinue our stockpiling, with the result that we will either avoid an atomic war or remain unwilling to surrender our national sovereignty."

Rebuttal of destructive dilemma: "If you had a good lawyer, then there is nothing wrong with our legal system, and if you were justly treated, then you were regarded as equal before the law; but either there is something wrong with our legal system or you were not regarded as equal before the law; consequently, either your lawyer was a poor one or you were unjustly dealt with."

On the contrary: "If I did not have a good lawyer, then I am still regarded as equal in the eyes of the law; and if I was simply treated unjustly, then there is nothing wrong with our legal system. I agree, however, that either something is wrong with the system or I was not regarded as an equal. What is to be concluded, however, is that I was justly treated or my lawyer was not a poor one."

EXERCISES

Check the validity of each of the following arguments. When the argument is valid, supply the name of its form, and when invalid, select the proper fallacy. Use this key:

Valid forms

1. Modus Ponens.
2. Modus Tollens.
3. Alternative Syllogism (weak).
4. Alternative Syllogism (strong).
5. Biconditional.
6. Hypothetical Syllogism.
7. Constructive Dilemma.
8. Destructive Dilemma.
9. Disjunctive Syllogism

Fallacies

a. Denying antecedent.
b. Affirms consequent.
c. Violates weak alternation by affirming alternatives.
d. Violates weak alternation by denying both alternatives.
e. Violates weak alternation by affirming one alternative and denying the other.
f. Violates strong alternation by affirming both alternatives.
g. Violates strong alternation by denying both alternatives.
h. Invalid dilemma.
i. Invalid hypothetical.
j. Invalid biconditional.
k. Invalid disjunctive.

1. To disarm unilaterally is equivalent to the certainty that there will be world peace; so if we are to be certain of world peace, we must disarm unilaterally.
2. Either we must be willing to fight an atomic war or we must be willing to surrender our national sovereignty, and we cannot do both. However, although we are unwilling to fight an atomic war, it follows that we still can be unwilling to surrender our national sovereignty.
3. A submarine must be sunk in the vicinity, because there is a bathyscaphe there, and wherever there is a sunken sub, a bathyscaphe is present.

4. Since a government is worthy of the loyalty of its citizens if it is not a tyranny, and the Slobvian Government is obviously worthy of such loyalty, it follows that it is not a tyranny.

5. A nation will be attacked by its enemies if it disarms. Therefore this nation will not be attacked, since it has not disarmed.

6. A parolee deserves to go back to prison if he violates his parole; so, since this prisoner does not deserve to go back to prison, he obviously failed to violate his parole.

7. Our friends must be at home, since their door is not locked, and when their door is locked they are away.

8. The painting in question is obviously a work of art, since a painting is a work of art if it has economic value, and this painting is a priceless treasure.

9. Either you did not pass the final or you passed the course; so, since you passed the course, you must have passed the final.

10. Either we shall go to Holland or we shall go to Denmark, and we shall not have time to visit both places; so, since we shall not fail to go to Holland, Denmark is out of the question.

11. Where there is cancer filters are useless, and if cigarette smoking is heavy there will be cancer; so, whenever cigarette smoking is not light, filters are not useless.

12. Wherever the patient does not have cancer there has been no cigarette smoking, but if the patient has cancer then filters are useless; so when filters are not useless, there has been no cigarette smoking.

13. To increase our nuclear weapons is equivalent to the certainty that there will not be a third world war; so if we are to be certain that there will not be a third world war, we must increase our nuclear weapons.

14. There must be a riot at the ball park, because the riot squads are there, and whenever there is a riot the riot squads are present.

15. Either you did not flunk the final exam or you passed the course; so, since you did pass the course, you obviously passed the final exam.

16. Our teacher must be at school, since his office is not locked, and when his door is locked he is not at school.

17. A criminal deserves to be executed if he kills a guard; so, since

the criminal does not deserve to be executed, he obviously did not kill a guard.

8. Slobvakia will be attacked only if it is unprepared, and it will be defeated only if it is unwilling to fight. But, since Slobvakia is either prepared or willing to fight, it follows that either Slobvakia will not be defeated or it will be attacked.

19. I'll not have a good time if I study, and I won't be able to stay in school if I don't study; so it is impossible for me to both have a good time and stay in school.

20. We shall go either to the World Series or to the UN, and we shall not have time to do both; so, since we will not miss the World Series, the UN is out of the question.

21. If I'm late then I'll miss the party, and I'll miss the party only if I'm late; but since I won't be late, I can't miss the party.

22. Taxes can be lowered only if government expenditures are cut; so, since taxes will be lowered, there will be a cut in governmental expenditures.

23. It is impossible to be selfish and socially minded; so, since you are not selfish, you must be socially minded.

24. Whoever gives to the poor is generous, so anyone who is not generous fails to give to the poor.

25. A person cannot practice medicine unless he has the ability; so, since Jones cannot practice medicine, he obviously lacks the ability.

26. Either we must disengage our forces from armed conflict or the military appropriations will increase; so, since we shall disengage our forces from such conflict, our military appropriations will not increase.

27. It's impossible to be a good student and fail to study six hours every day; so, since you never study that much, you can't be a good student.

28. No one would approve of the proposal under discussion unless he favored lower tariffs; so, since Smith does not favor lower tariffs, he obviously disapproves of the proposal in question.

29. The loss of Southeast Asia will follow if we withdraw from that area; but obviously we shall not lose it, since we do not plan to withdraw.

30. Our actions would at least be partially predictable if we were

completely determined by forces and laws outside of ourselves; so, since we can partially predict our actions, we must be completely determined in the sense indicated.

31. Either the defendant was fully aware of the consequences of his acts or he is not responsible for them. So, since he was fully aware of their consequences, he is responsible for them.

32. We cannot end price supports, since a depression would occur if we did, and we cannot possibly allow a depression.

33. Depressions are never inevitable, since they are never determined, and only what is inevitable is determined.

34. Since whatever is important is of interest to you, it follows that whatever is not of interest to you is unimportant.

CHAPTER TWELVE

Extended Arguments

"I see nobody on the road," said Alice.
"I only wish I had such eyes," the King remarked in a fret-
ful tone. "To be able to see Nobody! And at that distance too!
Why, it's as much as I can do to see real people, by this light!"

*Through the Looking Glass—*LEWIS CARROLL

From dealing with categorical syllogisms, enthymemes, sorites, dilemmas, and conditional and hypothetical argument forms, it is apparent (1) that the conclusion of a valid argument necessarily follows from the premises; (2) in the case of a valid argument, it is impossible to accept its premises and deny the conclusion, whereas one can accept the premises of an invalid argument and still deny the conclusion; (3) an invalid argument may have true premises and a false conclusion. Since every argument is either valid or invalid, when we know that an argument cannot be invalid, then it must be valid. An *argument is invalid whenever its conclusion is false and its premises can still be true.* The very nature of a valid argument provides an indirect test of validity.

1. Indirect Test of Validity

Consider the argument "All scientists are careful investigators, since they utilize logic, and anyone who utilizes logic is a careful investigator."

Let S = scientists.
Let P = careful investigators.
Let M = utilizers of logic.
The argument is of the form BARBARA:

$$\frac{\begin{array}{l} MaP \\ SaM \end{array}}{SaP}$$

Note carefully that S, P, and M stand for classes and that the premises and conclusion of the argument are simple propositions. Certain basic argument forms studied in Chapter XI apply to compound conditional propositions. We can translate BARBARA into a different form, using x to stand for the expression, "for every x," and using Mx to stand for "x is an M," Px to stand for "x is a P," and Sx to stand for "x is an S." BARBARA can now be rewritten:

1. (x) (Mx ⊃ Px)
2. (x) (Sx ⊃ Mx) / ∴ (x) (Sx ⊃ Px)

The major premise now reads, "For every x, if x is an M then x is a P"; the minor: "For every x, if x is an S then x is an M"; and the conclusion is, "For every x, if x is an S then x is a P." Our original major premise categorically asserted that all utilizers of logic are careful investigators. Now, since the statement is universal affirmative, an assertion is made about every individual within the extension of the class of logic utilizers. This enables us to select the letter x to stand for anything at all, no matter what it is. The symbol x is here a variable. It stands for anything. Now, if it should turn out that x happens to fall within the extension of M, if it is a logic user, then it must be a careful investigator. However, the expression x *utilizes logic* is not yet a proposition; it is neither true nor false. The x here is like a blank in a questionnaire; it must be filled in. Such an expression, containing the variable x, becomes a proposition when we replace the variable x by something definite, by a constant. The situation is analogous to finding an unidentified corpse. We are not satisfied until we name it John Doe. When needed, we shall use lower-case x, y, and z to stand for variables but shall use lower-case a, b, and c to stand for the names of individuals—of what has a definite, constant referent. To translate simple categoricals into compound propositions, we need to proceed further, utilizing here the principle of Universal Instantiation (UI). For example, by letting a stand for the name of an individual, namely, Albert, we can replace the variable x, and what was a propositional function, an expression capable of becoming a proposition, now becomes a proposition. Instead of talking about x using logic, we now are able to talk about Albert. Our translation is now complete. The argument is now written:

1. Ma ⊃ Pa
2. Sa ⊃ Ma / ∴ Sa ⊃ Pa.

It now reads: "If Albert is a user of logic then he is a careful investigator, and if Albert is a scientist then he uses logic; therefore, if Albert is a scientist then Albert is a careful investigator."

Now, do not worry where Albert came from. It does not matter. We just picked him off the street; there he was lying in the gutter. We are not saying that Albert is a user of logic; we are not saying that he is a careful investigator—of gutters, for example. We are saying that if he is a user of logic, then he is a careful investigator. Albert was simply chosen at random.

The principle of Universal Instantiation is actually assuming that for every x, if x has a certain property phi (ϕ), then a, where a is an individual, also has the property phi (ϕ), which may be abbreviated:

$$\frac{(x)\ \phi\,x}{\therefore\ \phi\,a}.$$

At times it is helpful to utilize a principle of reasoning which is the reverse of universal instantation; namely, Universal Generalization [1] (UG). Here we select a certain essential element or prop-

---

[1] An I proposition is individuated by Existential Instantiation (EI): "Some S is P" means there is an x, such that x is an S and x is a P, $(\exists x)(Sx \cdot Px)$, which is rewritten $(Sa \cdot Pa)$ by Existential Instantiation. An O proposition is rewritten, $(\exists x)(Sx \cdot \sim Px)$, there is an x such that x is an S and x is not a P, which becomes $(Sa \cdot \sim Pa)$, a is an S and a is not a P, where a is an individual not previously referred to in the same context. The reverse of Existential Instantiation is Existential Generalization (EG). If a has the property phi, where a is an individual, then x has the property phi.

$$\frac{\phi\,a}{\therefore (\exists x)\ \phi\,x.}$$

erty of an individual (ϕ) and assume that every x has the property ϕ:

$$\frac{\phi \, a}{\therefore (x) \, \phi \, x}.$$

If you are skeptical, let us now try to prove that this argument is *invalid*—that its conclusion can be false when its premises are true. Let us make this assumption and see if the premises (Ma ⊃ Pa) and (Sa ⊃ Ma) can still both be true. If Sa is assumed to be true in the minor premise, and since a true antecedent necessarily implies a true consequent, Ma must also be true; but on the assumption that Ma is true, the major premise (Ma ⊃ Pa) cannot possibly be true unless we *contradict* ourselves, for we have already assumed that Pa is false. The conditional statement (Ma ⊃ Pa) is false when Ma is true and Pa is false. Thus, to make (Ma ⊃ Pa) and (Sa ⊃ Ma) both true when (Sa ⊃ Pa) is false requires that we assume that Ma is true in the minor premise and false in the major premise. Such an assumption violates the principle of noncontradiction and is therefore absurd. To assume that the argument (Ma ⊃ Pa) (Sa ⊃ Ma) ∴ (Sa ⊃ Pa) is invalid, that its premises can both be true when its conclusion is false, thus ends in the absurdity of assuming that Ma is true and that Ma is false, which is impossible.

To those who are still skeptical about selecting Albert at random, what we have done is simply to show that if the conclusion of the argument is denied, the premises cannot be accepted. Let us go over it again, in words this time. To deny the conditional statement "If Albert is a scientist then he is a careful investigator" is to affirm that "although Albert is a scientist, he is not a careful investigator." The denial of (Sa ⊃ Pa) is

$$\sim (Sa \supset Pa) \equiv (Sa \cdot \sim Pa).$$

To indicate that we have denied the truth of the original conclusion, let us place a T under the expression *Albert is a scientist* and an F under the expression *Albert is not a careful investigator:*

$$\frac{Sa \supset Pa}{T \qquad F}.$$

We must remain consistent with our denial of this conclusion. Can we still accept the premises? An argument is invalid when its conclusion can be denied and its premises can still be true. What we are trying to do here is to show that the argument is invalid; if we cannot possibly find a set of true premises when the conclusion is false, the argument must then be valid. Let us continue with our example. Consider the major premise, "If Albert utilizes logic then he is a careful investigator." We have already assumed in our denial of the conclusion that Albert is not a careful investigator:

$$\frac{Pa}{F}.$$

We must be consistent in the major premise:

$$\frac{Ma \supset Pa}{F}.$$

For the major premise to be true, we must here deny that Albert utilizes logic:

$$\frac{Ma}{F}.$$

Remember that a simple conditional is false when the antecedent is true and the consequent is false; in all other cases it is true. By assuming that Albert does not use logic, the major premise can be accepted as true:

$$\frac{Ma \supset Pa}{F\ t\ F}.$$

But here is the difficulty: we must remain consistent in the minor (Sa ⊃ Ma). But we have already committed ourselves. In the conclusion we assumed Albert is a scientist, and in the major premise we assumed he did not utilize logic:

$$\frac{Sa \supset Ma}{T\quad F}.$$

This is impossible. We have assumed that anyone who is a scientist utilizes logic. Now we are brought to the conclusion that Albert is a scientist and yet he does not utilize logic. The only way out would be to deny that Albert is a scientist:

$$\frac{\text{Sa}}{\text{F}} \, .$$

This means that we are inconsistent, for in refusing to accept the conclusion (Sa ⊃ Pa), we assumed that Albert is a scientist. It is thus impossible to deny the conclusion (Sa ⊃ Pa) and accept the premises (Ma ⊃ Pa) and (Sa ⊃ Ma). To do so entails the acceptance of the absurdity that Albert is and is not a scientist.

What we have done is to show that when the argument in question is valid, the assumption of its invalidity leads to a contradiction or an absurdity. Whatever implies an absurdity cannot itself be assumed. By letting V = an argument is valid and A = something which is contradictory and therefore absurd, we can abbreviate the *principle of reduction to absurdity:*

$$
\begin{array}{ll}
1. & \sim\text{V} \supset \text{A} \\
2. & \sim\text{A} \\
\therefore & \text{V}.
\end{array}
$$

What implies an absurdity cannot itself be the case.

This principle can be used to test the validity of any argument, no matter how many premises are involved. Consider the argument: "Armed intervention is necessary if we are to avoid the spread of hostile influences in this hemisphere; and since we must choose between the necessity of armed intervention and not taking unilateral diplomatic action, we cannot escape the distasteful conclusion that such unilateral action must be taken if we are to avoid the spread of the aforementioned hostile influences."

Let A = Armed intervention is necessary.

Let S = We are to avoid the spread of hostile influences in this hemisphere.

Let U = Unilateral diplomatic action.

The argument, shorn of all verbiage, can now be written:

$$
\begin{array}{ll}
1. & (\text{S} \supset \text{A}) \\
2. & (\text{A} \, \text{v} \sim\text{U}) \, / \therefore \, (\text{S} \supset \text{U}).
\end{array}
$$

To test its validity indirectly, we need simply to deny the conclusion (S ⊃ U) by assuming that S is true and U is false, that the spread of hostile influences is avoided without unilateral diplomatic action. In the second premise $(A \lor \sim U)$, since we have already assumed we need not take unilateral action, $\sim U$ is true,

$$(A \lor \underset{t}{\sim U}) \; ,$$

so no matter what we may decide about A, about armed intervention, the compound proposition just stated is true. The premise $(S \supset A)$ must be treated in a manner consistent with the assumptions we have already made in handling the conclusion, where we have already assumed that S is true, that the spread of hostile influence is to be avoided. This forces us to assume that A is true, that armed intervention is necessary, and thus shows the invalidity of the argument. What we have done can be summarized:

$$1. \; \underset{\;\; t}{(\underset{T}{S} \supset \underset{T}{A})}$$

$$2. \; \underset{t \;\; T}{(A \lor \sim U)} \; / \therefore \; \underset{\;\;\;\;\; T \;\;\; F}{(S \supset U)}.$$
$$\underset{f}{}$$

First we denied the truth of the conclusion, and then while remaining consistent with that denial we tried to make assumptions that would still enable us to accept the premises as true. Our success, our ability to accept the premises while rejecting the conclusion, shows that the argument is *invalid*. For, as previously stated, an argument is invalid whenever its conclusion is false and its premises can still be true.

Consider the more complicated argument: "To hold that a society is the sole source of moral standards is equivalent to the denial of the existence of a God who is a moral lawgiver, and obviously Eichmann acted morally correctly in obeying the positive law of his society if, and only if, a society is the sole source of all moral standards. Now either a society is the sole source of all moral standards and the positive laws are the sole source of right and wrong or a society is neither the source of all moral standards nor is positive law the sole source of right and wrong. Consequently, either Eichmann was morally correct in obeying the positive law of his society and there is no God who is a moral lawgiver or Eichmann was not morally correct in his obedience to such positive law and God is a moral lawgiver."

Let S = A society is the sole source of moral standards.

Let G = The existence of a God who is a moral lawgiver.

Let E = Eichmann acted morally correctly in obeying the positive law of his society.

Let P = Positive laws are the sole source of right and wrong.

The argument can now be written in abbreviated form.

1. $S \equiv \sim G$
2. $E \equiv S$
3. $(S \cdot P) \vee (\sim S \cdot \sim P) / \therefore (E \cdot \sim G) \vee (\sim E \cdot G)$.

By remembering that equivalence $P \equiv Q$ means

$$(P \supset Q)(Q \supset P)$$

or $(P \cdot Q) \vee (\sim P \cdot \sim Q)$, we can substitute $S \equiv P$ for the more complicated expression in the third premise and can likewise simplify the conclusion to $(E \equiv \sim G)$, thus enabling us to rewrite the argument to

1. $S \equiv \sim G$
2. $E \equiv S$
3. $S \equiv P / \therefore E \equiv \sim G$.

The argument is invalid if, and only if, the premises can be true *whenever* the conclusion is false. Since the conclusion is a biconditional, there are two instances when it is false; namely, when E is true and $\sim G$ is false and when E is false and $\sim G$ is true. It is necessary to try *both cases* where the conclusion is false, unless the first case that we happen to try is successful in showing that the argument is invalid. In this particular argument, an absurdity results when we assume E is true and $\sim G$ is false and when we assume that E is false and $\sim G$ is true.

In the first premise, when E is true and $\sim G$ is false, S must also be false, since it is equivalent to $\sim G$.

1. $S \equiv \sim G$
   F   F

However, when E is true, the only way the second premise can be true is by assuming that S is true.

$$2.\ E \equiv S$$
$$T\quad T'$$

but this is to make the absurd assumption that S is false in the first premise and true in the second. Consequently, in the first case it is not possible to deny the conclusion (E $\equiv$ $\sim$G) without ending in a contradiction. The second instance, where E is false and $\sim$G is true, will yield the same results; namely, a case where the assumption of invalidity leads to an absurdity. Thus, since the argument cannot be invalid, it must be valid. In other words, the assumption that Eichmann acted morally correctly in obeying the positive law of his society, and yet there still is a God who is a moral lawgiver, requires that in the second premise we affirm that a society is the sole source of moral standards, since if E is true S must also be true. And yet by assuming that there is a God who is a moral lawgiver—namely, that $\sim$G is false—the first premise (S $\equiv$ $\sim$G) requires that S is false, that a society is not the sole source of moral standards.

Thus, by assuming (E $\cdot$ G), we arrive at (S $\cdot$ $\sim$S), which is impossible. Therefore, we cannot assume (E $\cdot$ G). Either E is false or G is false.

More briefly,

1. (E $\cdot$ G) $\supset$ (S $\cdot$ $\sim$S)
2. $\sim$(S $\cdot$ $\sim$S) principle of noncontradiction.
$\therefore$ $\sim$(E $\cdot$ G) 1, 2, Modus Tollens.

The *substitution technique* utilized to test the validity of an argument may be briefly summarized.

Step I. Assume *all* the conditions under which the conclusion of the argument would be false.

Step II. Assume the conditions under which every premise would be true (be consistent with the assumptions made in Step I with respect to the conclusion).

Step III. Interpretation: If you can find an instance when all the premises are true even though the conclusion is false, the argument is *invalid,* and you need make no further test.

The argument is *valid,* however, if you are forced to be inconsistent in your assumptions. But before concluding that an argument is *valid,* you must try to make the premises true in *every possible instance* where the conclusion is false. (Note, for example, that an alternative conclusion (P v Q) is false only when both P is false and Q is false, so you need make only one test; but a conjunction (P · Q) is false when both conjuncts are false, when the first is false, and the second true, and when the first is true, and the second false, so you must make three tests before concluding an argument is valid. You may stop checking after the first or second test if, and only if, you show that the argument is *invalid.* A valid argument is valid in every case; it takes only a single instance for an argument to be invalid.)

Further analysis discloses why the argument is valid,

$$1. \ S \equiv \sim G$$
$$2. \ E \equiv S$$
$$3. \ S \equiv P \ / \ \therefore \ E \equiv \sim G$$

can be written as follows:

$$1. \ (S \supset \sim G)(\sim G \supset S)$$
$$2. \ (E \supset S)(S \supset E)$$
$$3. \ (S \supset P)(P \supset S) \ / \therefore \ (E \supset \sim G)(\sim G \supset E).$$

By utilizing the principle of simplification (that in the case of a conjunction, since both conjuncts are true, either one is true, namely, (P · Q) ∴ P or (P · Q) ∴ Q, we can simplify the first premise and utilize (S ⊃ ~G), since there is an implicit conjunction between (S ⊃ ~G)(~G ⊃ S) ; and for the same reason we can separately utilize (E ⊃ S) in the second premise. The combination of (E ⊃ S) and (S ⊃ ~G) enables us to conclude (E ⊃ ~G) by means of a hypothetical syllogism; and by again utilizing a part of the first premise (~G ⊃ S) together with a part of the second premise (S ⊃ E), the conclusion (~G ⊃ E) can again be drawn by a hypothetical syllogism. The combination or conjoining of (E ⊃ ~G) with (~G ⊃ E) yields what we set out to demonstrate: that E ≡ ~G.

Written more succinctly, with the reasons given to the right of each step, the demonstration of the validity of the original argument is as follows:

1. $S \equiv \sim G$
2. $E \equiv S$
3. $(S \cdot P) \lor (\sim S \cdot \sim P) / \therefore (E \cdot \sim G) \lor (\sim E \cdot G)$
4. $(S \supset \sim G)(\sim G \supset S)$ from 1, Definition of material equivalence (Equiv.)
5. $(E \supset S)(S \supset E)$ from 2, Definition of material equivalence (Equiv.)
6. $(E \supset S)(S \supset \sim G)$ from 5,4, simplification (Simp.)
7. $E \supset \sim G$ from 6, Hypothetical Syllogism (HS)
8. $(\sim G \supset S)(S \supset E)$ from 4,5 by simplification (Simp.)
9. $\sim G \supset E$ from 8, by Hypothetical Syllogism
10. $E \equiv \sim G$ from 7, 9, Definition of material equivalence
11. $(E \cdot \sim G) \lor (\sim E \cdot G)$ from 10, Definition of material equivalence

2. Reduction to Absurdity

When we are sure that an argument is valid, we can utilize the principle of reduction to absurdity (abbreviated RA) as a part of our demonstration.

Consider the following argument: "Additional medical benefits can be guaranteed by the Federal Government if the basis of the social security assessment is increased. And if such benefits are guaranteed, retired citizens need not fear poverty due to medical expenses. The removal of such fears will result in a decrease in the number of illnesses among the aged due to anxiety; so, since the basis of the social security assessment will be increased, we can rest assured that the number of illnesses among the aged due to anxiety will decrease."

Let A = The basis of the social security assessment is increased.

Let B = Additional medical benefits can be guaranteed by the Federal Government.

Let C = Retired citizens need not fear poverty due to medical expenses.

Let D = Decrease in number of illnesses among aged due to anxiety.

The argument can now be abbreviated:

1. A ⊃ B
2. B ⊃ C
3. C ⊃ D
4. A / ∴ D

That the argument is valid can be shown first by assuming that D is false. From the third premise (C ⊃ D) and ~D by Modus Tollens, ~C can be inferred, which, when combined with the second premise (B ⊃ C), yields the conclusion ~B by Modus Tollens, which, together with (A ⊃ B) from the first premise, yields ~A, again by Modus Tollens. However, A is given as true in Premise 4, so that if we assume ~D, we end in the absurdity of being able to infer (A · ~A), which is impossible. In other words:

1. ~D ⊃ (A · ~A)
2. ~(A · ~A) principle of noncontradiction.
3. ∴ D 1, 2, MT.

Written more succinctly:

1. A ⊃ B
2. B ⊃ C
3. C ⊃ D
4. A / ∴ D
5. ~D   Reduction to absurdity
6. ~C   3, 5, MT.
7. ~B   2, 6, MT.
8. ~A   1, 7, MT.
9. A · ~A absurd
  ∴ ~ ~D or D.

From a contradiction, any conclusion follows with formal validity. This is what makes an undetected contradiction so dangerous to sound reasoning, for after a contradiction is smuggled into a discussion, the reasoning can subsequently be formally valid.

Suppose contradictory premises P and not P are admitted. We can infer from the *principle of addition* that from any true simple proposition a compound true alternative proposition may be formed by the addition of any proposition, no matter whether the latter is true or false. When P is true, the compound proposition (P v Q) will be true, no matter whether Q is true or false, since an alternative proposition is false if, and only if, both alternants are false.

Thus (P ∴ P v Q) is true by addition, abbreviated "add." Given two premises:

1. P
2. ~P

we can formally demonstrate the grossest nonsense. From 1. P by addition we can conclude (P v M), and from 2. ~P, by an alternative syllogism, M can be inferred. That is:

Given: 1.   P
2.   ~P / ∴   M
3. P v M   1, add.
4. M   3, 2, Alternative Syllogism.

Thus it is possible, although not necessary, to continue the preceding argument. To the fourth premise A, D can be added in Step 10, and D can be inferred in Step 11, from 10, and 8 by an alternative syllogism .

10. A v D   Addition
11. D   10, 8, AS.

The principle of reduction to absurdity can be summarized as a means of demonstration as follows:

1. Add the contradiction of the conclusion of the original argument to its premises.

2. Show by means of elementary logical steps that such an addition leads to an absurdity, thereby indirectly demonstrating that the original conclusion validly follows from the original set of premises.

Note carefully that when the assumption of the falsity of the conclusion does not lead to an absurdity, the argument is invalid. An argument is invalid, in other words, whenever its premises can be shown to be true, even though its conclusion is assumed to be false.

3. Conditional Proof

The introduction of the *principle of exportation* enables us to simplify further our demonstration of an argument's validity.

The meaning of the statement "If there is perpetual world peace, and justice is not forgotten, then Utopia will have arrived" is not changed when it is rewritten "If there is perpetual world peace, then if justice is not forgotten, Utopia will have arrived." The two expressions assert the same proposition; they are equivalent. Written more succinctly,

$$(P \cdot Q) \supset R \equiv P \supset (Q \supset R)$$

are equivalent expressions. Notice that if the right-hand side of the expression is false when P is true, Q, true, and R, false, then the left-hand side will also be false.

$$(P \cdot Q) \supset R \equiv P \supset (Q \supset R)$$
$$\text{T T} \quad \text{F} \quad \text{t} \quad \text{T} \quad \text{T} \quad \text{F}$$

The following complete truth table discloses in the final ($\equiv$) column that there are no cases when these expressions do not mean the same thing.

(P	·	Q)	⊃	R	≡	P	⊃	(Q	⊃	R)
T	T	T	T	T	T	T	T	T	T	T
F	F	T	T	T	T	F	T	T	T	T
T	F	F	T	T	T	T	T	F	T	T
F	F	F	T	T	T	F	T	F	T	T
T	T	T	F	F	T	T	F	T	F	F
F	F	T	T	F	T	F	T	T	F	F
T	F	F	T	F	T	T	T	F	T	F
F	F	F	T	F	T	F	T	F	T	F
	1		2		Final		4		3	

This principle of exportation can be used in demonstrating the validity of an argument the conclusion of which is a conditional proposition.

In the following arguments, for example, a *conditional proof* may be given by adding the antecedent of the conclusion $\sim$Q to the premises in Step 4.

1. $(P \supset Q)(R \supset S)$		6. R	2, 5, AS
2. $(P \lor R)$		7. S	1, 6 MP
3. $S \supset T / \therefore \sim Q \supset T$		8. T	3, 7 MP
4. $\sim$Q Assumption (conditional		9. $\sim Q \supset T$	4, 8 CP
proof, CP)			
5. $\sim$P 1, 4, MT			

On the assumption of $\sim$Q, T follows in Step 8, so that Step 9 simply notes that when $\sim$Q is assumed, T does follow, which is what we set out to prove. Conditional proof may be used more than once in an argument.

Consider the following: "If we disarm unilaterally we shall be at the mercy of any aggressor, and we shall encourage aggressors to attack us if we continue our policy of appeasement. Moreover, if we disarm unilaterally or fail to fight an atomic war, and either encourage an aggressor to attack us or are weakened further by a lack of determination, then it is unlikely that we shall survive as a nation and it is probable that we shall be overrun by Communism. Consequently, if we continue our policy of appeasement, then if we disarm unilaterally it is probable that we shall be overrun by Communism."

The argument can be rewritten more succinctly and demonstrated by using the following abbreviations:

D = We disarm unilaterally.
M = We shall be at the mercy of any aggressor.
E = We shall encourage aggressors to attack us.
C = We continue our policy of appeasement.
F = We fail to fight an atomic war.
W = We are weakened further by a lack of determination.
U = Unlikely that we shall survive as a nation.
O = Probable that we shall be overrun by Communism.

1. $D \supset M$
2. $C \supset E$
3. $[(D \lor F) \cdot (E \lor W)] \supset (U \cdot O) / \therefore C \supset (D \supset O)$
4. C   Assumption $/ \therefore (D \supset O)$

5. E	2, 4, Modus Ponens
6. D	Assumption / $\therefore$ O
7. D v F	6, addition
8. E v W	5, addition
9. (D v F) · (E v W)	7, 8, conjunction
10. (U · O)	3, 9, Modus Ponens
11. O	10, simplification
12. C ⊃ (D ⊃ O)	Conditional proof.

Practice is necessary to become proficient in utilizing argument forms. Here is another example: "We shall have an educational explosion if the student population continues to increase at the present rate. Such an explosion will result in Federal aid or increased tuition. But the latter alternative will deprive many deserving students of a college education, while Federal aid will lead to higher taxes. It is obvious that we are not going to deprive any deserving student of a college education, so if the student population continues its present rate of increase, higher taxes are inevitable."

Step 1. Construct a dictionary.

Let E = We shall have an educational explosion.
Let I = Student population continues to increase at present rate.
Let F = Federal aid.
Let T = Increased tuition.
Let H = Higher taxes.
Let D = Many deserving students will be deprived of college education.

Step 2. Rewrite the argument, utilizing the dictionary.

1. I ⊃ E
2. E ⊃ (F v T)
3. T ⊃ D
4. F ⊃ H
5. ~D / $\therefore$ I ⊃ H

Step 3. Give a demonstration of the validity of the argument in as few steps as possible.

6. I / $\therefore$ H Conditional proof. (Assume I for the sake of the argument.)

7. E   by using premise 1, 6, Modus Ponens.

8. F v T   2, 7 Modus Ponens.

9. ~T   3, 5, Modus Tollens.

10. F   8, 9, Alternative syllogism.

11. H   4, 10 Modus Ponens.

12. (I ⊃ H)   In Step 6, we assumed I conditionally. In Step 11, we saw that on the assumption of I, the conclusion H could be drawn, so in Step 12 we merely stated that if we assume I then H follows, and this is what we set out to show.

4. Summary of Basic Argument Forms

At this point it is well to summarize succinctly the basic argument forms that have been introduced, together with equivalences that are useful in reducing an argument to a simpler form.

4.1 Basic argument forms

I $P \supset Q, P \,/\therefore Q$ Modus Ponens, MP

II $P \supset Q, \sim Q \,/\therefore \sim P$ Modus Tollens, MT

IIIa. $(P \lor Q), \sim P \,/\therefore Q$ Alternative Syllogism, AS
    b. $(P \lor Q), \sim Q \,/\therefore P$

IV $(P \supset Q)(R \supset S), (P \lor R) \,/\therefore (Q \lor S)$
                          Constructive Dilemma, CD

V $(P \supset Q)(R \supset S), (\sim Q \lor \sim S) \,/\therefore (\sim P \lor \sim R)$
                          Destructive Dilemma, DD

VI $(P \supset Q)(Q \supset R) \,/\therefore (P \supset R)$
                          Hypothetical Syllogism, HS

VII $P \,/\therefore P \lor Q$ Addition, Add.

VIIIa. $P \cdot Q \,/\therefore P$ Simplification
     b. $P \cdot Q \,/\therefore Q$ Simplification

IX $\dfrac{(x)\ \phi x}{\phi a}$ Universal Instantation, UI

X $\dfrac{(\exists x)(\phi x)}{\phi a}$ Existential Instantation, EI, where *a* stands for an individual not previously occurring in the context.

XI $\dfrac{\phi\,a}{(x)\ \phi\,x}$ Universal Generalization, UG, the reverse of Universal Instantation, may be utilized in such instances where the assumption is warranted that what is true of an arbitrarily selected individual is also true of anything whatsoever. (Not to be used when *a* is introduced by Existential Instantation.)

XII $\dfrac{\phi\,a}{(\exists x)\ \phi\,x}$ Existential Generalization, EG, the reverse of Existential Instantation. If an individual has a certain property ϕ, then something has the property.

The additional of UI, UG, EI, EG, enables us to transform simple propositions into compound propositions, to which the basic argument forms I–VIII are applicable.

4.2   Interdefinitions

1. $\sim(P \cdot Q) \equiv (\sim P \lor \sim Q)$ Interchangeables

2. $\sim(P \lor Q) \equiv (\sim P \cdot \sim Q)$ Interchangeables

3. $(P \supset Q) \equiv (\sim P \lor Q)$ Interchangeables

4. $(P \supset Q) \equiv \sim(P \cdot \sim Q)$ Interchangeables

5. $(P \equiv Q) \equiv (P \supset Q)(Q \supset P)$ Interchangeables

6. $(P \equiv Q) \equiv (P \cdot Q) \lor (\sim P \cdot \sim Q)$
          Interchangeables

4.3   Further useful equivalences

7. $(P \cdot Q) \supset R \equiv P \supset (Q \supset R)$ Exportation

8. $(P \supset Q) \equiv (\sim Q \supset \sim P)$ Transposition

9.*a.* $P \lor (Q \cdot R) \equiv (P \lor Q) \cdot (P \lor R)$
Distribution, Dist.

b. $(P \lor Q) \cdot R \equiv (P \cdot R) \lor (Q \cdot R)$
Distribution, Dist.

c. $P \supset (Q \cdot R) \equiv (P \supset Q)(P \supset R)$
Distribution, Dist.

d. $(P \lor Q) \supset R \equiv (P \supset R) \cdot (Q \supset R)$
Distribution, Dist.

10. $P \lor P \therefore P$ Tautology, Taut.

11.*a.* $(P \cdot Q) \equiv (Q \cdot P)$ Commutation

b. $(P \lor Q) \equiv (Q \lor P)$ Commutation

12. $\sim\sim P \equiv P$ Double Negation, DN

4.4 *Basic logical laws*

1. $P \supset P$ Law of identity
2. $\sim(P \cdot \sim P)$ Law of noncontradiction
3. $P \lor \sim P$ Law of excluded middle

By means of this list it is possible to handle a wide variety of lengthy arguments. It is necessary, however, to be extremely cautious in transforming simple propositions into compound propositions. From two particular categorical propositions a valid categorical syllogism cannot be constructed.

1. MiP
2. SiM / $\therefore$ SiP

contains an undistributed middle term. To transform the latter, the following procedure must be used.

1. $(\exists x)(Mx \cdot Px)$
2. $(\exists x)(Sx \cdot Mx) / \therefore (\exists x)(Sx \cdot Px)$.

In a universe of discourse that has at least two individual members, *a* and *b,* the argument can be written:

    1. (Ma · Pa) v (Mb · Pb)
    2. (Sa · Ma) v (Sb · Mb) / ∴ (Sa · Pa) v (Sb · Pb).

But this argument is now clearly invalid, since it is possible by our *substitution technique* to show that its premises can be true even when its conclusion is false. By assuming that Pa and Sb are false in the conclusion, the conclusion is false, but if Sa and Ma are true in the second premise, the second premise will be true, and if Mb and Pb are true in the first premise, that premise will be true. Thus, the conclusion may be false when the premises are true, so the argument is invalid.

    1. (Ma · Pa) v (Mb · Pb)
            T   T
    2. (Sa · Ma) v (Sb · Mb) / ∴ (Sa · Pa) v (Sb · Pb)
      T   T   F   F   F

The premises of the preceding arguments consist of definite compound propositions. In contrast, consider the following argument:

"Incompetent public officials are always disrespectful of the constitutional rights of citizens, and anyone guilty of such disrespect encourages violence. Moreover, whoever encourages violence undermines constitutional government, and whoever undermines constitutional government is always responsible for bomb-throwing and violence. Whoever encourages violence and undermines constitutional government is undoubtedly responsible for the murder of innocent women and children. And since it is unfortunately true that there is at least one governor who is an incompetent public official, the conclusion that at least one incompetent public official is responsible for the murder of innocent women and children is inevitable."

Here the premises and the conclusion are general statements, consisting of simple propositions, which must be translated into compound propositions before the basic argument forms listed above (paragraphs 4.1, 4.2, 4.3) are applicable to them.

Let us use the following abbreviations:

Ix —x is an incompetent public official.
Dx—x is disrespectful of the constitutional rights of citizens.
Ex —x encourages violence.
Ux—x undermines constitutional government.

Bx —x is responsible for bomb-throwing and violence.
Rx—x is responsible for the murder of innocent women and children.
Gx—x is a governor.

The original argument can now be rewritten.

1. $(x)(Ix \supset Dx)$
2. $(x)(Dx \supset Ex)$
3. $(x)(Ex \supset Ux)$
4. $(x)(Ux \supset Bx)$
5. $(x)(Ex \cdot Ux) \supset Rx)$
6. $(\exists x)(Gx \cdot Ix) / \therefore (\exists x)(Ix \cdot Rx)$

In its present form, however, the component parts of the premises are propositional functions. In the first premise, for example, the expressions *x is an incompetent public official* and *x is disrespectful of the constitutional rights of citizens* are neither true nor false; they are not propositions. Propositional functions become propositions when the variable *x* is replaced by an individual instance, in this case by a concrete member of the class of incompetent public officials.

Let us employ the letter *w* to stand for the name of a concrete individual, that is, Mr. W. By employing the principles of Universal Instantiation, Existential Instantiation, and Existential Generalization, the validity of the argument can now be demonstrated.

1. $(x)(Ix \supset Dx)$
2. $(x)(Dx \supset Ex)$
3. $(x)(Ex \supset Ux)$
4. $(x)(Ux \supset Bx)$
5. $(x)(Ex \cdot Ux) \supset Rx)$
6. $(\exists x)(Gx \cdot Ix) / \therefore (\exists x)(Ix \cdot Rx)$
7. $Iw \supset Dw$ 1, UI
8. $Dw \supset Ew$ 2, UI
9. $Ew \supset Uw$ 3, UI
10. $Uw \supset Bw$ 4, UI
11. $(Ew \cdot Uw) \supset Rw$ 5, UI
12. $Gw \cdot Iw$ 6, EI
13. Iw 12, Simp.
14. Dw 7, 13, MP

15. Ew	8, 14, MP
16. Uw	9, 15, MP
17. Ew · Uw	15, 16, Conjunction
18. Rw	11, 17, MP
19. Iw · Rw	13, 18, Conjunction
20. (∃x) (Ix · Rx)	19, EG

There is no substitute for practice in the handling of extended arguments.

EXERCISES

Symbolize the following arguments. Check their validity; if they are valid, give a formal proof, using the dictionary suggested.

A. *Key:*

A = Prices drop.
B = The market will be flooded.
C = There will be a recession.
D = There will be a tax cut.

1. Either prices do not drop or the market will be flooded. And if there is no recession the market will be flooded, but if there is a recession there will be a tax cut. Therefore, if prices drop there will be a tax cut.
2. If prices drop the market will be flooded, and if there is a recession there will be a tax cut; so if it is not the case that prices do not drop and there is no recession, then either the market will be flooded or there will be a tax cut.
3. If the dropping of prices implies that the market will be flooded, then there will be a recession, and if the flooding of the market implies that prices will drop, then there will be a tax cut; so if the dropping of prices is equivalent to the flooding of the market, then there will be both a recession and a tax cut.
4. Either prices will drop and the market will be flooded or prices will not drop and the market will not be flooded. But since we know that either prices will drop or the market will be flooded, we are certain that the market will be flooded and prices will drop.

5. If the market is not flooded, then prices will not drop, and either the market is not flooded or there is a recession. Moreover, it is impossible that there can be both a recession and not a tax cut. So, since there will not be a tax cut, there will not be a drop in prices.

B. *Key:*

A = One of the servants committed the crime.
B = The crime was an inside job.
C = There was no accomplice on the outside.
D = One is forced to lose confidence in domestic help.
E = It is impossible to be too careful.
F = The criminal will be apprehended.
G = Robbery was the motive.
H = The police are called.
I = The door was left open.
J = Someone was careless.

1. Either one of the servants committed the crime or the crime was an inside job. And if the door was left open, then robbery was the motive. But if one of the servants committed the crime, one is forced to lose confidence in domestic help, and it is impossible to lose confidence in domestic help. However, if robbery was the motive, the police will be called, so at least we know that the police will be called.

2. If the crime was an inside job, there was no accomplice on the outside, and if the latter was the case, robbery was certainly the motive. But if robbery was the motive, one is forced to lose confidence in domestic help, and if one is forced to lose confidence in domestic help, then it is impossible to be too careful. Now either the crime is an inside job or someone was careless. No one was careless. So it is impossible to be too careful.

3. If one of the servants did not commit the crime, then the crime was not an inside job. And if the crime was not an inside job, then the door was left open. But if the door was left open, then someone was careless. And if someone was careless, then one is forced to lose one's confidence in domestic help. So either one

of the servants did not commit the crime or one is forced to lose one's confidence in domestic help.

4. If one of the servants committed the crime, the crime was an inside job, and if a servant did not commit the crime, there was an accomplice on the outside. But if either the crime was an inside job or there was no accomplice on the outside, then if robbery was the motive and the police are called then the criminal will be apprehended. Of course, robbery was the motive and the police will be called, so the criminal will be apprehended.

5. Either one of the servants committed the crime and it was an inside job or one of the servants did not commit the crime and it was not an inside job. But if it was an inside job implies that one of the servants committed the crime, then robbery was not the motive, and if the latter is the case, the police will not be called, and if they are not called, the criminal will not be apprehended; so the criminal will not be apprehended.

C. *Key:*

    R = We trust the Russians.
    T = We will conclude a nuclear arms test ban.
    D = We shall disarm.
    L = We have learned from history.
    C = We trust China.
    K = Khrushchev will bury us.

1. Either we do not trust the Russians or we will conclude a nuclear arms test ban, but if we do not disarm, then we do not trust China. We do not both trust the Russians and trust China. To trust the Russians implies we have not learned from history. Khrushchev will not bury us if we have learned from history. Therefore, either we do not trust the Russians or Khrushchev will bury us.

2. We shall not conclude a nuclear test ban unless we disarm. But if we disarm, we must trust both the Russians and China. If we trust both of them, we have not learned from history. Our failure to learn from history will result in Khrushchev's burying us. So if we disarm, Khrushchev will bury us.

3. It is impossible for us to not disarm and not to have learned from history. Nor can we both disarm and not trust China. Either we have not learned from history or we trust the Russians. But if we trust the Russians, then Khrushchev will bury us. So if we do not trust China, Khrushchev will bury us.

D. *Key:*

A = Continue price supports.
B = Increase surplus.
C = Support food for peace.
D = Give food away to needy nations.
E = Destroy the domestic market.
F = Farmer will suffer tremendous economic losses.
G = Our own national economy will undergo a recession.

1. If we continue to support farm products, the food surplus will increase, and if we discontinue such support, the farmer will suffer tremendous economic losses. If the farmer suffers such losses, our own national economy will undergo a recession. Since we cannot increase our surplus, our national economy will undergo a recession.

2. It is not possible to not increase our surplus without supporting food for peace. But if we support food for peace, we shall then give food away to needy nations. And if we do that, we destroy their domestic market. But we cannot afford to destroy their domestic markets, so our own surplus will increase.

3. Either the farmer will suffer tremendous economic losses and we do not continue price supports or the farmer does not suffer such losses and we do continue them. Tremendous economic losses suffered by the farmer will result in a national economic recession, which in turn will put an end to the giving of food to needy nations. So if we discontinue price supports, we can then no longer give food to needy nations.

E. *Key:*

S = European civilization will survive.
E = Economic unity.
A = Aggression is at an end.

C = Spread of Communism is arrested.
P = Western civilization will perish.

1. European civilization will not survive if, and only if, there is no economic unity, but either European civilization will survive or there will be economic unity. However, if Europe does not survive and there is no economic unity, then aggression is not at an end or the spread of Communism is not arrested. And if it is not the case that both aggression is at an end and the spread of Communism is arrested, then Western civilization will perish. Therefore, Western civilization will perish.

Symbolize and test the validity of each of the following arguments. If invalid, name any fallacies you detect, and if valid, construct a formal proof of this validity. Use the following dictionary for each of the four following hat problems:

F. *Key:*

P = Al saw a green hat on both Bill and Charlie.
Q = Al would have known the color of his own hat.
R = Bill saw a green hat on Charlie.
S = Bill would have known the color of his own hat.
T = Charlie would have known that his own hat is not green.

1. If Al saw a green hat on both Bill and Charlie, then Al would have known the color of his own hat. And if Bill saw a green hat on Charlie, then Bill would have known the color of his own hat. Moreover, if Al did not see a green hat on both Bill and Charlie, and if Bill did not see a green hat on Charlie, then Charlie would have known that his hat is not green. But Charlie obviously did not know his own hat is not green and Al did not know the color of his own hat, so Bill must have known the color of his own hat.

2. If Al saw a green hat on both Bill and Charlie, then Al would have known the color of his own hat, and if Bill saw a green hat on Charlie, then Bill would have known the color of his own hat. But, since neither Al nor Bill knew the color of their own hats, and if Al did not see a green hat on Charlie, then

Charlie knew his own hat is not green. Therefore Charlie knew his own hat is not green.

3. If Al saw a green hat on both Bill and Charlie, then Al would have known the color of his own hat. And if Bill saw a green hat on Charlie, then Bill would have known the color of his own hat. Moreover, since either Al or Bill knew the color of his own hat, and if either Al saw a green hat on both Bill and Charlie or Bill saw a green hat on Charlie, then Charlie knew his own hat is not green. So Charlie knew his own hat is not green.

4. If Al saw a green hat on both Bill and Charlie, then Al would have known the color of his own hat. And if Bill saw a green hat on Charlie, then Bill would have known the color of his own hat. And it is not the case that Al saw a green hat on both Bill and Charlie and that Bill saw a green hat on Charlie. And if either Al did not know the color of his own hat or Bill did not know the color of his own hat, then Charlie knew his hat was not green. Therefore, Charlie knew his hat was not green.

Assuming that cheaters always lie and noncheaters always tell the truth, symbolize the following arguments by using the following dictionary. Test their validity, and if valid construct a formal proof.

G. *Key:*

A = Albert is a cheat.
S = Albert said he is not a cheat.
L = Albert lied when he said he is not a cheat.
B = Bill is a cheat.
F = Bill lied when he said Albert said that he (Albert) is not a cheat.
C = Charlie is a cheat.
E = Charlie lied when Charlie said, "Albert is a cheat."

1. Either Albert is a cheat or he would say that he is not a cheat. And if Albert is a cheat, then he would say that he is not a cheat. Of course, either Albert is a cheat or he is not, so in any case he would deny that he is a cheat.

2. If Albert said he is not a cheat, then Bill lied when Bill said that Albert said that he (Albert) is not a cheat. And if Bill were

himself a cheat, he would have been lying, but Bill was not lying. So Bill obviously is not a cheat.

3. Now if Charlie is a cheat, then Charlie lied when he said, "Albert is a cheat," and Albert is not really a cheat. But if Charlie is not a cheat, then Charlie did not lie when he said that Albert was, and Albert is really a cheat. Of course, Charlie either is or is not a cheat, so we can conclude that Charlie lied in saying Albert is a cheat and Albert is not a cheat or Charlie did not lie in saying Albert is a cheat and Albert is a cheat.

4. Now if Charlie lied when he said Albert is a cheat, then Charlie is himself a cheat, and if Charlie did not lie on this occasion, then of course Albert is really a cheat, so since either Charlie lied or he didn't, Charlie or Albert is a cheat.

H. Make your own dictionary and determine which of the following arguments are valid by the substitution technique. When they are valid, give a formal proof of their validity.

1. To introduce censorship implies that our freedom is restricted, but if we are to guarantee protection against libel, there must be censorship, and we must offer such protection, so our freedom is bound to be restricted.

2. If Thrasymachus' definition of justice as the interest of the stronger is correct, then the moral dimension of human experience is identical with the legal system of a nation. To affirm the latter to be the case implies that morality is relative to a given society. But either morality is not relative to a given society or the sole basis for valuing a free democracy above a tyranny is a cultural preference, and if such be the case, a Hitler is as "good" a man as a Churchill. Such a conclusion is unacceptable, so Thrasymachus' definition is incorrect.

3. Either we shall continue with our present policies or we must withdraw from world leadership, but if we continue, we shall become involved in an armed conflict, and if we withdraw, we shall retreat into a prewar isolationism. Such an isolationism will lead to an end of civilization as we now know it. But if we become involved in an armed conflict, the result will be an atomic holocaust, which in turn will put an end to civilization

as presently known. Unfortunately, therefore, we are forced to conclude that civilization as now known will end.

Arguments on the resumption of the bombing of North Vietnam.

I. *Key:*

R = The bombing of North Vietnam is to be resumed.

M = The morale of the South Vietnamese Government is maintained.

D = The enemy is denied immunity from the cost of aggression.

E = North Vietnam will be convinced that war is not worth the economic price.

W = The present war in Vietnam will end.

P = There will be a long land war in Asia.

I = There will be an increase in the determination of the enemy.

A = The number of American troops is increased in Vietnam.

B = Goods from North Vietnam are blocked from the south.

G = Expansion of present war to global war of nuclear proportions.

1. An increase in American troops in Vietnam will result in the maintenance of the morale of the South Vietnamese Government and the bombing of North Vietnam need not be resumed. It is not possible to fail to resume the bombings and to have a long land war in Asia. If we do not have the latter, the determination of the enemy will not increase, and without such an increase, the war will not expand into a global war of nuclear proportions. So if we increase American troops in Vietnam, we shall not have such a global war.

2. If we do not block the flow of goods from the north to the south, the enemy is not denied immunity from the cost of aggression. And if the enemy is not denied such immunity, North Vietnam will not be convinced that the war is not worth the economic price. And if North Vietnam remains unconvinced, the war will not end. And if it does not end, the enemy's determination will increase. And if the latter happens, the number of American troops present will increase. Such an increase in American troops will result in global warfare of nuclear proportions, so

the failure to block the flow of goods from north to south will result in such a global war.

3. If we do not resume the bombings, the morale of the South Vietnamese will crumble, and if we resume the bombings, the determination of the enemy will increase. An increase in such determination or the shattering of South Vietnamese morale either will not end the war or there will be a long land war in Asia. The failure to end the war or a long land war in Asia will result in global war of nuclear proportions. Dreadful as such a consequence may seem, it is inevitable.

4. An increase in the number of American troops will result in a decrease in the enemy's determination. Such an effect implies that there will not be a long land war in Asia. And if there is not, the present war will end. And if it does, there will not be a global war. So a global war will be avoided if we increase the number of American troops.

5. It is impossible to resume the bombings and not increase the determination of the enemy. An increase in the latter will result in a long land war in Asia. Unfortunately, it is impossible to become engaged in such a long land war without sparking a global war of nuclear proportions. Under no circumstances can we permit such a global war. So the bombing of North Vietnam is not to be resumed.

J. *Key:*

T = Bureaucrats tend to increase their own importance.
H = Bureaucrats hire unneeded personnel.
J = Bureaucrats justify themselves.
C = Creation of work is required.
S = Bureaucrats must send memos to themselves.
N = The need for useless personnel increases.
E = Further expansion results.
I = The necessity of increased spending follows.

1. It is impossible for the chief bureaucrats of a bureaucracy to tend to increase their own importance and not to hire unneeded personnel. And it is not possible for them to hire unneeded personnel without justifying themselves. However, such justification

requires the creation of work. To create work, such bureaucrats must send memos to themselves. By sending memos to themselves, they then increase the need of useless personnel, and further expansion results. The necessity of increased spending follows from the need of useless personnel and from such expansion. Consequently, the tendency on the part of such bureaucrats to increase their own importance inevitably results in the necessity of increased spending.

2. If bureaucrats do not hire unneeded personnel, then they need not send memos to themselves. And if they do not tend to increase their own importance, then the creation of work is not required. Unfortunately it is impossible for bureaucrats to refrain from both the sending of such memos and the creation of work. Bureaucrats do not tend to increase their own importance. But if they do hire unneeded personnel, it is to justify themselves. So they do justify themselves.

K. Make your own dictionary and symbolize the following arguments. Check their validity, and if they are valid, give a demonstration of their validity.

1. Someone is either not human or he is created free and equal. Anyone so created is, of course, endowed with inalienable rights, and whoever has such rights ought to be treated fairly. So it is impossible to be human and not deserve fair treatment.

2. Whoever is endowed by his Creator with inalienable rights ought to be given his due and treated fairly; so anyone who ought not to be treated fairly is not endowed with such inalienable rights.

3. Anyone who is treated justly ought to be treated like anyone else. To be treated like anyone else implies that what is accidental is not to be confused with a person's essential nature. When such confusion is avoided, there is equal opportunity. So when everyone is treated justly, there is equal opportunity.

4. Either we are not created free and equal or we ought to be given equal opportunity. Anyone given such opportunity can realize his potential only if he has a right to life, liberty, and the pursuit of happiness. He can have the latter only if what is accidental is not confused with his essential nature. And since we

are created free and equal, the accidental is not to be confused with our essential nature.

L. *Key:*

I = Inflation results.
D = Demand exceeds the supply.
C = Credit is too easy.
S = There is a shortage of skilled labor.
E = There is excessive government spending.
T = Taxes are too low.

1. Either the demand does not exceed the supply or there is a shortage of skilled labor. But if there is such a shortage, the result will be inflation; so either the demand does not exceed the supply or there is inflation.

2. It is impossible for the government to spend excessively without the demand exceeding the supply. And if credit is too easy, the demand will exceed the supply; so if the demand exceeds the supply, the government spends excessively.

3. Whenever credit is too easy, the demand exceeds the supply, and if credit is not too easy, the government does not spend excessively; so the demand exceeds the supply only if there is excessive government spending.

4. Either taxes are not too low or inflation results, and there is inflation only if credit is too easy; so if credit is not too easy, taxes are not too low.

5. Either the demand does not exceed the supply or taxes are too low. But if inflation is not to be the result, then taxes are not too low and there is a shortage of skilled labor. But since it is not possible for the demand not to exceed the supply and still have a shortage of labor, inflation is bound to result.

6. If there is a supply exceeded by the demand, then there will be a shortage of skilled labor. And if the demand does not exceed the supply, then taxes are not too low. But if there is a shortage of labor or taxes are not too low, there will not be an inflation. So there will not be an inflation.

7. Either credit is not too easy or there is inflation. But if credit is not too easy, then taxes are too low. However, if there is either

inflation or taxes are too low, the result will be both excessive government spending and demand exceeding supply. So we can conclude that the supply will be exceeded by the demand.

8. If credit is too easy, then taxes are too low, and if credit is not too easy, there will not be an inflation. If there is inflation or taxes are too low, then the demand does not exceed the supply, so the demand does not exceed the supply.

9. Since the demand exceeds the supply and credit is too easy, or the demand does not exceed the supply and credit is not too easy, we can conclude that the demand exceeds the supply if credit is too easy.

10. Inflation results when the demand exceeds the supply. Such excess of demand is caused by any one of the following factors, whether they occur individually or in combination: too easy credit, a shortage of skilled labor, excessive government spending, and too low taxes. It is possible to tighten credit, and we can overcome any shortage of skilled labor. But the raising of taxes simply increases the government's excessive spending, so that the latter cannot be eliminated. Consequently, we cannot avoid inflation.

REVIEW

Given as *true:* "No one favoring escalation is willing to risk war with China," what can you infer about each of the following?

1. No one that fails to favor escalation is unwilling to risk war with China.   T   F   U

2. Anyone unwilling to risk war with China does not favor escalation.   T   F   U

3. No one willing to risk war with China fails to favor escalation.   T   F   U

4. A few of those who do not favor escalation are not willing to risk war with China.   T   F   U

5. Only those who do not favor escalation are willing to risk war with China.   T   F   U

6. A few people that are unwilling to risk war with China favor escalation.   T   F   U

7. Several of those willing to risk war with China do not favor escalation.   T F U

8. Those who do not favor escalation are never willing to risk war with China.   T F U

9. Few of those who are unwilling to risk war with China favor escalation.   T F U

10. No one who is unwilling to risk war with China favors escalation.   T F U

11. Few people that are unwilling to risk war with China favor escalation.   T F U

12. A few that fail to favor escalation are unwilling to risk war with China.   T F U

13. Many who are unwilling to risk war with China fail to favor escalation.   T F U

14. Only those favoring escalation are unwilling to risk war with China.   T F U

15. No one who is unwilling to risk war with China fails to favor escalation.   T F U

16. Few of those who do not favor escalation fail to be willing to risk war with China.   T F U

17. Several who fail to favor escalation are willing to risk war with China.   T F U

18. Those who do not favor escalation are always unwilling to risk war with China.   T F U

19. Everyone who does not favor escalation is willing to risk war with China.   T F U

20. Few of those unwilling to risk war with China fail to favor escalation.   T F U

CHAPTER THIRTEEN

Informal Fallacies

"How is bread made?"

"I know that!" *Alice cried eagerly. "You take some flour——"*

"Where do you pick the flower?" the White Queen asked. . . .

"Well, it isn't picked *at all," Alice explained: "it's* ground——"

"How many acres of ground?" said the White Queen. "You mustn't leave out so many things."

Through the Looking Glass—LEWIS CARROLL

To err is human; no one is infallible; everyone makes mistakes, and yet errors in reasoning are often dangerous to our own well-being. Mistaken beliefs and opinions may lead to actions which, while pleasant at first, may finally end in misery.

On the personal level the rejection of moral standards, the repudiation of religion, the adoption of radical attitudes in politics, whether on the extreme right or the extreme left, are frequently the result of fallacious or erroneous reasoning—of pseudointellectual fallout. For a fallacious argument usually appears plausible; it seems to offer evidence and is therefore persuasive, even though it is defective and should not persuade anyone. When as the result of defective reasoning errors are made the basis of social or political action, havoc is wrought on a wide scale.

Not every dispute is the result of fallacious reasoning; there are genuine differences due to a different interpretation of certain states of affairs; however, many tensions in our personal and group experience are the direct consequence of sloppy reasoning. Either we do not get the facts straight—we misinterpret them—or our limited experience may be hastily generalized in terms compatible with our preconceived biases and lack of interest in what is true. The love of wisdom—the desire to believe and to act upon only what is true—is a habit that requires cultivation; an error or a lie can be equally or even more satisfying. Error appeals to our natural perverseness, and even a love of truth and a desire to avoid error are not a sufficient safeguard against the many pitfalls of reasoning, for fallacies are very clever in disguising themselves as sound arguments. "Here we are," they say; "don't we look like sound pieces of reasoning? Take our hand; we'll go far together in persuading others; we can sell many products, undermine established institutions, wreck lives, and destroy nations. While we destroy virtue and integrity, we are useful in the acquisition of power and wealth, in seduction, sedition, and the spread of confusion."

In short, fallacies are faulty instances of reasoning which gain their persuasive force by masquerading as sound arguments. They appear to offer evidence in support of a position when they do not.

There are many ways of making mistakes, and there is no universally accepted way of classifying error. Whereas our study of valid argument forms intended to provide instruments that will enable us to reason correctly, our study of fallacies is meant to familiarize us with mental snags, lest we run aground on the shoals of irrationality. We study valid argument forms to be able to use them; we study fallacies to avoid them. The best safeguard against improper reasoning is the habit of reasoning well, and our knowledge of improper or fallacious reasoning can help us to avoid some of the common ways people fall into error.

We are now familiar with fallacies due to an improper form of argumentation, such as an improper conversion, an illicit major or minor term, an undistributed middle, or an affirmed consequent. Little attention has been given to content. Our primary concern has been with the form of valid arguments, rather than with their material. In what follows we shall be concerned with soundness as well as validity, with content as well as form.

The simplest errors in reasoning, the ones most easy to detect, originate in linguistic confusion due to the ambiguity of words, inattention to syntax, and shifts in usage.

Sometimes we slide into verbal pitfalls, mental traps, by tumbling into linguistic snares, buzzing as it were like a fly in a bottle, in a verbal maze, in a crisscross of confusion arising in part, at least, from inattention to the meaning, structure, and use of our language.

A second class of mistakes rests primarily on a mistaken notion of relevance; and what is relevant to a given argument often depends on nonverbal states of affairs. A third category of errors, and the most difficult to detect, is occasioned by questionable, if not unwarranted, assumptions, frequently metaphysical in character; for instance, about the nature of God, man, and the world. Whether an argument is judged fallacious will here partially depend on a philosophical outlook. Differences of interpretation may result if someone holds or denies that the meaning of words determines the meaning of facts, that the cause of phenomena resembles phenomena, that the order and connection of ideas are identical with the order and connection of things, that the world is created, or that the world is all that there is.

Metaphysical positions are often uncritically assumed and dogmatically held. Many an argument can be shown to be circular and therefore fallacious when its suppressed metaphysical assumption is made explicit.

It is, of course, quite possible for the same argument to commit more than one fallacy. In classifying arguments we shall simply try to locate the error which is most readily evident.

1. Verbal Fallacies

1.1 Equivocation

The fallacy of equivocation occurs in an argument when the impression is given that a key word or expression is used univocally (in a single sense) when it is actually being used equivocally (in two different senses). As long as the equivocal shift in meaning remains undetected, the argument appears valid; but when a careful definition of the ambiguous term is given, it becomes apparent that the conclusion has not been established by sufficient evidence, and the argument then loses its probative force.

An equivocal argument may appear to be of the valid form $(P \supset Q)(Q \supset R) \therefore (P \supset R)$, when it is really of the invalid form $(P \supset Q)(Z \supset R) \therefore (P \supset R)$. When equivocation occurs in a syllogism, the shift in meaning is frequently in the middle term, so that instead of

$$\begin{array}{l} \text{MaP} \\ \underline{\text{SaM}} \\ \therefore \text{SaP} \end{array}$$

a pseudo syllogism with four terms is introduced:

$$\begin{array}{l} \text{MaP} \\ \underline{\text{SaN}} \\ \text{SaP} \end{array}$$

Arguments in which vague expressions are used are prone to equivocate.

Consider, for example, the following:

1. Any country which holds elections is a democracy.
2. Russia holds elections.
∴ Russia is a democracy.

The expression *holds elections* in the major premise implies a choice between candidates who are chosen without compulsion, whereas the choice of candidates offered in a Soviet election is dictated by a single political ideology.

Again, the following:

The rights of the individual should be guaranteed by the government, and since everyone has the right to own property, the government should guarantee that everyone is a property owner.

Key: guarantee: Used in first sense to indicate that government should protect what an individual has a right to. Used in second sense that government should be the instrument by which a privilege is attained, a legitimate goal achieved.

Many equivocal arguments arise because of a failure to distinguish between negations and opposites. Voluntary actions and involuntary actions are contrary: the same act cannot both be voluntary and involuntary; but the negation of a voluntary action is an act performed under overwhelming compulsion.

Consider the following fallacious argument:

> Since a person is not responsible for what he does involuntarily, the accused ought to be acquitted because he never intended to injure; his action was not performed voluntarily.

Key: involuntarily: used in the sense of under compulsion, of being overcome by violence. "Not voluntarily" here simply implies a lack of intention on the part of the accused. A person is responsible for the consequences of his action, whether or not a particular result is intended.

A similar error can be detected in the ambiguous use of *ignorance:*

> Since no one is responsible whose actions are the result of ignorance, and my client was ignorant that what he did was against the law, my client is not responsible.

In its first usage the attorney appeals to the principle that when ignorance is the inescapable cause of an act, there is no personal responsibility; the second sense simply asserts that the accused was in a subjective state of being unaware of the law; it does not show that this condition of being in ignorance was invincible or justifiable.

1.2 Amphiboly

The fallacy of amphiboly occurs in an argument when the meaning intended by a phrase is not clear because of the grammatical structure of the sentence in which it is used. An amphibolous sentence permits a double interpretation, one view of which may be true and the other false. The ambiguity is not due to an equivocal use of words, but rather to the syntactical arrangement of the sentence. Careless writing replete with dangling modifiers, pronouns with ambiguous antecedents, and improper punctuation frequently gives rise to amphiboly.

For example, had Hitler consulted an astrologer, he might have been told that "if he invaded Russia a mighty nation he would destroy." What does this sentence assert? Is Russia to be destroyed, or is Germany to be destroyed?

Consider the will which states: "I do hereby bequeath $10,000 to my dog and my cat." Does each animal receive $10,000, or is the $10,000 divided between them? And how much is twice 13 plus 8? Is it $(2 \times 13) + 8 = 34$, or is it $2 \times (13 + 8) = 42$?

1.3 Accent

The fallacy of accent refers primarily to an error in reasoning due to a misplaced emphasis on a word or phrase in a sentence. The same sentence may have an entirely different meaning—even ironical or sarcastic—when its several parts receive different stresses. Certain intonations of voice, facial expressions, and gestures add to the meaning of words. By accentuating a different phrase in a sentence you can make a direct quotation convey an entirely different meaning from the one originally intended by its author. Such a disregard for balance permits the unfair slanting of the material of an argument.

Consider the patient who is told by a physician, "I cannot recommend a diet *too highly*," but understands the sentence to stress, "*I cannot recommend a diet* too highly." Does the sentence "We should not do evil to our friends" assert that anyone else is fair game? It makes a difference whether you stress the expression "*We should not do evil* to our friends" or lay the stress on the expression *our friends*; that is, "We should not do evil to *our friends*."

A more dangerous and misleading form of the fallacy of accent is when a whole sentence or paragraph is *lifted out of context* and given a significance that was never intended originally.

For example, the speaker who carefully lists the conditions under which an atomic war is morally permissible may be reported in the headlines thus: "Noted Authority Advocates ATOMIC HOLOCAUST."

1.4 Division

The fallacy of division occurs either when what is true of a whole is predicated of its constituent parts or when what is predicated of a class or collection is predicated distributively of each member of that class. It does not follow that because a Rolls-Royce is an expensive car, each of its parts is expensive or that because a law firm is a good law firm, each lawyer who belongs to it is a good lawyer. To argue to the contrary is to ascribe to its constituent parts certain properties which belong to the whole, thereby committing the fallacy of division. Likewise, what is true of a class of objects taken collectively need not be true of each individual member of that class. That mountain lions are rapidly becoming extinct does not permit the inference that a particular lion in a zoo is rapidly becoming extinct; that horses are found throughout the United States does not mean that each member of the extension of the term *horses* is to be found throughout the United States. The fallacy of division can be a contributing factor in the formation of prejudice. For even if it is admitted that a particular group of people collectively possess an undesirable quality with greater frequency than certain other groups, this would still not permit the inference that each individual member possessed the quality in question.

1.5 Composition

Whereas the fallacy of division erroneously draws an inference from a whole to its constituent parts or from a class to each of its members, the fallacy of composition either ascribes the properties of the constituent parts of a whole to the whole itself or predicates of a class of individuals such properties as belong solely to its individual members. Division and composition are thus related conversely.

The same word, when applied to an individual or a component part, may have a different significance when applied to a class of individuals or to a whole. Wise individual faculty members do not guarantee a wise faculty; strong individual soldiers do not guarantee a strong regiment; individual star players do not insure an outstanding team performance. To argue that because each part has a certain characteristic, the whole has the same characteristic, or to argue from a distributive sense of a term to its collective sense, is to commit the fallacy of composition.

1.6   Figure of Speech

The fallacy of figure of speech occurs when words or expressions that are similar in form are understood to be similar in meaning. The argument that, because something is audible when capable of being heard and visible when capable of being seen, therefore something is desirable when desired, derives its apparent force from the similar structure of the words *audible, visible,* and *desirable,* overlooking the shift from *being capable of* in the first two instances to *ought to be* in the case of what is desirable.

When interpreted more broadly, the fallacy of figure of speech may include a variety of serious errors. Abstract terms, analogical expressions, and metaphors may be hypostatized or taken literally. Familiar words and expressions which have an intelligible sense in one context may have no literal meaning in another context. The literal use of metaphors often diverts and obscures the real issue: it is responsible for many clichés and pompous prestige jargon.

Such terms as *the state, society, sex, nature, science, right, wrong, justice, the unconscious, life, evolution, democracy,* are frequently spoken of as if they enjoyed an independent existence.

2. Fallacies of Relevance

Errors in reasoning frequently arise because what is submitted as evidence is simply beside the point at issue. A conclusion may be drawn which is irrelevant to or does not follow from the reasons given; relevant evidence may also be neglected, and factors may be introduced which divert or camouflage the real issue. To turn away from the subject at hand, to exaggerate an opponent's position, to misuse humor, and to make picayune distinctions of no importance may be useful devices in the hands of the propagandist, but are obstacles in the way of sound reasoning.

2.1   Neglected aspect

To present evidence in support of one side of an issue to the exclusion of relevant evidence to the contrary is to commit the fallacy of neglected aspect. The withholding of evidence hostile to the conclusion at hand may be malicious and intentional or due to stupidity. Contrary evidence is frequently neglected by oversimplification or by the presentation of two alternatives as though they were the only options available.

The slogan which offers a choice of being *Red or Dead* overlooks a third possibility, the option of being *Alive and Free*.

To argue for or against a major health insurance program, pointing solely to its advantages or its disadvantages while failing to consider revelant alternative proposals, is an error of omission.

A full and fair treatment of an issue does not require an endless parade of repetitious facts. It is seldom possible to marshal every shred of evidence and every single argument on both sides of an issue. However, within reasonable limitations a student in a classroom, for example, has the right to expect that his professor will remain within his field of competence and that counterevidence will not be neglected.

2.2 *Non sequitur*

The fallacy of *non sequitur* is an argumentative leap to a conclusion which does not follow from the premises presented in evidence. The conclusion drawn is irrelevant. The premises adduced may be quite true, but they simply do not constitute grounds for the conclusion attached beneath them. There may be other premises that would lead to the proposed conclusion; however, the fallacy of *non sequitur* is most dangerous when the required premises are patently false or at least highly questionable. By supposing the false or questionable premises, you give an illusion of demonstration, whereas no evidence has actually been brought forth. What is asserted as a conclusion may be consistent with the premises presented, but it is not deducible from them. If, instead of concluding $(P \supset T)$ from the premises $(P \supset Q)(Q \supset R)(R \supset S)(S \supset T)$, one concludes $(P \supset Z)$, the latter is simply irrelevant to the premises presented.

From the premises "Anyone who favors an increase in government controls is willing to restrict individual freedom to gain greater security, and liberals do favor an increase in government controls" the conclusion "therefore, liberals are in favor of totalitarianism" simply does not follow. The only conclusion that can be drawn is that

liberals are willing to restrict individual freedom to gain greater se
curity. To draw any other conclusion from these premises is to fal
into a *non sequitur*.

2.3   *Ignoratio elenchi*

The fallacy of *ignoratio elenchi* is frequently more subtle than a
non sequitur, for whereas the latter simply asserts a conclusion tha
does not follow from the premises presented, the former does give a
valid demonstration of a conclusion. The error of *ignoratio elenchi*
lies in an ignorance of refutation, in an evasion of the issue at hand
To refute the assertion of a universal affirmative proposition SaP, i
is necessary to establish the truth of its contradictory SoP. To
offer a demonstration of any other conclusion is simply beside the
point.

More broadly interpreted, any argument that seeks to prove a
conclusion other than the one demanded may be considered an
ignoratio elenchi. Suppose, for example, that the issue is whether the
Soviet Union can be trusted to keep its treaty agreements, and someone were to prove that the Soviet Union has made great industrial
progress; suppose the issue is whether a particular religious dogma is
true, and someone were to demonstrate that it is useful to maintaining the social order; or suppose the issue is whether alcoholic beverages are morally permissible, and you were to demonstrate that
most students would welcome their exhilarating effect upon their
studies; such argumentation, even when valid, would simply serve
to establish a conclusion irrelevant to the issue at hand.

2.4   *Ad hominem*

Besides diverting attention from an issue by establishing an irrelevant conclusion, it is possible to appear to give evidence by arguing
against the motives and the character of the person advancing an
argument. While the testimony of a gangster who appears before a
Senate Investigating Committee is either true or false, the character
of such a witness is not totally irrelevant; it may cast doubt on the
credibility of certain parts of his testimony, especially if there is no
corroborative evidence. However, the mere fact that the witness is
"an aging, two-bit punk—once a thief, a dope pusher, a willing killer

for syndicate chiefs, now turned stool pigeon" does not of itself necessitate that his entire testimony is false.

More clearly, however, the arguments advanced against alcoholism are not refuted by pointing out that the person formulating them is himself an alcoholic. To discredit a person does not necessarily discredit his argument; to shift away from the point at hand to the person, to vilify his character, or to show that he is himself engaged in the activity which he condemns is simply beside the point. The evidence for the objective truth of a position is to be considered on its own merits. To commit the *ad hominem* fallacy is to introduce the person of the opponent when it has little or no bearing on the point of debate.

2.5 *Ad ignorantiam*

A further example of irrelevance, frequently combined with the *ad hominem* fallacy, ignores the principle that the burden of proof rests on the person who makes the assertion. A position is not established simply because no one can refute it.

In a court of law the prosecution is required to offer evidence sufficient to establish guilt beyond a reasonable doubt. It is not the responsibility of the accused to demonstrate his own innocence; in fact, he is accorded the privilege of remaining silent. To shift the burden of proof by appealing to the ignorance of one's opponent as evidence for one's own position is to commit the fallacy of *ad ignorantiam*. Instead of establishing that a given position P is true by offering evidence in support of P, the argument is advanced that P is true since no one has shown that P is false.

To argue that man is completely determined by his environment because no one can prove that he is not, that God does not exist because no one can prove He does, that morality is relative to society because no one can prove it is not, or that death is the end of human existence because no one can prove it is not is to fall into a trap of reasoning.

2.6 *Erroneous appeal to authority (ad verecundiam)*

The complexity of social life and the various domains of knowledge requires specialization and the cultivation of special fields of competence. Certain people are authorities in certain fields; few people are authorities in every field. To appeal to a genuine authority as evidence in support of a particular position is not fallacious if the authority cited has expert competence in the area under discussion. Frequently, however, the experts disagree, and other evidence besides their testimony is usually required. The testimony of the physician in matters of health, of the ballistic expert in identifying a weapon, of the fingerprint expert in matching a set of prints, of the physicist in physics, the biologist in biology, or the businessman in business is to be considered in situations where their special fields are relevant to the issue at hand.

An illegitimate and fallacious appeal to authority, an *argumentum ad verecundiam*, takes place when someone who is not an authority in the area under consideration is appealed to as though he were an authority. Usually a person who has obtained prominence in a single field has acquired a certain rightfully earned respect and prestige. Genuine competence in a worth-while activity is worthy of admiration, but to transfer the prestige acquired in one domain to an area where a person is not an expert but an amateur is a very serious form of irrelevance.

The baseball player who testifies on the merits of a particular razor blade as though he were an expert on steel and the movie star who endorses a particular cigarette filter as though an expert on lung cancer are rather trivial examples of this fallacy. It is far more serious when the pseudo expert is sincerely unaware of his own ignorance and incompetence.

An authority in the field of natural science may pose as an expert on economics, ethics, and politics, or a theologian may utter authoritative pronouncements on detailed scientific questions. Of course, a natural scientist may also know theology, and a theologian, natural science. The judgment of the scientist in theology is not to be respected because he knows science, but because he knows theology. And likewise the judgment of the theologian in natural science is to be credited to the extent that he is expert in that field.

An erroneous appeal to authority is encouraged by advertising media and the popular press, which seek out people prominent in one field and treat them as though they were expert in every field. Beware of the *expert* that knows what he knows but does not know what he doesn't know.

2.7   Irrelevant appeal to emotion and sentiment

Further irrelevancies are frequently introduced into argumentation by appealing to popular sentiments of long standing, some of which are legitimate in themselves, such as patriotism, love of family, and respect for proper authority, while others are illegitimate, such as bias, prejudices, and weakness of character; but whether legitimate or illegitimate, feelings and sentiments are not a substitute for reasons. Fear and compassion, love of the good, and hatred of injustice are a part of human nature. And there is a proper place for an appeal to emotion. The threat of the legitimate use of force, for example, by the proper authority can be evoked as a deterrent to certain actions. However, the guilt or innocence of the accused is not determined by our feelings of compassion for his aged suffering parents; the morality of an action is not determined by the threat of coercion; the feasibility of a practice is not necessarily reinforced by an appeal to its frequency, by repeated assertion, or by association with generally accepted popular sentiments.

The use of highly emotional terms or question-begging epithets and the introduction of needless technical jargon, popular clichés, and slogans, obfuscate rather than clarify, and then distract from the issue. In Shakespeare's *Julius Caesar*, Mark Antony's funeral oration never deals with whether Caesar was a tyrant deserving assassination. That Caesar had brought fame to Rome and treasure to its coffers and left his fortune to the populace evoked a feeling of pride and gratitude which incensed the mob and diverted their attention from the question of the guilt or innocence of the assassins.

In debating the wisdom of the Senate's ratification of the nuclear test ban treaty, Senator Dirksen was quoted by the magazine *Time*. After citing Chinese philosophy and Abraham Lincoln, Dirksen said that what bothered him was the searing memory of Hiroshima:

For the first time, the whole bosom of God's earth was ruptured by a man-made contrivance that we call a nuclear weapon.

Oh, the tragedy. Oh, the dismay. Oh the blood. Oh, the anguish. When the statisticians came to put the cold figures on paper, they were as follows: as a result of one bomb—66,000 killed, 69,000 injured, 62,000 structures destroyed. That was the result of one bomb, made by man in the hope of stopping that war. Little did he realize what this thermonuclear weapon would do, and the anguish that would be brought into the hearts of men, women, and children.[1]

Whether Dirksen's speech insured the ratification of the treaty is beside the point. The quoted passage simply does not deal with the issue in question: whether the interests of the United States are jeopardized by the suspension of nuclear tests. That the horrors of warfare increase with the use of modern weapons is questioned by no one. There would have been no point in developing or dropping a nuclear bomb if we had not known what it would do. That it succeeded in bringing the war to an end is seldom questioned. But what does Hiroshima have to do with a treaty which in no way decreases the existing stock pile of thermonuclear weapons? Will the treaty lessen the anguish of the victims of Hiroshima? Does the argument answer the treaty's critic that Russia is ahead in the race toward a defensive weapon which the United States cannot develop without further tests, so that the treaty increases the possibility of nuclear war? Such argumentation simply appeals to a popular sentiment, a horror of war, neglecting to mention the horror of a life under a Communist regime.

3. Fallacies of Unwarranted Assumption

While there need be no sharp line of demarcation between the kinds of fallacies, the primary source of many errors in reasoning is the tacit or explicit introduction of unwarranted or highly questionable assumptions. The mistake is not so much a matter of relevance or ambiguity as of presupposing what is at issue or of assuming false or highly debatable premises.

3.1   The fallacy of the general rule

To presuppose that what is true in general, under normal conditions, is true under all circumstances without exception is to make an unwarranted assumption. To apply a general rule to situations for which it was never properly intended is a serious source of error. Exercise is beneficial to healthy people, but it may kill someone with

[1] Vol. 82, No. 12 (September 2, 1963).

a weak heart. The rule of the majority as a principle of sound government is applicable only in situations where the rights of the minority are also guaranteed. Obedience to the authority of a government is morally permissible only when that government is just and allows redress for grievances. That the press ought to be free to publish all the news or that individual property rights ought to be guaranteed does not apply in times of national emergency when our life as a country is threatened. Freedom of religion and freedom of speech do not give license to offer human sacrifice and to incite to riot and sedition. Such general rules were never intended to apply to all circumstances and to operate under all conditions. Each right, each privilege, presupposes a corresponding obligation; to refuse the obligation is to forfeit the right. The right to life, liberty, and the pursuit of happiness is forfeited by the criminal who does not feel obliged to accord the same right to others.

3.2 Hasty generalization

To commit the fallacy of hasty generalization is to formulate a general rule or a universal principle on the basis of evidence which warrants a particular conclusion. It is to assume that what is relatively true under certain conditions is true under all conditions. Frequently our sense of the dramatic, our proneness to bias, and our tendency to oversimplify lead us to formulate sweeping statements.

From our experience that in many cases an extreme position is to be avoided and that a compromise can be found we might conclude that we ought always to compromise, even when to do so would be morally reprehensible. General rules cannot be formulated from accidental or exceptional situations.

The fallacies of the general rule and of hasty generalization are not to be mistaken for those of division and composition. The latter are the result of a confusion between a collective whole and its component parts, between the collective and distributed use of "all," or between class inclusion and class membership, whereas the fallacy of the general rule applies a general principle to situations where it is inapplicable, and that of hasty generalization formulates a general principle on the basis of insufficient evidence.

3.3   False cause

The tendency to generalize too quickly may lead to belief that we have discovered the cause of a phenomenon when we have not. P is the cause of Q if, and only if, the presence of P necessitates Q. The mere conjunction of two states of affairs does not require that there be a causal connection between them. It might just happen that A and B are coincidentally both true. The fallacy of false cause may occur when a given effect E is erroneously thought to be caused by A, when in fact its real cause is C.

A reversal of the causal relation may also be the source of error: E may be thought to be the cause of C, when the opposite is the case. Frequently, a false cause is assumed simply because two phenomena A and B occur together simultaneously or because A precedes B temporally. Such concurrence or priority may simply be coincidental. It is quite possible that without there being any causal connection between A and B, both A and B are themselves the effect of an identical cause, or each is the effect of two or more distinct causes.

Further erroneous identification of causes results when what is the necessary condition of a phenomenon is mistakenly identified with what is both necessary and sufficient or when reciprocal relations are mistaken for strict causal relations. That a reduction in taxes is followed or accompanied by a rise or fall in the stock market, that a patient recovers or dies after the administration of a drug, or that it begins to rain after a tribal dance does not necessarily imply causal connections.

Theories concerning human behavior which leave no room for the performance of voluntary morally responsible acts usually derive their plausibility by fallaciously assuming that what is a necessary condition for responsible behavior is both a necessary and sufficient condition. Human acts do not occur apart from a social structure; we are born into a family, into a religious community, and into a state or nation at a particular period in history and with a complex set of hereditary factors. In short, our physical and social environment constitutes the necessary conditions or framework in which we act. We are not born into a vacuum, and we do not live and act in a vacuum. But it begs the question to assume that the set of con-

itions, without which we could not act, causally determines our
cts so that we are not morally responsible for them.

3.4 False analogy

Structural and functional similarities between things and events
re useful in classifying, in forming concepts and hypotheses, and in
roviding an interpretation of what is conceptually remote. Two
hings may be like each other in certain respects.

The term *healthy* is applicable to Mr. Jones and to his complexion,
ut not in the same sense. It is Mr. Jones who is healthy. *Healthy*
when attributed to Mr. Jones's complexion is used in the sense that
is complexion is a sign of health in Mr. Jones. Terms such as *life*
an also be used analogously. We can legitimately speak of the life
f a cabbage and the life of an elephant; but here, too, we must remember that the expressions *life of a cabbage* and *life of an ele-
hant* differ in meaning to the extent that what cabbages are differs
rom what elephants are.[2]

The failure to understand the analogical usage of language can
esult in a misuse of analogy. To call a lion a king of the beasts is a
seful and suggestive metaphor, but to attribute real kingly powers
o a lion is to be misled by an analogy.

To argue on the basis of superficial resemblances, neglecting basic
ifferences, can result in false analogies. There is little similarity be-
ween a complex modern state and a living organism or between
hysical exercise and modern warfare, and yet one might per-
uasively argue that just as exercise benefits the body, war is beneficial
o the State.

Even when the resemblance between two things or situations is not
uperficial, it still does not follow that because they are alike in some
espects they are alike in every respect. The same apparent condi-
ions may not always produce the same results. A farmer may not
ntend to feed a turkey the day before Thanksgiving.

Structural and functional similarities do not permit the inference
hat things alike in some respects are *necessarily* alike in every re-
pect.

To argue on the basis of a false analogy is to conclude that since

[2] Cf. E. L. Mascall, *Existence and Analogy* (London, Longmans, Green,
949), p. 101 ff.

two objects or situations S_1 and S_2 are known to resemble each othe
by sharing a common property P_1, they *necessarily* share a secon
property P_2, although there is no known connection between P_1 an
P_2.

3.5 *Hypothesis contrary to fact*

To commit the fallacy of hypothesis contrary to fact is to appl
a speculative assumption which is contrary to actual states of affair:
It is not possible to reach a definite conclusion by presupposing
state of affairs contrary to what actually did occur. On the basis c
what did not happen, we can speculate about what *might* have beer
but we cannot reach a certain conclusion as to what *would* hav
been. It is hardly possible to consider all the alternatives in a situa
tion with any degree of complexity. It is fallacious to argue that i
Hitler had never been born, there would not have been a secon
world war. Of course, without Hitler the course of events would mos
likely have been somewhat different; however, the conclusion tha
can be reached is that there might not have been a second world wa
if Hitler had not been born.

3.6 *Poisoning of the wells*

To commit the fallacy of poisoning the wells is to preclude in ad
vance the possibility of any evidence to the contrary. A position i
assumed in such a manner that nothing can count as evidence agains
it. The very possibility of contradictory evidence is ruled out of cour
a priori. To dismiss arguments against the thesis that every act i
causally determined by membership in an economic class on the
grounds that counterarguments simply serve to demonstrate eco
nomic determinism is dogmatically to rule out the possibility o
counterevidence.

An objective, fair presentation of a position ought to specify wha
counts as evidence for the point of view being held and what woulc
count as evidence against the position taken. There is no point i
discussing a position when it is simply assumed that nothing can pos
sibly count against it.

3.7 *Complex question*

To pose a single question composed of two questions requiring separate answers is to commit the fallacy of a complex question. To demand a yes-or-no answer to such questions as "Are you going to stop cheating on exams?" "Do you intend to stop your reckless driving?" "Are you willing to discontinue your use of narcotics?" is to assume that a prior issue has already been decided; namely, that you cheat on exams, drive recklessly, and use narcotics. To avoid the fallacy, such questions must first be divided. If the questions "Do you cheat on exams?" "Do you drive recklessly?" "Do you use narcotics?" are answered affirmatively, it is then fair to ask, "Are you going to stop?"

3.8   Contradictory premises

The assumption of contradictory premises is an extremely dangerous error, since once they are assumed, any conclusion can be demonstrated with formal validity. The question "Can God create a stone so large that He cannot lift it?" demands the exercise of omnipotence and the denial of omnipotence. The question "What happens when an irresistible force meets an immovable object?" demands that there be something irresistible and that there be something which is not irresistible. To ask "What lies beyond the end of space?" is to assume that you have reached a terminal point which is not a terminal point. To ask "What happens at the end of our existence?" is to presuppose that our existence comes to an end and that it does not come to an end. Such questions conceal contradictions and lead to absurdity.

3.9   Genetic fallacy

To commit the genetic fallacy is to assume that the truth or falsity of a proposition or the adequacy or inadequacy of a hypothesis or theory can be determined by tracing its source or origin. Instead of examining the evidence in support of a proposition, reference is made to the way it came to be held; and if the source of origin is regarded in an unfavorable light, the proposition in question is dismissed without further ado.

To reject the truth claims of Islam, for example, solely on the grounds that the Koran was written at a time prior to the technological advances of the twentieth century is among other things to confuse the nature of something with how it came into being.

The genetic fallacy may also be committed by assuming an *a prior* connection between the logical and the temporal order, thereb necessitating the conclusion that the course of social developmen proceeds from the simple to the complex. The truth of a propositio depends on whether the relation of identity asserted by it accuratel; designates things as they are. It does not depend on the motives o character of the person making the assertion nor upon the time anc place at which the proposition was first uttered.

The circumstances and the character of witnesses offer clues fo further lines of investigation, but the present nature of something i not to be made dependent on its origin, unless it can be shown tha there is an intrinsic causal connection between the way in whicl something came into being and the way it now is. For example, tc raise questions concerning the source and origin of the modern in stitution of the Papal Office within the Roman Catholic Church i: not irrelevant, since the claim now made to Papal authority is in part dependent on historical antecedents. But to dismiss the morai principles of distributive justice on the ground that it was first developed by Aristotle at a time when people wore sandals instead of shoes is to argue fallaciously, since questions of justice do not change simply because of a change in technology.

3.10   Begging the question

The fallacy of begging the question occurs in many forms and is perhaps the most subtle form of fallacious reasoning. What is to be proved in the conclusion may simply be stated in a disguised form in the premises.

> A favorable response to higher taxes always results in providing better education, since a favorable response to higher taxes always results in better classroom buildings, and what does not result in providing better education is an unfavorable response to higher taxes.

The argument is thus of the form

$$\bar{P}a\bar{S}$$
$$\frac{SaM}{\therefore \ SaP} \ .$$

The contrapositive of the conclusion is restated as a premise, thus making the argument circular.

Still again, the truth of one of the premises of an argument may itself require the truth of the conclusion.

Consider the argument:

$$
\begin{array}{cc}
\text{M} & \text{P}
\end{array}
$$
1. To accept the authority of Genesis is to accept a myth.
$$
\begin{array}{cc}
\text{S} & \text{M}
\end{array}
$$
2. To believe in the doctrine of creation is to accept the authority of Genesis.
$$
\begin{array}{cc}
\text{S} & \text{P}
\end{array}
$$
∴ To believe in the doctrine of creation is to accept a myth.

$$
\begin{array}{l}
1.\ \text{MaP} \\
2.\ \text{SaM} \\
\hline
∴\ \text{SaP}
\end{array} \ .
$$

Now, suppose that reasons are demanded for the first premise MaP, and it is now argued:

$$
\begin{array}{ccc}
\text{S} & \text{a} & \text{P}
\end{array}
$$
1. To believe in the doctrine of creation is to accept a myth.
$$
\begin{array}{ccc}
\text{M} & \text{a} & \text{S}
\end{array}
$$
2. To accept the authority of Genesis is to believe in the doctrine of creation.
$$
\begin{array}{ccc}
\text{M} & \text{a} & \text{P}
\end{array}
$$
∴ To accept the authority of Genesis is to accept a myth.

$$
\begin{array}{l}
\text{SaP} \\
\text{MaS} \\
\hline
∴\ \text{MaP}
\end{array} \ .
$$

The argument is circular, since the premise MaP itself assumes the conclusion SaP.

The first party of a dispute may also ask the second party to admit what is contradictory to the latter's thesis or to admit a principle that could be established only if the contradictory were true. Such circular arguments are very deceptive when stated at length, especially in book form. The real issue may never be stated, or it may simply be regarded as having been settled, thereby shifting attention to secondary issues.

3.11   Reduction fallacy

The fallacy of reduction is a form of question-begging, since it assumes uncritically that the various domains of experience are reducible to each other. Differences in philosophical positions necessitate different interpretations of God, man, and the world. However, when a metaphysical assumption, critical to the reduction in question, is simply taken for granted without mention or defense, the most important question is then simply dogmatically regarded as settled.

The fullness and richness of the world is distorted when its diversity is reduced to a part. Historical events, for example, cannot be adequately explained solely in terms of their physical aspects: sacrificial love is not adequately understood solely in terms of biological concepts, nor are the norms of ethics and aesthetics to be unquestioningly reduced to feeling. And it is uncritical simply to assume that the moral propriety of an event is to be judged solely in terms of the period and the positive law of the society in which it occurred.

EXERCISES

Critically analyze the following.
1. For Sale: Antique table suitable for gentleman with wooden legs.
2. The commandment "Thou shalt not covet thy neighbour's wife" does not apply to the case in question, as the woman involved is the wife of a total stranger.
3. Dogs are friendly animals, so this animal must be friendly, since it is a dog.
4. Since everyone has a right to his own opinion, to argue that the moral principles of our society are right, and that contrary standards adopted in other societies are wrong, is to fall into a bourgeois provincialism.
5. *Question:* How do you prevent an elephant from *charging?*
   Answer: You take away his credit card.
6. Science is aware of the difficulties.
7. The State can do no wrong.
8. The present rate of population growth will result in a scarcity of food within a few hundred years.

9. Conservatives wish to turn back the clock of history, since they are opposed to an increase in government interference in private affairs, and anyone who does that is against Federal aid to public education.

10. To hold that some students approve of cheating is obviously false, since most students have expressed their disapproval.

11. The freedom of speech is guaranteed by the Constitution, so that it is unconstitutional to impose any restriction upon expression by censorship.

12. Died John Doe, old-time grid star at University of Playball when Yarvard and Hale Colleges ruled the roost of kidney disease.

13. Negroes in the United States have acquired less economic wealth than non-Negroes. ∴ Mr. Doe must be poorer than his neighbor, since he is a Negro.

14. *Question:* How do you make an elephant *float?*
    Answer: With two scoops of ice cream, an elephant, and some root beer.

15. Adjustments in our moral standards with respect to premarital sexual intercourse are long overdue, since recent surveys have shown that the practice is widely adopted.

16. Mr. Smith is not an atheist, since it can be shown that he goes to church regularly.

17. To refute the allegation that taxes should be lowered, one need only note the rapid economic growth under the present administration.

18. Do you still beat your wife?

19. How do you explain the fact that you are responsible for your acts when you are not responsible for them?

20. Aid to Hungary during the uprising in 1956 would have resulted in an atomic war, since it would have angered the Russians, and an atomic war was avoided by our failure to aid Hungary.

21. Miracles violate the laws of nature and are therefore impossible.

22. Man is nothing but protoplasm.

23. God does not exist, because no one ever saw him.

24. What do you mean we should have invaded Cuba? You've never been in the Army!

25. When did you first abandon your respect for the rights of others?

26. The Communist system has worked quite well in Red China, as is evidenced by the increase in literacy throughout the entire nation.

27. Born to John Doe bespectacled balding cinemite a fifth child.

28. What did God do before time began?

29. Social scientists are ethical relativists, since they study society, and those who are not ethical relativists are not social scientists.

30. Russia is a Communist country, so Mr. Petrov must be a Communist, since he is a Russian.

31. Nature is aware of the difficulties involved.

32. The recent decisions of the Supreme Court regarding prayer in the public schools are not contrary to the original intent of the Constitution, since it can readily be shown that they have been widely accepted by religious leaders.

33. For Sale: Yacht; $5,000 below cost.

34. The dream of Utopia is an illusion, since it first arose in a pre-atomic age.

35. Censorship ought to be abolished, since it violates the principle that everyone ought to be guaranteed the freedom of expression.

36. That it is morally right to legalize abortion is supported by the fact that many prominent lawyers are in favor of doing so.

37. A failure to vote Yes on this amendment will result in your losing the support of the political bosses in the next election.

38. Men are smarter than women, since no one has proved the contrary.

39. The patient is sick, because he has a high temperature.

40. Your attempt to show that belief in democracy is not simply an emotion of fear is itself due to an emotion of fear, and you thus verify rather than refute my thesis.

41. The accident would never have occurred if the driver of the other car had not been drinking.

42. Mother Nature will look after her offspring.

43. Nature destroys the weak, and the strong alone survive; so, too, a nation ought to purge itself of its weaker members.

44. Germany would have won World War II if Hitler had only invaded England instead of Russia.

45. The advocates of capital punishment are easily refuted, since recent studies have shown that states which have abolished it do not have a higher incidence of crime.

46. There would have been no domestic difficulties if the husband had not lost his job.

47. Your arguments against my thesis that whatever we do is determined by sex drive are themselves determined by sex drive and thus simply confirm rather than count against the position which I am defending.

48. When a part of the human body is cancerous, you remove it by surgery; when a segment of society is sick, it should be destroyed.

49. To refute the notion that artificial contraceptives are immoral, one need only note the tremendous increase in the world's population.

50. Wearing a hat she carried her dress in her arms.

51. What made you decide to lead a life of crime?

52. Evolution is an established fact, since it is widely accepted, and change is certainly not unestablished.

53. No wonder you're against our present administration! You lost your job, didn't you?

54. How do you account for the fact that you are a loyal American when in fact you are a traitor?

55. The United States would have remained neutral during World War II if Japan had not attacked Pearl Harbor, and if the U.S. had remained neutral, the Allies would have lost the war.

56. It is evident that the sole way to solve the farm problem is to continue price supports, since no one is able to prove the contrary.

57. Belief in a personal God is out of date, since Julian Huxley, a great scientist, disbelieves in one.

58. When you consider the anguish of the innocent wife and children and the war record of the accused, I can only ask that the jury vote acquittal.

59. The members of Group *x* that live in our town are dirty, slov-

enly, lazy, and dishonest, from which it follows that everyone in the country from which they came is also dirty, slovenly, lazy, and dishonest.

60. The claims of Marxist economic theories can be dismissed simply because they were developed at a time when labor unions did not exert a mitigating influence upon management.

61. The universe is chemistry.

62. The accused undoubtedly committed the act in question; however, when his family background is considered, together with his early history, it is impossible to hold him responsible; he could not have acted otherwise.

63. Our candidate deserves your vote: he's a hundred per cent American, a native son, with a long record of charity, one of your own friends and neighbors.

64. Life after death is impossible.

65. What will you think about when you cease to be?

66. Conservatives cannot win an election, since they are sneered at by liberals, and conservatives are unable to win an election.

67. The paintings of Rembrandt are nothing but oil splashed on canvas.

68. A man is what he eats.

69. The Biblical doctrine of creation can be discarded because it was first held to by a nation that did not know the latest scientific theories.

70. Are you still unwilling to admit that our quarrel is your fault?

71. Red China ought not to be seated in the United Nations, since the government on Formosa strongly objects.

72. Are you ready to stop being disrespectful to your parents?

73. Whatever you do in adult life depends on your unconscious experience as a child; you are causally determined by your environment from the moment of your birth, if not before.

74. Those tried at Nuremberg were treated unfairly, since they were prosecuted for obeying the laws of their country.

75. It is clearly evident that you are a thief, since you cannot prove that you are not.

76. Just as exercise is good for the human body, exercise is also good for the body politic.

77. Art is frozen emotion.

78. You need have no fear of the patient's life; he has received many injuries, but none of them is serious when considered individually.

79. There must be life on other planets, since no one has been able to show that there isn't.

80. The American students that were on the boat were a noisy bunch of drunks. I can only conclude that American students must always behave improperly.

81. Since to increase the national debt promotes prosperity, an increase in my personal debts will make me more prosperous.

82. The rightness or wrongness of homosexuality depends on the standards of the group in which it is practiced.

83. Man is his body.

84. Eichmann did not commit any crime, since he simply obeyed the laws of the country in which he was a citizen.

85. Physical survival is the only norm to measure the moral correctness of an act.

86. Religion is man's feeling of awe.

87. Pleasure and pain are the final test of morality.

88. God is a feeling of dependence.

89. Murder is the result of an improper environment.

90. Since every member of the band is an outstanding musician, how can you say that their rendition was atrocious?

91. The theory of evolution must be true, since no one has disproved it.

92. Man is determined by his heredity and is therefore not morally responsible for what he does.

93. Alcoholism is nothing but a disease.

94. The businessman is not bound by the same moral norms in his business as he is in his private life. The sole question to be asked in a business transaction is whether it will make money.

95. The soul is mythical, since it is metaphysical, and what is other than mythical is other than a soul.

96. What is good for General Motors is good for the country.

97. "One night in their cell Genovese said to Valachi: 'You know you buy a barrel of apples and one of them is touched. That apple has to be removed, or it'll touch the rest of the apples.' Then Genovese kissed Valachi. It was the Mafia's 'kiss of

death,' to let Valachi know he was the apple to be removed."
—*Time*, October 4, 1963.

98. All religions are in danger of becoming intolerant. Christianity is a religion. So Christianity is false.

99. An atomic bomb has more destructive power than the bombs used in World War II; so if one is dropped, more people will be killed than were killed in World War II.

100. Who are you to say that cheating is wrong; weren't you kicked out of school for it?

101. Since each article of clothing worn was quite stylish, she must have been well dressed.

Foreign Relations

102. *The Senate Consents.*

"The outcome was never in serious doubt—only the size of the majority. Last week, after nearly three weeks of hearings and eleven days of formal debate, the U.S. Senate gave its consent to the nuclear test ban treaty with Russia by an 80 to 19 margin. President Kennedy hailed the vote as 'a welcome culmination of this effort to lead the world once again to the path of peace.'

"*A Real Stinker.* In its final hours, the debate produced sparks. The day before the ratification vote, dissenting Senators sought to tie a spate of qualifications to the pact—any one of which could have put the whammy on the whole works. 'If reservations are attached to the treaty,' New York Republican Jacob Javits had warned, 'it will mar for the world and all the nations which are signing the treaty the statesmanship which dedicated it in the first place.'

"Despite the warning, Arizona Republican Barry Goldwater introduced a reservation that would have made the treaty conditional on the withdrawal of Soviet men and materiel from Cuba. 'If you must vote for this treaty,' said Goldwater, who had no intention of doing so, 'demand at least this single, honorable, appropriate and meaningful price.' Fuming, Majority Leader Mike Mansfield accused Goldwater of seeking 'not to build the treaty but to bury it.' Besides, added Arkansas Democrat J. William Fulbright, 'the Russians would laugh at us.' Barry lost, 75 to 17."—*Time,* October 4, 1963.

03. Psychologists do not believe in the soul, since psychologists are behaviorists, and those who believe in the soul are other than psychologists.

04. What do you mean that he's being treated unfairly? Would you want him as a member of your own family?

05. There is no use in listening to what you have to say; everyone knows you're on the radical right.

06. No one should even bother to listen to your arguments against inflation; everyone knows you are in business and stand to lose by wage increases.

CHAPTER FOURTEEN

Induction

" 'O Oysters,' said the Carpenter,
'You've had a pleasant run!
Shall we be trotting home again?'
But answer came there none—
And this was scarcely odd, because
They'd eaten every one."

Through the Looking Glass—LEWIS CARROLL

1. The Nature of Induction

The preceding chapters have been primarily concerned with the formal validity of inferences. Little attention has been devoted to the questions "How do we get our premises?" and "Where do they come from?" Many of our most important premises are presupposed, either because we cannot do without them or because the assumption of their contradictory requires greater credulity and may even lead to absurdity. The basic principles of logic—the laws of noncontradiction $\sim(P \cdot \sim P)$, of excluded middle $(P \, v \sim P)$, and of identity $(P \supset P)$—are presupposed in our every experience; to deny them leads to chaos.

To assume that there is a reason why things are as they are—for example, that cancer and babies have a cause—is inevitable if we are to understand the world in which we live. Some of our assumptions—the least important—are shared by nearly everyone, since they are supported by our observations and experience. However, there is no universal acceptance of such basic presuppositions as "Our sensory experience yields knowledge of a world, independent of our knowing it," "The world is the creation of an omnipotent being," "Man is a morally responsible creature of God"; and yet such assumptions may prove unavoidable and tremendously influential in the acquisition of certain kinds of knowledge. Not every assumption that we make is true: some are contradictory, while others fail to explain; they are overly complex and multiplied unnecessarily. Moreover, we have seen that the formal validity of an argument is not a sufficient ground for its acceptability. A sound argument requires that its premises be true.

A part of the logician's task is to point out the different kinds of things to be known, the extent to which they are knowable, and the way that each can be known. From our limited experience, whether direct or indirect, public or private, we seek to formulate universal propositions which then become the premises of valid arguments. It is noteworthy that a valid argument cannot be drawn from two particular categorical premises. Since all direct experience of observation is of particulars, we are faced with the difficulty of attaining universal premises. The process by which we seek to establish general propositions from singular experiences is a part of what is known as *induction*. Such reasoning may attempt to formulate hypotheses, offer explanations, make predictions, and discover causal connections. Induction draws inferences from what is known directly to what is known indirectly. That a phenomenon is observed to occur in some individual instances leads to the conclusion that it will occur in all parallel instances essentially like the observed instances. The method of the sciences is a combination of the deductive procedures we have studied with what is usually called the method of induction.

From a formal point of view, induction may be expressed in several ways; first, in what is known as an Inductive Syllogism:

1. Washington, Jefferson . . . Eisenhower, were Protestants
2. Washington, Jefferson . . . Eisenhower, are all the Presidents before Kennedy

∴ All the Presidents before Kennedy were Protestants

or more simply:

$$\frac{\text{W, J, . . . E, were P}}{\text{W, J, . . . E, are all the M's}}$$
∴ All M is P.

Such induction by complete enumeration requires that all particulars be mentioned.[1]

Such a form of argument is not always considered to be induction, and yet it clearly serves a useful service by summarizing in a general formula what is contained in its premises.[2] What may be problematic is the premise which asserts that W, J, . . . E, are all the M's.

Nevertheless, such an induction attempts to establish a universal proposition by exhaustively enumerating all the instances subsumable under it.[3]

$$\frac{\begin{array}{l}1.\ \ a, b, c, \text{ are B's}\\ 2.\ \ a, b, c, \text{ are all the A's}\end{array}}{∴\ \ \text{All A is B.}}\ .$$

A second case of induction infers from the fact that all observed members of Class A are in possession of Property B that all the unknown members of Class A also possess Property B. Here a general conclusion is reached on the basis of experience with particulars: *a, b, c,* are individual members of A, and *a, b, c,* possess B; therefore the conclusion is reached that all A are B. (We have already used a similar line of reasoning in our elementary argument form Universal Generalization, UG.)

One might argue, for example, that since Fido, Rover, and Becky are dogs and they bark, therefore all dogs bark. Such an inference is justified if the characteristic noted is a property of the kinds of things under discussion; however, one cannot argue that because Fido, Rover, and Becky have black and white spots, all dogs have black and white spots; for being spotted is accidental to being a

[1] H. W. B. Joseph, *An Introduction to Logic,* 2nd ed. (Oxford, Clarendon Press), p. 380.

[2] See George Hendricks von Wright, *The Logical Problems of Induction* (New York, Macmillan, 1957), p. 9.

[3] See Morris R. Cohen and Ernest Nagel, *An Introduction to Logic and Scientific Method* (New York, Harcourt, Brace, 1934), p. 275.

dog. The problem is, of course, to know how to distinguish what is essential from what is accidental.

It is possible, moreover, to draw the conclusion that because *a, b, c,* are individual members of A and have a certain essential element B, then all A's are B's and whatever has the essential element B is also an A; that is, all A's are B's and all B's are A's. For example, one might infer that since Tom, Dick, and Harry are men and have essential elements *x. y,* and *z,* then all men have the elements *x, y, z* and whatever has elements *x, y, z* is a man.

Obviously not all inductive generalizations are true. To argue that because bad tempers are characteristic of certain individuals with red hair, therefore all redheads are ill-tempered, is factually false. Nevertheless, because certain generalizations that we make are false, it does not follow that all of them are. And to know that it is false that "All A's are B's" is to know the truth of the proposition "Some A's are not B's."

Of course, the problem is again to distinguish true from false generalizations. When the members of a class are in fact homogeneous with respect to the characteristic in question, generalizations in terms of the latter will be true. Theoretical certainty is seldom attainable, and the generalization may then take the form that since *a, b, c,* are A, and *a, b, c,* possess a characteristic B, and no other member has ever been observed that lacks B, it is to a degree certain that all A's are B. The degree of certainty depends partially on the nature and the purpose of the generalization. A generalization is theoretically certain if its denial is an absurdity; it is certain beyond a reasonable doubt if its denial leads to a contradiction when conjoined with other propositions accepted without question; it is practically certain when it provides a sufficient basis for action by serving as the most reliable guide that is available under existing conditions. Whenever there is a degree of doubt connected with a generalization, such doubt may vary in terms of a scale of probability. The conclusion then reached may, for example, be of the form that, nine chances out of ten, all A's are B's, or there is a 50–50 chance that all A's are B's, or when there is still a strong doubt, there is a small chance (1 out of 10, for example) or it is possible that . . . all A's are B's.[4]

[4] *Ibid.,* pp. 277–279.

Some logicians hold that the evidence for generalizations that deal with matters of fact can never be more than probable, the degree of their probability depending on the fairness of the sample and the state of knowledge attainable in the field in which the generalization is made. Others hold that by abstraction it is possible to move from a sensory awareness of particulars to an intellectual apprehension of their stable natures or essences; that is, through the instrumentality of the concept, the essence of the particular is apprehended, and an essential predicable relationship between the subject and a predicate is made evident.[5]

Our immediate concern, however, is not to decide the theoretical issues raised about induction, but to describe the more formal aspects of inductive inferences. From this perspective, we have noted three forms of inference, where lower-case letters are individual members and A is a class, while B is an essential characteristic or property.

1. (1) a, b, c, are B.
   (2) a, b, c, are all the A's.
   ∴ All A is B.

2. (1) a, b, c, . . . are A's.
   (2) a, b, c, . . . are B.
   ∴ All A is B.

3. (1) a, b, c, are A's.
   (2) a, b, c, are B.
   ∴ All A is B and All B is A.

Inductive generalizations need not be concerned with the properties or characteristics of single individuals, but they may be made with respect to the relations that members of Class A have to each other. In other words, if x is a member of A and y is a member of A, then x sustains a certain relation R to y. This relation R between x and y may, of course, be of any kind; that is, symmetrical, asymmetrical, nonsymmetrical, and so forth. Formally stated, the fourth kind of inductive generalization may be written:

[5] See Francis H. Parker and Henry B. Veatch, *Logic as a Human Instrument* (New York, Harper, 1959), pp. 285 ff.

4. $(x)(y)(Ax \cdot Ay) \rightarrow Rxy$), or more simply:

1. x is an A.
2. y is an A.
∴ x is related to y.

Other conclusions might have been reached; for example, when R is symmetrical,

$$(x)(y)(Ax \cdot Ay) \rightarrow (Rxy \cdot Ryx);$$

when R is asymmetrical,

$$(x)(y)(Ax \cdot Ay) \rightarrow (Rxy \cdot \sim Ryx);$$

and when R is nonsymmetrical,

$$(x)(y)(Ax \cdot Ay) \rightarrow (Rxy \cdot Ryx) \text{ v } (Rxy \cdot \sim Ryx).$$

A fifth form of inductive inference may take the form that for every x and for every y, where x and y are individuals, if x sustains a certain relation R to y, then if x is an A then y is a B, where A and B are the names of classes or properties.

$$(x)(y)(Rxy \rightarrow (Ax \rightarrow By)).$$

Such a generalization R may, of course, be of any kind; that is, symmetrical, transitive, reflexive, and so on.

The inductive generalizations with which we have dealt have been universal in character. Of course it is possible to formulate statistical generalizations inferring that something will be true of a certain proportion rather than of every member of a class.[6] However, we need not here concern ourselves with statistical inductions, and for the most part our further interest will center around the more simple form of inductive generalization which infers that because the observed members of a Class A have a property or essential element B, therefore all the unobserved members of A also have the same element or property. That is:

a, b, c, are A's.
a, b, c, are B.
∴ All A is B.

[6] See Von Wright, *op. cit.*, p. 4 ff.

The term *induction* means many things to many authors. The questions "What is induction?" and "Under what conditions is induction possible?" are regarded as among the main questions of logical theory, since the discovery of all truths, other than what is self-evident, and the acquisition of all knowledge, other than what is intuitive, depend exclusively on some form of experience and on inductions and their interpretations. Induction is the operation of discovering and proving general principles, the mental process by which the inference is drawn that what is true in a particular case is true in all the cases that resemble it in certain notable respects; a process that infers that what is true of certain individuals of a class is true of the whole class; that what is true on certain occasions will in similar circumstances be true on every occasion. Strictly speaking, logical operations which do not contain an element of inference, from the known to the unknown, are not a part of what is meant by induction. Induction is not the mere shorthand registration of what is already known; it is not a mere collection of known facts; [7] nor is it preoccupied with the mere description of the facts; it is rather concerned with their explanation and prediction, with the establishment of the conditions under which similar facts may be expected to recur. Such generalizations from experience are held to be warranted on the assumption that the very constitution of the universe requires that what happens once will happen as often as there is a recurrence of the same circumstances. The assumption of the uniformity of the course of nature, although itself a generalization from experience, is the ultimate major premise of all inductions. The course of nature is, however, infinitely varied, so that it is not always legitimate to assume that the unknown will be like the known. The conclusion that something is universally true, simply because we have never experienced contrary instances, is warranted to the degree that there is reason to hold that if such contrary instances had occurred, they would have been observed.

The study of our world of experience is the study of many uniformities, of many different law spheres, not of a single law. [8] How-

---

[7] John Stuart Mill, *A System of Logic* (London, Longmans, Green, 1925), p. 188 ff.

[8] The question "What is the ultimate origin of the world we experience, of its laws and structures, of its unity and diversity" lies beyond the scope

ever, great care must be exercised to distinguish the kinds of uniformities that have hitherto been found to be perfectly invariable in nature from those that vary with changeable circumstances.

Our experience discloses uniformities which, as far as any human purpose is concerned, may be regarded as certain and universal and as constituting a basis for the evaluation of other inductive inferences. A logic of induction is possible because less certain inductive inferences can be compared with those about which we are certain. By showing that the falsity of a questionable inference necessitates the abandonment of an induction about which there is certainty, the weaker induction is at least raised to a higher level of certainty.

The whole theory of induction is based on the principle of causation. It is an assumption of common sense that every fact which has a beginning has a cause. The latter is sometimes understood as an ultimate metaphysical principle, or simply as the invariability of succession between every fact in nature and some other fact which preceded it. A cause is an invariable antecedent; an effect, the invariable consequent of a phenomenon; and the universality of the law of causation simply notes the connection between every consequent and some particular antecedent or set of antecedents. John Stuart Mill, for example, was not concerned with establishing a cause which *actually* produces the effect; his concern was with the establishment of an invariable order of succession to which end rules or canons may be formulated.[9] A consequent, however, is

___

of a course in logic. And yet in dealing with the problem of induction, such general philosophical issues cannot be avoided. Are the "laws of nature" identical with the laws formulated in the sciences? Are the uniformities of the external world ultimately caused by an omnipotent being? Are they the results of a chance universe that had no beginning? Are they the product of the human mind? Do they become at least partially known to the mind? The answers to such questions frequently influence what is written on induction and the nature of science. They need not concern us in dealing with the formal aspects of induction.

[9] The problem of the nature of causality is not a part of an elementary course in logic. It belongs to the discipline known as metaphysics. To affirm that there is causal order in the cosmos is not to assume that the lawlike statements formulated in the special sciences have discovered this order. The laws of science are not to be equated with the "laws of nature." The question of the character and origin of the laws of nature is frequently answered by assuming that nature is "God," in the sense of being all that there is, or by assuming that there is a God who is the author of nature and nature's laws.

not the effect of a single antecedent; it is rather a set of antecedents which determine an invariable sequence. The mere fact that a given phenomenon *has been* preceded by a certain antecedent, or that a certain antecedent *has* always been followed by a particular consequent, does not establish a causal relation. An antecedent does not necessarily cease with the appearance of its effects, nor does an effect necessarily cease with the cessation of its cause; however, the conditions necessary for the first production of a phenomenon may be necessary for its continuance. An effect may even occur simultaneously with its cause, and a single cause may be productive of heterogeneous effects.

In most cases, several causes are at work in the production of an effect; their joint effect is usually, but not always, identical with the sum of their separate effects. As a general rule, causes in combination produce the same effects as when they act singly, but the composition of causes may bring about a change in the laws in question and result in an entirely new set of effects.

"Induction is the process by which we conclude that what is true of certain individuals of a class is true of the whole class, or that what is true at certain times will be true in similar circumstances at all times." [10]

Such a process of inference proceeds from the known to the unknown. It may lack the theoretical certainty and the necessity of deductive inference. However, from a practical point of view, inductions are frequently indubitable, and the generalizations proceeding from them are held with psychological conviction until a counterinstance is discovered. Few, if any, doubt that the sun will rise tomorrow; it is, of course, not logically necessary that it do so. The world may come to an end. Who knows? And yet here it is not necessary to enter into the question as to the legitimacy of inductive procedures.[11] The fact is that inductions are made. Our present task is to show how induction is used to formulate a theory to explain the observed facts.

There is always a possibility of error in the pursuit of knowledge. The results of inductive processes lead to contingent, not absolutely

[10] Mill, *op. cit.*, p. 118.
[11] For a detailed discussion of the problem of justifying induction, see Von Wright, *op. cit.*

necessary, results. Unless we assume that our mind is incapable of knowing the world as it is,[12] we are to some extent able to know things as they are. If we can form concepts of and about the nature of the world in which we live, then it is not necessary to justify the formulation of universal statements from an experience of particulars. We are in principle able to make this transition because we can differentiate what is essential and what is accidental to particulars. Such inferences are not infallible. We need not always be right in our judgments in order to be right sometimes.

Induction is a part of the method of science; it is a part of logic —a part that differs from deduction, without being opposed. The sciences seek to explain the "facts"—facts that are observed. Such "facts" are particular in nature. We cannot observe everything. By abstracting what is essential to the particular, the effort is made to explain what is observed in complete generality. The scientist seeks to explain what he saw and what he expects to see. The generalizations that are made are universal in form and can, therefore, serve as the basis of logical deductions about the future.[13]

We have repeatedly stated that logic is the instrument of human knowledge; that it is the method of the sciences, as well as being indispensable to everyday affairs. In the broadest sense, man is truly a rational being; he forms concepts, makes judgments, and reasons deductively in every aspect of experience. His concepts may be vague and inadequate, his judgments may be expressed in false propositions, and his reasoning may be invalid; but the mere fact that he engages in such activity is accurately described by the term *rational*.

What we have studied about the nature of concepts and propositions is of importance to the process of induction. By abstracting the essential nature of particulars through the instrumentality of

[12] Such an assumption is rather odd, since it is difficult to understand how we could know that we cannot know. If we are able to arrive at the knowledge that we cannot know, why not employ the same "method" in order to know some other things as well.

[13] Although there is no uniformity of procedure in the actual workings of the scientist, an approximate pattern can sometimes be noted. An hypothesis, when verified to a certain degree of probability, may attain the status of a theory. Theories which receive general acceptance are sometimes spoken of as laws. Choices between theories are usually made on the basis of simplicity; that is, on the basis of their explanatory power.

concepts, we come to know what things are. When our concepts are combined into judgments, expressed in propositions, we discover certain identities or nonidentities in the nature of things.

Among other things, the inductive process enables us to formulate hypotheses, expressed in hypothetical propositions. A hypothesis is held tentatively. It may be discarded when predictions made on the basis of it are not fulfilled. A new hypothesis is sought when certain predictions are not verified by a series of observations. Induction enables us to proceed from original observations to hypotheses. The latter frequently permit us to make deductions in the form of predictions. A third step of verification may be taken in such areas as permit further observations and experiments. This cycle starts with particular observable facts which are then described in complete generality, enabling predictions to be made (by deduction). When possible, the predictions are checked against the facts, and the cycle from facts to facts is completed. Certain theories, of course, do not lend themselves to immediate verification. Whether there is a conscious existence after death, for example, is verifiable only in the sense that this will be known in the future, if there is conscious existence after death.

The process of induction may lead immediately from our sensory awareness of particulars to an apprehension of the nature or essence in the particulars. We need not examine every individual human being to know that man is capable of being rational. To know what the nature of particulars is, it is, of course, necessary to have recourse to observation.

2. Mill's Canons of Experimental Inquiry

Our experience warrants the assumption that there are parallel cases in nature: that under the same conditions what happens once will happen again. At times our observations are directed to particular events or instances that occur in nature. We then find a ready-made instance suited to our purposes. On other occasions, we make an artificial circumstance in order to abstract from it the nature of what is observed. Such an artificial arrangement may take the form of an experiment. The latter enables us to produce the kind of circumstances that we want in order to check our hypotheses and to discover the law governing the phenomenon in question.[14]

Experiments enable us to examine combinations of circumstances not found in nature. By inductive inquiry we probe into the effects of a given cause or we seek to ascertain the causes of a given effect.

2.1 The method of agreement

The first canon of experimental inquiry, as formulated by Mill, compares different instances in which a given phenomenon occurs.

If two or more instances of the phenomenon under investigation have only one circumstance in common, the circumstance in which alone all the instances agree is the cause (or effect) of the given phenomenon.

Suppose we observe the occurrence of a given phenomenon on four different occasions A, B, C, D, and that in the case of A there are the following relevant circumstances, c, e, f, g; in the case of B, we note c, h, i, j; in that of C, we observe c, k, l, m; while in that of D, we note c, n, o, p; the canon enables us to conclude that c, the only circumstance common to A, B, C, D, is either the cause or the effect of the given phenomenon.

Of course, our conclusion presupposes that we know which circumstances are relevant to a given phenomenon, so that the effectiveness of the canon presupposes a certain previous state of knowledge. Otherwise we may not be dealing with circumstances that have any bearing on the phenomenon in question. The person who becomes intoxicated on different occasions by putting ice cubes in gin, vodka, whisky, wine, and beer had better do more than give up ice cubes, although on the surface this was all that the various drinks had in common.

There is always the abstract possibility that the actual cause is multiple and that there is some unknown factor which, together with c, is actually the cause. It may even be the case that c is accidental to the phenomenon in question.

Consider the all too frequent phenomenon of academic failure:

Student A. Product of large high school, male, eighteen years old, part-time job, lacks interest in studies.

[14] For what immediately follows, see Mill, *op. cit.*, pp. 250–284.

Student B. Attended small high school, female, not employed, nineteen years old, lacks interest in studies.

Student C. Interested in sports, married, graduated from private school, lacks interest in studies, twenty-one years old.

Student D. Army veteran, twenty-five years old, exceptionally high I.Q., lacks interest in studies.

It would be easy to conclude that the lack of interest was the cause or the effect of the academic failure. However, there is no reason why the cause is the same in each instance. Student A may simply be poorly prepared to do college work; hence the lack of interest. Student B may be on the verge of a nervous breakdown, Student C may be spending too much time in sports or may have marital problems, and Student D may have financial difficulties.

Mill's canon of agreement is more readily applicable to a controlled experiment, but here, too, there may be unknown factors which mitigate against its effectiveness. The lack of perfection and the difficulties in isolating the relevant circumstances in no way detract, however, from the usefulness of experiment, as is attested by the number of technical achievements and discoveries attained. The usefulness of the method of agreement is enhanced when it is supplemented by noting differences as well as similarities or identities.

2.2   The method of difference

The second canon as formulated by Mill states:

If an instance in which the phenomenon under investigation occurs and an instance in which it does not occur, have every circumstance in common save one, that one occurring only in the former; the circumstance in which alone the two instances differ is the effect, or the cause, or an indispensable part of the cause, of the phenomenon.

The method of agreement seeks to find instances agreeing in a single relevant circumstance while differing in every other relevant circumstance. The method of difference seeks to find two instances resembling each other in every circumstance, except that the phenomenon under study is present or absent. For example, if when A is placed in a set of ascertained circumstances A, B, C, we note the effect *a, b, c,* whereas when B, C, are present without A, we then note only *b, c,* we then conclude that A is the cause of *a.* Of course, we may begin with an effect and seek to discover its cause. If we then choose an instance *a, b, c,* known to be the consequents of antecedents A, B, C, and find a condition where *b, c,* is the known effect of B, C, we can then conclude that A is the cause or a part of the cause of *a.* Our conclusion is the result of comparing an instance of the occurrence of a phenomenon with an instance where the phenomenon does not occur. Instead of noting the points of agreement, however, we here concentrate on the difference between the case where the phenomenon occurs and the occasion where it does not occur.

A similar kind of reasoning takes place in ordinary experience. Suppose you are sitting at your desk and are suddenly startled by the shattering of glass. You look up, see a broken window, and then find a baseball on the floor. The baseball was not there before; it is the only thing that has changed—that and the broken glass. You would hardly conclude that the broken glass produced the baseball.

The method of difference can be effectively used in a controlled situation. Nature seldom provides two instances where we can be sure that they differ in only one single important respect. It is difficult, if not impossible, to find instances exactly similar except in one important circumstance. Nevertheless, the canon is of practical consequence.

Consider two instances:

Instance A: The phenomenon of boiling water is present. The conditions under which this occurs are: A heavy aluminum pan; room temperature of 72°F.; ordinary tap water in pan; at sea level; pan on gas stove; heat fully turned on under pan.

Instance B: The phenomenon of boiling water is absent. The conditions under which this occurs are: A heavy aluminum pan; room temperature 72°F.; ordinary tap water in pan; at sea level; pan on gas stove; heat barely turned on under pan.

It is here readily evident that the amount of heat is the cause of the boiling water.

2.3 *Joint method of agreement and difference*

The effectiveness of the two canons is greatly enhanced by combining the method of agreement and the method of difference into a third canon:

If two or more instances in which the phenomenon occurs have only one circumstance in common, while two or more instances in which it does not occur have nothing in common save the absence of that circumstance, the circumstance in which alone the two sets of instances differ is the effect, or the cause, or an indispensable part of the cause of the phenomenon.

By comparing various instances in which a occurs and discovering that the circumstance a alone is common, we are able to establish a connection between A and a. By leaving A out, we can strengthen our conviction that A is the cause or a part of the cause of a, if when A is absent a does not occur. Of course, it may not be possible to attain certainty that the instances where a occurs agree solely in the fact that A is present and that the instances where a does not occur agree in nothing except that A is absent. But the fact that we do not obtain theoretical certainty does not detract from the usefulness of the canon.

The joint method of agreement and difference notes positive instances and negative instances. The positive instances, where the phenomenon occurs, have a single circumstance in common, and in the case of the negative instances, where the phenomenon does not occur, nothing is in common except the absence of the circumstance common to the positive instances.

The application of the canon may be schematically represented.

Positive Instances

Phenomenon is present: *Relevant circumstances under which*
Instance A: a, b, c, d *phenomenon is present.*
Instance B: a, e, f, g

Negative Instances

Phenomenon is not present: *Relevant circumstances under which*
Instance D: k, l, m, n *phenomenon is absent.*
Instance E: o, p, q, r

A concrete example:

Positive Instances

Phenomenon present: *Circumstances under which phenomenon occurs:*

Instance A: Shattering of glass   Flying aircraft breaking sound barrier, clear sky, midwinter, thermopane windows.

Instance B: Shattering of glass   Flying aircraft breaking sound barrier, rainy day, summer, plain window.

Negative Instances

Phenomenon absent: *Circumstances under which phenomenon does not occur:*

Instance C: No shattering of glass   Springtime, old house, storm window, near railroad.

Instance D: No shattering of glass   Modern church, on major highway, autumn, stained-glass windows.

2.4   *The method of residues*

The canons of experimental method can be supplemented by a fourth. If from previous inductions we know that A and B are the cause of *a*, *b*, and on the occasion A, B, C, we note *a*, *b*, *c*, we can subduct A, B, and conclude that C is the cause of *c*.

As stated by Mill:

Subduct from any phenomenon such part as is known by previous inductions to be the effect of certain antecedents, and the residue of the phenomenon is the effect of the remaining phenomenon.

This method of residues presupposes, of course, that we know which antecedents are relevant. The degree of certainty attained will be enhanced if C can subsequently be shown to be the cause of *c*, independently from its occurrence with A and B. Schematically represented:

The phenomenon is present: Where A is known previously to be the cause of *a* and B to be cause of *b*.

Antecedents

Instance 1:	A, B, C	followed by a, b, c
Instance 2:	B, C	followed by b, c
(by removing, subducting, A)		
Instance 3:	C	followed by c.

Thus the conclusion is reached that C is the cause of c.

The method of residues is concretely in evidence in the noting of changes in weight or temperature.

For example, consider the temperature of a classroom at 80°F. If the contribution of the body temperature of forty persons is known previously to contribute 2° and the heat of the radiators 72°, the conclusion can be drawn that the remaining 6° is due to the heat of the sun shining through the window.

2.5   The method of concomitant variation

A fifth canon, the final one formulated by Mill, states:

Whatever phenomenon varies in any manner whenever another phenomenon varies in some particular manner, is either a cause or an effect of that phenomenon, or is connected with it through some fact of causation.

The mere fact that two phenomena occur together is not sufficient to warrant the conclusion that there is a causal relationship between them, for both may be the effects of a common cause. The introduction of controlled variation, however, assists us in distinguishing effects from causes.

For example, by increasing the heat of a body, we note an increase in its bulk, but by increasing its bulk we do not increase its heat. The introduction of variations is especially useful together with the method of difference; that is, after we have determined that a certain object produces a certain effect. For, assuming that A is the known cause of a, we may then note that when A changes in quantity, a changes in quantity. We may then predict beyond the limits of our observation that the same numerical relation will hold. Such predictions, however, cannot yield deductive certainty. The methods of experiment yield hypotheses and permit deductions to be made.

Experimental methods are not to be thought of as a panacea or a way of solving all problems. Not only are there areas of human knowledge where controlled experiments are not possible (for example, mathematics and history), but, as already noted, the methods themselves have limitations.

The methods suggest that something cannot cause a phenomenon if it is not found in all instances where the phenomenon occurs; that for something to be the cause of a phenomenon, the phenomenon must occur whenever the alleged cause occurs. The methods suggest lines of inquiry, corroborate hypotheses, and eliminate irrelevant circumstances. Moreover, by following them we refuse to accept something as the cause of a phenomenon unless there is a variation in the phenomenon when there is a variation in the alleged cause and no variation in the phenomenon when there is an absence of variation in the cause.[15]

The very utilization of experiments presupposes a hypothesis which is brought to the experiment. Given a certain phenomenon P, we may then formulate alternative hypotheses H_1, H_2, H_3, as possible causes of P. Our alternative hypotheses are limited to what we consider to be relevant to the phenomenon in question. The situation may be formalized:

"Ideally we would like to ascertain that the phenomenon P occurs if, and only if, H_1 v H_2 v H_3 occurs, that is, $P \equiv (H_1$ v H_2 v $H_3)$.

By applying the canons under the conditions of a controlled experiment, we may eliminate H_1 by showing that P occurs in the absence of H_1 or by showing instances of H_1 without P. A variation in H_1 may fail to produce a variation in P, or a variation may occur in P without a variation in H_1. By eliminating H_1, we may then assume $P \equiv H_2$ v H_3. Subsequent experiments or observations may then eliminate H_2, leaving us with $P \equiv H_3$. The difficulty is that we cannot be certain that $P \equiv H_3$ because there may be other unknown facts H_4 v H_5 which actually cause P, and we have simply failed to eliminate H_3. The most we can do is to assume that within the limits of our observation $(H_3 \supset P)$. The fact that P does occur does not enable us to deduce with certainty that H_3 is the cause of P. From the deductive point of view, the argument $(H_3 \supset P) \cdot P / \therefore H_3$ affirms the consequent. The canons of deduction are simply not applicable to the verification of a hypothesis. Strictly speaking, the

[15] See Cohen and Nagel, *op. cit.*, pp. 245–269.

absence of P in the presence of H_3 does not entirely eliminate H_3 as being connected with the phenomenon, for the argument $(H_3 \supset P) \cdot {\sim}P /\therefore {\sim}H_3$ overlooks the actual situation.

A hypothesis H_3 is always formulated with a host of tacit assumptions T; for example, the laboratory conditions are the same, our measuring devices are operating properly, we have not overlooked relevant circumstances, and so on. Consequently, the situation is actually $[(H_3 \cdot T) \supset P] \cdot {\sim}P /\therefore {\sim}(H_3 \cdot T)$, which means $({\sim}H_3 \vee {\sim}T)$; that is, either our hypothesis is wrong or our tacit assumptions are wrong, and possibly both are wrong.

The difficulties and limitations of the experimental and inductive methods do not suggest that induction and experiments are to be dispensed with. Induction is not to be judged by the canons of deduction. The two are different; both are necessary. The one supplements the other.

In concluding, it should be evident that logic is the instrument of human knowledge. By abstracting from what we observe in different areas of experience, we form different kinds of concepts. Our concepts are then combined into different kinds of propositions (such as categorical and hypothetical), and we then formulate arguments to show why such and such is so and so. When we are not certain, our arguments are conditional in form. When we are certain, they are categorical. That we frequently err and speak categorically when we should speak conditionally, that we confuse contingencies with necessities and regard what is possible as impossible, simply illustrates the frailty of our human situation.

However, the alternative between omniscience or omni-ignorance is a weak disjunction. We know some things, not everything, and not nothing. At this point it is to be hoped that the student knows some logic.

EXERCISES

1. How can we establish general propositions from singular experiences?
2. What is meant by induction by complete enumeration?
3. What do you understand by causation? Is it essential to induction?

. State Mill's Canons of Experimental Inquiry. What is the strength and weakness of each?

. Describe several situations to which Mill's Canons of Experimental Inquiry are applicable.

INDEX

Index